USING

microsoft®
powerpoint®
2010

Patrice-Anne Rutledge

que®

800 East 96th Street, Indianapolis, Indiana 46240 USA

Using Microsoft® PowerPoint® 2010

Copyright © 2011 by Pearson Education, Inc.

ISBN-13: 978-0-7897-4294-0
ISBN-10: 0-7897-4294-2

Library of Congress Cataloging-in-Publication Data

Rutledge, Patrice-Anne.
  Using Microsoft PowerPoint 2010 / Patrice-Anne Rutledge.
    p. cm.
  Includes index.
  ISBN 978-0-7897-4294-0
  1. Presentation graphics software. 2. Microsoft PowerPoint (Computer file) I. Title.
  T385.R8953 2011
  005.5'8—dc22
                          2010020536

Printed in the United States of America
First Printing: August 2010

Trademarks

Warning and Disclaimer

Bulk Sales

Que Publishing offers excellent discounts on this book when ordered in quantity for bulk purchases or special sales. For more information, please contact

U.S. Corporate and Government Sales
1-800-382-3419
corpsales@pearsontechgroup.com

For sales outside of the U.S., please contact

International Sales
international@pearson.com

Associate Publisher
Greg Wiegand

Acquisitions Editor
Michelle Newcomb

Development Editor
Deadline Driven Publishing

Managing Editor
Kristy Hart

Project Editor
Lori Lyons

Copy Editor
Apostrophe Editing Services

Indexer
Lisa Stumpf

Proofreader
Water Crest Publishing, Inc.

Technical Editor
Geetesh Bajaj

Publishing Coordinator
Cindy Teeters

Book Designer
Anne Jones

Compositors
Jake McFarland
Nonie Ratcliff

Contents at a Glance

Media Files Table of Contents

To register this product and gain access to the Free Web Edition and the audio and video files, go to quepublishing.com/using.

Table of Contents

About the Author

Patrice-Anne Rutledge is a business technology author and consultant who specializes in teaching others to maximize the power of new technologies. Patrice has used—and has trained others to use—PowerPoint for many years, designing presentations for meetings, seminars, trade shows, and worldwide audiences. She is also the author of four previous books about PowerPoint for Pearson Education. She can be reached through her website at www.patricerutledge.com.

Dedication

To my family, with thanks for their ongoing support and encouragement.

Acknowledgments

Special thanks to Michelle Newcomb, Geetesh Bajaj, Ginny Munroe, San Dee Phillips, and Lori Lyons for their feedback, suggestions, and attention to detail.

We Want to Hear from You!

As the reader of this book, *you* are our most important critic and commentator. We value your opinion and want to know what we're doing right, what we could do better, what areas you'd like to see us publish in, and any other words of wisdom you're willing to pass our way.

As an associate publisher for Que Publishing, I welcome your comments. You can email or write me directly to let me know what you did or didn't like about this book—as well as what we can do to make our books better.

Please note that I cannot help you with technical problems related to the topic of this book. We do have a User Services group, however, where I will forward specific technical questions related to the book.

When you write, please be sure to include this book's title and author as well as your name, email address, and phone number. I will carefully review your comments and share them with the author and editors who worked on the book.

Email: feedback@quepublishing.com

Mail: Greg Wiegand
             Associate Publisher
             Que Publishing
             800 East 96th Street
             Indianapolis, IN 46240 USA

Reader Services

Visit our website and register this book at quepublishing.com/register for convenient access to any updates, downloads, or errata that might be available for this book.

Introduction

Microsoft PowerPoint 2010 is part of Microsoft's latest suite of business software applications, Microsoft Office 2010. Using PowerPoint, you can quickly create a basic slideshow or you can delve into sophisticated features to create a customized presentation. Because it's part of the Microsoft Office suite of products, you'll find PowerPoint to be intuitive and very familiar if you already use any other Office applications, such as Word or Excel.

Using Microsoft PowerPoint 2010 is designed to get you up and running on PowerPoint as quickly as possible. This book starts with presentation basics and then introduces you to PowerPoint 2010's many new features that can give your presentation the wow factor, enable you to collaborate with colleagues around the world, and extend the power of PowerPoint with third-party applications. Because knowing how to use the software is just part of creating a successful presentation, *Using Microsoft PowerPoint 2010* also provides numerous tips on presentation design, content, rehearsal, and delivery. For now, turn to Chapter 1, "Introducing PowerPoint 2010," to get started with this powerful presentation tool.

Who This Book Is For

This book is for you if...

- You want to become productive with PowerPoint as quickly as possible and are short on time.

- You want to move beyond a basic bulleted list presentation and make the most of PowerPoint's many design features.

- You're a visual learner and want to *see* how to use PowerPoint in addition to reading about it.

Using This Book

More than just a book, *Using Microsoft PowerPoint 2010* is tightly integrated with online video tutorials, audio insights, and other web-based content, which is designed to provide you with a media-rich, customized learning experience not available through any other book series today. *Using Microsoft PowerPoint 2010* is a thorough resource at your fingertips.

This book enables you to customize your own learning experience. The step-by-step instructions in the book give you a solid foundation in using PowerPoint, while rich and varied online content, including video tutorials and audio sidebars, provide the following:

- Demonstrations of step-by-step tasks covered in the book
- Additional tips or information on a topic
- Practical advice and suggestions
- Direction for more advanced tasks not covered in the book

Here's a quick look at a few structural features designed to help you get the most out of this book.

- **Chapter roadmaps:** At the beginning of each chapter is a list of the top-level topics addressed in that chapter. This list enables you to quickly see the information the chapter contains.
- **Notes:** Notes provide additional commentary or explanation that doesn't fit neatly into the surrounding text. Notes give detailed explanations of how something works, alternative ways of performing a task, and other tidbits to get you on your way.
- **Tips:** This element gives you shortcuts, workarounds, and ways to avoid pitfalls.
- **Cautions:** Every once in a while, there is something that can have serious repercussions if done incorrectly (or rarely, if done at all). Cautions give you a heads-up.
- **Cross-references:** Many topics are connected to other topics in various ways. Cross-references help you link related information together, no matter where that information appears in the book. When another section is related to one you are reading, a cross-reference directs you to a specific chapter in the book in which you can find the related information.

 LET ME TRY IT tasks are presented in a step-by-step sequence so you can easily follow along.

 SHOW ME videos walk through tasks you've just got to see—including bonus advanced techniques.

 TELL ME MORE audios deliver practical insights straight from the experts.

POINT-COUNTERPOINT audio debates compare alternative solutions—so you can pick one that's best for you.

Special Features

More than just a book, your USING product integrates step-by-step video tutorials and valuable audio sidebars delivered through the **Free Web Edition** that comes with every USING book. For the price of the book, you get online access anywhere with a web connection—no books to carry, content is updated as the technology changes, and the benefit of video and audio learning.

About the USING Web Edition

The Web Edition of every USING book is powered by **Safari Books Online**, allowing you to access the video tutorials and valuable audio sidebars. Plus, you can search the contents of the book, highlight text and attach a note to that text, print your notes and highlights in a custom summary, and cut and paste directly from Safari Books Online.

To register this product and gain access to the **Free Web Edition** and the audio and video files, go to **quepublishing.com/using**.

The author also has a website online at www.patricerutledge.com/books/power-point2010, where you can access book updates, news about PowerPoint features and tools, and other books and courses that might be of interest.

PowerPoint 2010 Basics

Introducing PowerPoint 2010

PowerPoint is powerful, easy-to-use presentation software that is part of the Microsoft Office suite of products. You can use PowerPoint to create presentations for a wide variety of audiences and for a wide variety of purposes. A presentation communicates information, and a good presentation can truly convince, motivate, inspire, and educate its audience. PowerPoint offers the tools both to create a basic presentation and to enhance and customize your presentation slides to meet your goals.

In this chapter, you explore the many features and benefits of using PowerPoint, including the new features introduced in PowerPoint 2010. You can also listen to tips on making the most of PowerPoint as a communication and design tool and watch videos that show you how to use the Ribbon tabs, use Backstage View, and work with PowerPoint presentation views.

Understanding What PowerPoint Can Do

One of PowerPoint's strengths is its flexibility. Using themes, templates, and other presentation building blocks, you can quickly create a basic presentation even if you have little or no design skills. If you are a designer, PowerPoint's advanced features and customization options give you complete creative control. With PowerPoint, you can

- Create a presentation using a template, using a theme, or from scratch. Another option is importing a presentation outline from another application such as Microsoft Word.

- Add text and tables to your presentation to convey basic information.

- Add visual content with charts, pictures, clip art, SmartArt graphics, and other shapes or objects.

- Bring multimedia into the picture using sound, video, and animation.

- Add interactivity with hyperlinks and action buttons.

- Create and print notes and handouts for you and your audience.

- Share and collaborate on presentations with others in your organization.

- Access PowerPoint using the PowerPoint web app or a mobile device.

- Deliver a presentation onscreen using a computer, broadcast it online, or create a presentation video that you can post on the web.

 TELL ME MORE   Media 1.1—Understanding What PowerPoint Can Do
Access this audio recording through your registered Web Edition at
my.safaribooksonline.com/9780132182553/media.

Exploring New PowerPoint 2010 Features

PowerPoint 2010 includes many new features that users of previous versions will enjoy. This new version of PowerPoint emphasizes visual creativity, usability, and collaboration. Some new features that might interest you include the following:

- **Animation Painter**—Apply the formatting of one animation to another animation. This button works in much the same way as the Format Painter button. See Chapter 14, "Working with Animation and Transitions," for more information.

- **Presentation Sections**—Divide your presentation into logical sections to simplify navigation and organization. See Chapter 5, "Formatting and Organizing Objects, Slides, and Presentations," for more information.

- **Video Editing**—Use professional video editing and formatting tools directly in PowerPoint without the need for an external application. See Chapter 13, "Working with Audio and Video," for more information.

- **Paste Preview**—Preview what pasted content will look like before you actually paste it. See Chapter 5 for more information.

- **Screenshot Captures**—Incorporate screenshots directly from PowerPoint. See Chapter 9, "Working with Images," for more information.

- **Backstage View**—Perform common file-related tasks such as creating, opening, saving, sharing, and printing presentations in fewer steps. See "Using Backstage View," later in this chapter for more information.

- **Merge and Compare**—Compare and reconcile multiple versions of the same presentation. See Chapter 8, "Reviewing Presentations," for more information.

- **Co-Authoring**—Collaborate with others on the same presentation in real-time. See Chapter 17, "Sharing and Collaborating on Presentations," for more information.

- **Broadcast Slide Show**—Broadcast your presentation to anyone on the web using either SharePoint Server 2010 or a free Windows Live account. See Chapter 15, "Presenting a Slide Show," for more information.

- **Create a Video**—Share your presentation with others as a high-definition, web-based, or mobile device video. See Chapter 13 for more information.

- **Document Sharing**—Share your document with colleagues real-time and communicate with them via instant messaging using Office Communicator 2007 R2. See Chapter 17 for more information.

- **PowerPoint Web App**—View and edit PowerPoint presentations on the web using the external PowerPoint web application. See Chapter 20, "Accessing PowerPoint on the Web and Mobile Devices," for more information.

In addition to these new features, PowerPoint 2010 also offers many enhancements, including

- An enhanced Ribbon that is available across all Office applications

- More Office themes

- More SmartArt graphics

- Easier access to animation tools

- Enhanced slide transitions, including 3-D effects

- Numerous new image editing features

- Powerful editing tools for mathematical equations

- Improved notes printing

- Improved slide show recording functions

- Enhanced language and translation tools

Using the Ribbon Tabs

Although the *Ribbon* isn't a new PowerPoint feature (it was introduced in PowerPoint 2007), it does represent a new experience for anyone upgrading from version 2003 or before.

SHOW ME   Media 1.2—Using the Ribbon Tabs
Access this video file through your registered Web Edition at
my.safaribooksonline.com/9780132182553/media.

The Ribbon, which replaces the menu structure found in previous versions of PowerPoint, provides an easy way to access common commands and buttons using the least space possible. The Ribbon is divided into tabs: Home, Insert, Design, Transitions, Animations, Slide Show, Review, View, and Add-Ins. Each Ribbon tab includes groups and buttons of related features.

Figure 1.1 shows the Home tab.

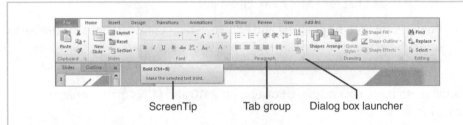

          ScreenTip   Tab group   Dialog box launcher

Figure 1.1   *Ribbon tabs are where you find all your PowerPoint commands.*

To quickly determine the function of tab buttons and commands, pause your mouse over each option to display a basic description in a ScreenTip. If a hotkey is available (such as pressing Ctrl+C to copy), it also displays in the ScreenTip.

Common Ribbon features include

- **Galleries**—Galleries offer a menu of visual choices that pertain to a selected ribbon button or command. For example, when you click the down arrow next to the Themes group on the Design tab, a visual gallery of theme images displays (see Figure 1.2).

- **Live Preview**—Most, but not all, PowerPoint galleries provide a live preview of each option before you actually apply it to your slide. As an example, the Themes gallery enables you to see how each theme appears on your presentation when you pause your mouse over it. That way, you can quickly try out several options before making any changes to your actual presentation.

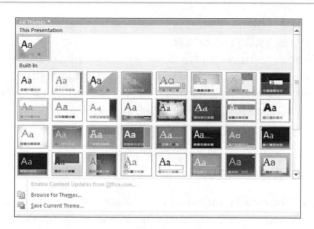

Figure 1.2 *Galleries offer a quick overview of potential visual effects.*

- **Dialog box launcher**—Clicking one of these small diagonal arrows in the lower-right corner of a group opens a dialog box of related options. For example, the Home tab includes dialog box launchers in the Clipboard, Font, Paragraph, and Drawing groups. The Clipboard dialog box launcher, interestingly enough, doesn't launch a dialog box, but rather a task pane. All the other launchers launch a traditional dialog box. See "Using Task Panes" later in this chapter, for more information about task panes.

- **Contextual tabs**—Although the main tabs always display on the Ribbon, PowerPoint also includes several contextual Ribbon tabs that appear only when performing specific tasks. For example, when you select a chart on a PowerPoint slide, the Chart Tools tab displays, which includes three subtabs: Design, Layout, and Format (see Figure 1.3). They remain as long as you work on your chart. When you click elsewhere on your slide, they disappear.

Figure 1.3 *PowerPoint opens additional contextual tabs depending on the task you perform.*

See Chapter 19, "Customizing PowerPoint," for more information about customizing the Ribbon tabs.

A few buttons include two sections: The upper portion performs a default action, and the lower portion (with a down arrow) opens a drop-down menu or gallery of options. For example, clicking the upper portion of the New Slide button on the Home tab automatically inserts a new slide using the default Title Slide layout. Clicking the lower portion opens a gallery of options.

Using Backstage View

PowerPoint 2010 introduces *Backstage View*, which enables you to perform PowerPoint's most common file-related tasks in one place. For example, Backstage View is now the place where you create, open, save, share, and print presentations.

 SHOW ME   Media 1.3—Using Backstage View
Access this video file through your registered Web Edition at
my.safaribooksonline.com/9780132182553/media.

To access Backstage View, click the File tab. Figure 1.4 shows Backstage View.

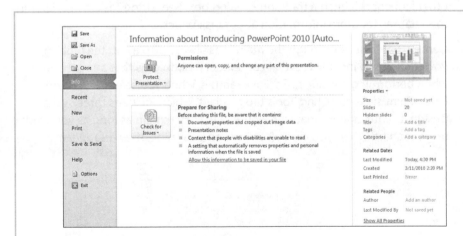

Figure 1.4   *Perform all your file-related tasks in one place: Backstage View.*

On the left side of the screen, you view a list of buttons and tabs. Clicking one of the buttons (Save, Save As, Open, Close, Options, and Exit) performs a command. Clicking one of the tabs (Info, Recent, New, Print, Save & Send, and Help) displays related content on the right side of the screen. Future chapters cover all the features available in Backstage View, including Chapter 2, "Creating a Basic Presentation."

Using Toolbars

Although PowerPoint 2010 uses far fewer toolbars than earlier versions of PowerPoint, you need to know about two types of toolbars: the Quick Access Toolbar and mini toolbar.

Using the Quick Access Toolbar

The *Quick Access Toolbar* is a small toolbar that displays in the upper-left corner of your screen (see Figure 1.5) and is available no matter which ribbon tab you select.

Figure 1.5 *Common commands are at your fingertips no matter what you're doing in PowerPoint.*

By default, this toolbar contains three buttons: Save, Undo, and Repeat, but you can customize it to include almost any PowerPoint command. See Chapter 19, "Customizing PowerPoint," for more information about customizing the buttons on this toolbar and moving it to another location.

Using Mini Toolbars

Mini toolbars are small contextual toolbars that appear when you perform specific tasks. For example, when you select text, a mini toolbar appears with options related to text formatting (see Figure 1.6).

Figure 1.6 *When you edit text, a mini toolbar appears with common text-editing commands.*

Although you can perform the same tasks using the commands on the main ribbon tab, using the mini toolbar moves these commands to a more convenient location.

Using Task Panes

A *task pane* is a window inside PowerPoint that lets you perform common PowerPoint tasks without covering your slide area. You can keep more than one pane open at time, but keep in mind that too many open task panes can clutter your screen. A sampling of PowerPoint's task panes include

- **Clip Art**—Search for image, audio, and video clips. Click the Clip Art button on the Insert tab to open this task pane, as shown in Figure 1.7.

Figure 1.7   *The Clip Art task pane is one of the most common PowerPoint task panes.*

- **Clipboard**—Collect and paste up to 24 different items. Click the dialog box launcher in the Clipboard group on the Home tab to open this task pane.

- **Animation**—Apply sophisticated animations to your slides or objects on your slides. Click the Animation Pane button on the Animations tab to open this task pane.

You can make the task pane wider or narrower if you prefer. To do so, pause the mouse pointer over the left edge of the pane until the pointer becomes a two-headed arrow. Click the mouse and drag the left edge to either the left or right until the task pane is the width you want.

To close a task pane, click the Close (x) button in the upper-right corner.

Understanding PowerPoint Views

PowerPoint includes several different *views,* which are arrangements of slides and tools on the screen that you use to work with and view your presentation. Which view you use depends on what you're doing. The View tab, shown in Figure 1.8, includes numerous view buttons in the Presentation Views group and the Master Views group.

Figure 1.8   *Select a view option on the View tab.*

 SHOW ME   Media 1.4—Understanding PowerPoint Views
Access this video file through your registered Web Edition at
my.safaribooksonline.com/9780132182553/media.

You can also click one of the view buttons in the lower-right portion of the PowerPoint window to display the Normal, Slide Sorter, Reading, and Slide Show views.

PowerPoint's views include

*   **Normal view**—This is the default view, as shown in Figure 1.9.

Slides and Outline tab

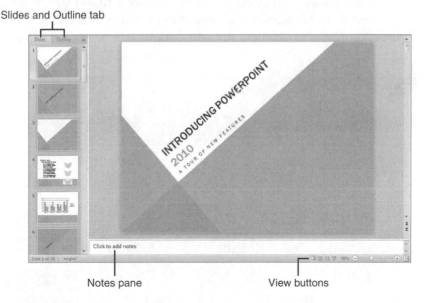

Notes pane   View buttons

Figure 1.9   *Normal view is PowerPoint's default viewing option.*

Normal view includes

- **Slide pane**—Located in the center of the screen. You can add text, graphics, tables, charts, and other objects to your presentation on the slide pane.

> Use the scrollbar on the right side of the Slide pane to navigate between presentation slides. You can also use the Page Up and Page Down keys to move among slides.

- **Slides tab and Outline tab**—On the left side of the screen. The Slides tab displays thumbnails of your slides. The Outline tab displays an outline of your presentation, including the initial text of each slide. You can use the tabs to rearrange and organize slides or to display a particular slide in the slide pane. See Chapter 7, "Outlining Presentations," for more information.

- **Notes pane**—Includes space for you to write speaker's notes or notes to yourself about your presentation.

  You can resize the panes in Normal view. To do so, drag the border between panes to a new location. If you want to hide the Slides tab and Outline tab, click the Close (x) button. You can always reopen them later by clicking the Normal view button.

- **Slide Sorter view**—This view, as shown in Figure 1.10, displays miniature previews of all the slides in your presentation, making it easier for you to organize them. See Chapter 7 for more information.

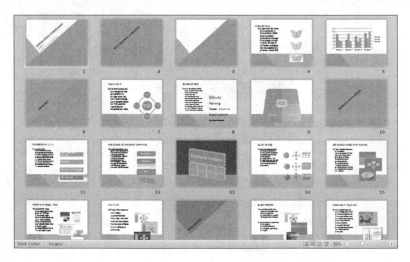

Figure 1.10   *Seeing miniature versions of your slides can help you rearrange them.*

- **Notes page view**—This view, shown in Figure 1.11, displays your notes in a full-page format, making it easier to view the content you enter on the notes pane.

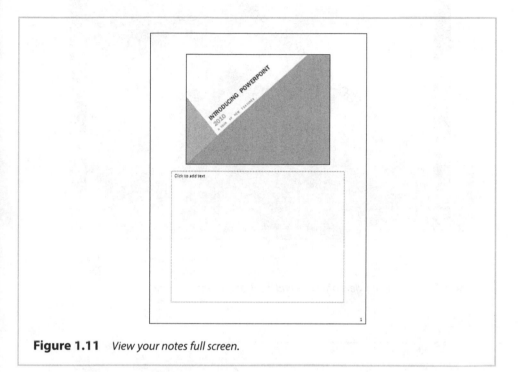

Figure 1.11   *View your notes full screen.*

- **Reading view**—Reading view (see Figure 1.12) displays your slides as they would appear in a slide show, full-screen, but with navigation buttons and menus in the lower-right corner.

Menu and Navigation Options

- **Slide Show view**—Slide Show view displays your slides as they would appear in an actual slide show, full-screen, without any menus, toolbars, or other features. Figure 1.13 shows this view. See Chapter 15, "Presenting a Slide Show," for more information.

- **Master views**—PowerPoint's three master views include the Slide Master, Handout Master, and Notes Master views. You use these views only when you customize your slide masters, including the placeholders, backgrounds, and colors that appear your slide layouts. See Chapter 19, "Customizing PowerPoint," for more information.

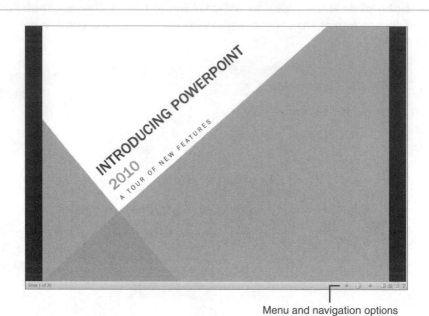

Menu and navigation options

Figure 1.12   *Reading view offers several ways to navigate full screen.*

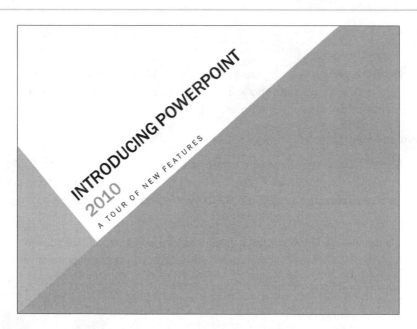

Figure 1.13   *Slide Show view demonstrates how your presentation will look when you present it.*

PowerPoint's default view is Normal view with the Slides tab selected. If you want to change this, click the File tab, select Options, and go to the Advanced tab in the Options dialog box, where you can specify your default view in the Display section.

Getting Help

Although PowerPoint is an intuitive program, there are times when you might need additional help in completing an in-progress task or figuring out how to do something. Fortunately, help is just a click away. Microsoft continuously updates its help system, so if you're connected to the web while you search for PowerPoint help, you'll always get the latest help content.

 LET ME TRY IT

Searching for Help

To search for help on a specific topic, follow these steps:

1. Click the Help button in the upper-right corner of the screen (a small question mark in a blue circle) or in the upper-right corner of a dialog box. Pressing F1 is another way to access help. Figure 1.14 shows the PowerPoint Help window, which opens.

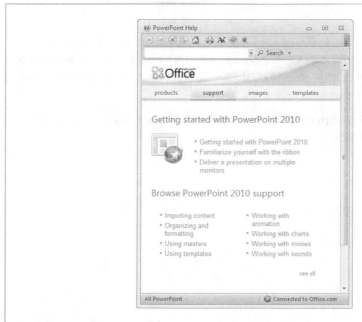

Figure 1.14   *The Help window displays detailed help on your selected topic.*

2. To search for help on a specific topic, enter keywords in the text box, For example, if you want to search for help on creating sections, you could enter "sections."

3. Click the Search button to initiate the search. The Help window displays a list of search result articles.

4. Click the article title that best matches your search to view the help content.

The top of the Help window includes the following buttons:

- **Back**—Return to previous help screen.

- **Forward**—Continue to next help screen.

- **Stop**—Halt the current search.

- **Refresh**—Refresh the help content.

- **Home**—Return to the main PowerPoint Help screen.

- **Print**—Print the open help article.

- **Change Font Size**—Make the help text larger or smaller.

- **Show Table of Contents**—Display a hyperlinked list of all PowerPoint help articles.

- **Keep on Top**—Maintain the help window on top of other applications, for easy access.

You can also receive help in Backstage View. To do so, click the File button and select Help. Figure 1.15 shows the Support page, which enables you to access the Help window, view a getting started guide on the web, contact the Microsoft support center, check for software updates, and more.

Microsoft Office Online (http://office.microsoft.com) also offers searchable help, tutorials, and downloads.

Figure 1.15 *Backstage View offers more help options.*

Creating a Basic Presentation

After you learn—or refresh your memory about—how to navigate PowerPoint, you can create a basic presentation. This chapter gets you up and running on presentation basics so that you can quickly move forward to more advanced and sophisticated PowerPoint techniques.

In this chapter, you explore the many ways to create a PowerPoint presentation that suits your needs. You can also listen to presentation tips and watch videos that show you how to create a presentation using a template, create presentation sections, and save your presentation.

Understanding PowerPoint Presentations

Before you start creating your first PowerPoint 2010 presentation, you need to understand *themes*, *templates*, and *slide layouts*, which are presentation building blocks.

 TELL ME MORE Media 2.1—Understanding PowerPoint Presentations
Access this audio recording through your registered Web Edition at my.safaribooksonline.com/9780132182553/media.

Understanding Themes

A *theme* is a standalone file with colors, fonts, and effects to use in a single presentation. Other Microsoft Office 2010 applications, such as Word and Excel, also support themes, enabling you to create a consistent look and feel between Office documents.

Each theme contains

- **Fonts**—A theme contains two fonts: one for headings and one for body text.

- **Colors**—PowerPoint color schemes include a set of 12 coordinated colors for text, backgrounds, accents, and hyperlinks.

- **Effects**—Office themes apply graphic effects to tables, text, charts, diagrams, shapes, and pictures.

Every presentation has a theme—even a blank presentation, which uses the Office theme. You can apply a theme when you first create your presentation or apply one at any time to an existing presentation.

See Chapter 3, "Customizing Themes and Backgrounds," for more information about themes.

Understanding Templates

A *template* is a starter document that you apply when you create a new presentation. Templates can include slide layouts; theme colors, fonts, and effects; background styles; and content for a specific type of presentation, such as for a project status meeting or training seminar. Your new presentation contains the template's content, layout, formatting, and theme. It's usually a good idea to apply a single template to a presentation for consistency, but you can apply multiple templates to a single presentation if you want. Figure 2.1 illustrates a sample presentation created with a template.

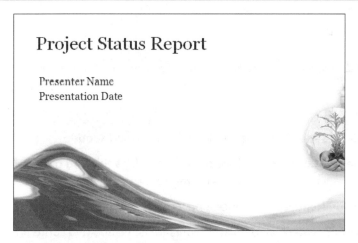

Figure 2.1   *Get a head start creating a project status presentation.*

Understanding Slide Layouts

In addition to themes and templates, the other important design feature you need to consider is a *slide layout*. A slide layout helps you add specific types of content to your slides, such as text, tables, charts, and pictures.

By default, PowerPoint offers nine choices of layout (see Figure 2.2), but you can create your own layouts as well. If you enabled support for Far East Asian languages, additional layout options are available.

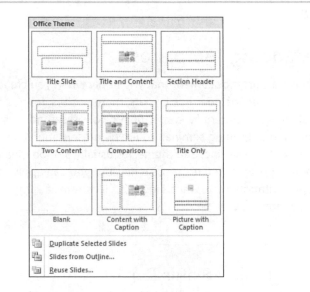

Figure 2.2   *Choose an existing layout or start from scratch.*

The layouts are

- **Title Slide**—Include placeholders for a title and subtitle.
- **Title and Content**—Include placeholders for a title and one content item, such as a table, chart, SmartArt graphic, picture, clip art, or media file.
- **Section Header**—Introduce a new presentation section.
- **Two Content**—Include placeholders for a title and two content items.
- **Comparison**—Include placeholders for a title and two content items, each with a text heading.
- **Title Only**—Include a placeholder for a title only.
- **Blank**—Include a completely blank slide.

- **Content with Caption**—Include placeholders for a brief title, text, and content item.

- **Picture with Caption**—Include placeholders for a large picture, title, and text.

If the predefined layouts don't suit your needs, you can modify a blank slide or modify one of the existing layouts by adding, moving, or deleting objects.

🕑 *See Chapter 4, "Working with Text," for more information about inserting text in placeholders.*

The Title and Content, Two Content, Comparison, and Content with Caption layouts include a content palette as a placeholder. This content palette includes six buttons:

- Insert Table

- Insert Chart

- Insert SmartArt Graphic

- Insert Picture from File

- Clip Art

- Insert Media Clip

On any slide that contains the content palette, you can also enter a bullet list using the starter bullet that displays in the upper-left corner of the slide area. If you click one of the buttons on the palette, this bullet disappears.

🕑 *Future chapters cover each of these options in more detail.*

Creating a Presentation

You can create a presentation in several different ways, depending on the amount of content and design assistance you need. You can create the following:

- **Presentation using a template**—Use one of PowerPoint's existing templates, a template you create yourself, or a template from Office.com's collection of templates.

- **Presentation using a theme**—If you don't need the content help of a template, creating a new presentation using a PowerPoint theme provides an initial design with coordinated colors, fonts, and effects.

- **New presentation using an existing presentation**—Using this option, you create a presentation by copying an existing presentation and then editing and modifying it. Doing this doesn't change the original presentation.

- **Blank presentation**—A blank presentation contains black text on a white background with no content suggestions. Create a blank presentation only when you are experienced with PowerPoint and want to create a custom design. Even if you want to create a custom presentation, it often saves you time to start with a similar existing design and then customize it.

> If you're going to create a complex presentation, it's often beneficial to create a storyboard before actually working in PowerPoint. A storyboard is a visual roadmap for your presentation. Begin by mapping out your complete presentation flow. By determining up front the order of your content and the best way to communicate your message (text, tables, charts, audio, video, or pictures), you can design your presentation faster and more effectively.

Creating a Presentation from a Template

Using a template is one of the easiest way's to create a new presentation. Be sure to customize your template to ensure that it meets the needs of your audience.

SHOW ME   Media 2.2—Creating a Presentation from a Template
Access this video file through your registered Web Edition at
my.safaribooksonline.com/9780132182553/media.

LET ME TRY IT

Creating a Presentation from a Template

To create a new presentation from a template, follow these steps:

1. Click the File tab, and then click New to open Backstage view (see Figure 2.3).

2. Select the template you want to use. You can do the following:
   - Click the Recent Templates button to select a template you recently applied.
   - Click the Sample Templates button to preview PowerPoint's default templates.
   - Click the My Templates button to select a template you created.

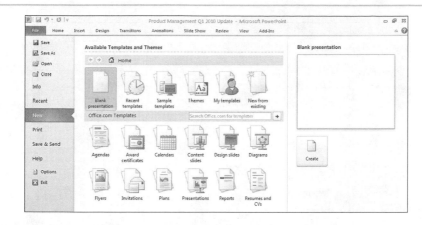

Figure 2.3   *PowerPoint includes many templates from which to choose.*

- Click one of the buttons in the Office.com Templates section. PowerPoint searches Office.com and displays matching templates.

3. Click the Create button to open your new presentation with the selected template. If you choose a template on Office.com, click the Download button instead. PowerPoint opens a new presentation based on your selected template.

4. From here, you can add content to your presentation, format it, and insert additional slides.

Creating a New Presentation with a Theme

Using a coordinated PowerPoint theme as a starting point is another good way to create a presentation.

 LET ME TRY IT

Creating a New Presentation with a Theme

To create a new presentation with a theme, follow these steps:

1. Click the File tab, and then click New to open Backstage view (refer to Figure 2.3).

2. Click the Themes button. PowerPoint displays a list of available themes, as shown in Figure 2.4.

3. Select the theme you want to apply to your presentation.

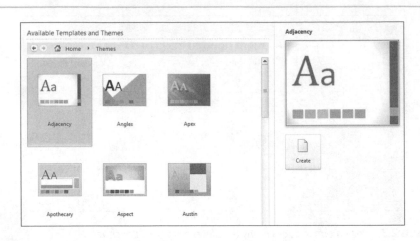

Figure 2.4   *Create a coordinated design using a theme.*

4. Click the Create button. PowerPoint opens a new presentation with a Title Slide layout.

Creating a New Presentation from an Existing Presentation

Another way to create a new presentation is simply to copy an existing presentation whose content and format are similar to what you want.

 LET ME TRY IT

Creating a New Presentation from an Existing Presentation

To create a new presentation from an existing presentation, follow these steps:

1. Click the File tab, and then click New to open Backstage view (refer to Figure 2.3).

2. Click the New from Existing button. The New from Existing Presentation dialog box opens, as shown in Figure 2.5.

3. Select the existing presentation on which you want to base the new one.

4. Click the Create New button. PowerPoint creates a copy of the original presentation, which you can modify.

Figure 2.5   *Creating from an existing presentation can save you a lot of time.*

Creating a Presentation from Scratch

If you have your own vision for your presentation and want to start with a blank slate, you can create a presentation from scratch.

 **LET ME TRY IT**

Creating a Presentation from Scratch

To create a blank presentation, follow these steps:

1. Click the File tab, and then click New to open Backstage view.

2. Double-click the Blank Presentation button to open a blank slide in Title Slide layout.

   Figure 2.6 illustrates a sample blank presentation.

3. From here, you can add more slides and adjust formatting to suit your needs.

Figure 2.6   *To have complete design control, you can use a blank presentation.*

Adding Slides to Your Presentation

To add a new slide to an open presentation, on the Home tab, click the lower portion of the New Slide button. From here, you can

- Select a layout from the gallery that appears (refer to Figure 2.2). See "Understanding Slide Layouts" earlier in this chapter for more information about layout options.

- Select Duplicate Selected Slides to insert duplicates of the slides selected on the Slides tab.

- Select Slides from Outline to create slides from an outline you created in another application, such as Microsoft Word. See Chapter 7, "Outlining Presentations," for more information.

- Select Reuse Slides to open the Reuse Slides task pane, as shown in Figure 2.7. You can reuse slides from another PowerPoint presentation or from a slide library. See Chapter 17, "Sharing and Collaborating on Presentations," for more information about slide libraries.

Alternatively, click the top portion of the New Slide button to add a slide in Title and Content layout automatically without opening the gallery. Pressing Ctrl+M also performs this same task.

Figure 2.7 *Reuse slides from a presentation on your computer or in a slide library.*

Adding Sections to Your Presentation

PowerPoint 2010 introduces the ability to add sections to your presentations. Sections are particularly useful for large presentations where it's easy to get lost in a sea of slides. You can use sections to define presentation topics or distinguish between speakers, for example.

You can also use the Section Header slide layout to further define presentation sections. See the "Understanding Slide Layouts" section earlier in this chapter for more information.

 SHOW ME Media 2.3—Adding Sections to Your Presentation
Access this video file through your registered Web Edition at
my.safaribooksonline.com/9780132182553/media.

 **LET ME TRY IT**

Adding Sections to Your Presentation

To add a section to your presentation, follow these steps:

1. In either Normal view or Slide Sorter view, select the slide that starts the section you want to insert.

2. On the Home tab, click the Section button, and select Add Section from the menu. PowerPoint inserts an untitled section, as shown in Figure 2.8.

Alternatively, right-click between two slides on the Slides tab where you want to insert a section, and from the menu that displays, click Add Section.

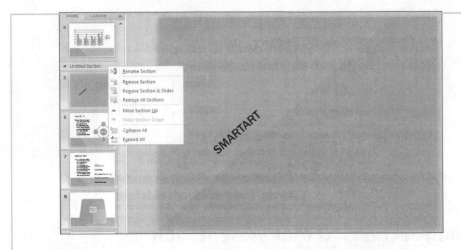

Figure 2.8   *Add sections to better manage large presentations.*

3. Select the untitled section, click the Section button again, and select Rename Section. Figure 2.9 shows the Rename Section dialog box, which opens.

Figure 2.9   *Give each section a meaningful name.*

4. Enter a Section Name, and click the Rename button.

You can follow this procedure to enter as many sections as you need in your presentation.

Collapsing and Expanding Sections

If you have a lot of slides and sections, you might want to collapse them for easier viewing on the Slides tab. To do so, click the Section button on the Home tab, and select Collapse All from the menu. You can also collapse sections by right-clicking a section and selecting Collapse All from the menu. Expand collapsed sections by selecting Expand All from these same menus.

Removing Sections

To remove a section, select it, click the Section button on the Home tab, and select Remove Section from the menu. To remove all sections, select Remove All Sections. You can also remove a section by right-clicking it and selecting Remove Section from the menu that appears.

When you remove a section, PowerPoint deletes the section marker but not the slides in that section. If you want to remove a section and its slides, right-click the section and select Remove Sections & Slides from the menu.

Saving a Presentation

After you create a presentation, you should save it. Table 2.1 lists the available file formats in which you can save your presentation.

Table 2.1   PowerPoint File Types

File Type	Extension	Result
PowerPoint Presentation	PPTX	Save as a PowerPoint 2010 or 2007 presentation (an XML-enabled format).
PowerPoint Macro-Enabled Presentation	PPTM	Save as a presentation with macros enabled.
PowerPoint 97–2003 Presentation	PPT	Save as a presentation you can open in PowerPoint 97 to 2003.
PDF	PDF	Save as a PDF (Portable Document Format) file.
XPS Document	XPS	Save as an XPS (XML Paper Specification) file.
PowerPoint Template	POTX	Save as a template that you can use as a starter for future presentations.
PowerPoint Macro-Enabled Template	POTM	Save as a template with macros enabled.
PowerPoint 97–2003 Template	POT	Save as a template you can open in PowerPoint 97 to 2003.
Office Theme	THMX	Save as a theme that includes colors, fonts, and effects.
PowerPoint Show	PPS, PPSX	Save as a slide show.
PowerPoint Macro-Enabled Show	PPSM	Save as a slide show with macros enabled.
PowerPoint 97–2003 Show	PPT	Save as a slide show you can view in PowerPoint 97 to 2003.
PowerPoint Add-In	PPAM	Save as an add-in that includes custom commands or VBA code.
PowerPoint 97–2003 Add-In	PPA	Save as an add-in that you can open in PowerPoint 97 to 2003.

Table 2.1   PowerPoint File Types

File Type	Extension	Result
PowerPoint XML Presentation	XML	Save in XML format for use in an XML information storage system.
Windows Media Video	WMV	Save as a video that you can play on the web or on a media player.
GIF Graphics Interchange Format	GIF	Save as a graphic for use on the web.
JPEG File Interchange Format	JPG	Save as a graphic for use on the web.
PNG Portable Network Graphics Format	PNG	Save as a graphic for use on the web.
TIFF Tag Image File Format	TIF	Save as a TIFF graphic image.
Device Independent Bitmap	BMP	Save as a bitmap graphic image.
Windows Metafile	WMF	Save as a 16-bit vector graphic image.
Enhanced Windows Metafile	EMF	Save as a 32-bit vector graphic image.
Outline/RTF	RTF	Save as an outline in Rich Text Format, which you can open in Microsoft Word.
PowerPoint Picture Presentation	PPTX	Save as a PowerPoint 2010 or 2007 presentation in which each slide is converted to a picture.
OpenDocument Presentation	ODP	Save in a format that you can open using applications that support ODP files, such as Google Docs or OpenOffice.

 SHOW ME   Media 2.4—Saving a Presentation

Access this video file through your registered Web Edition at
my.safaribooksonline.com/9780132182553/media.

 **LET ME TRY IT**

Saving a Presentation

To save an open PowerPoint presentation, follow these steps:

1. On the Quick Access Toolbar, click the Save button. Alternatively, press Ctrl+S. If this is the first time you've saved the presentation, the Save As dialog box displays, as shown in Figure 2.10.

2. Select the folder in which to save your presentation. PowerPoint automatically selects your default folder, but you can change this if you want. You can customize the default folder on the Save tab in the PowerPoint Options dialog box (choose Tools, Save Options from the Save As dialog box).

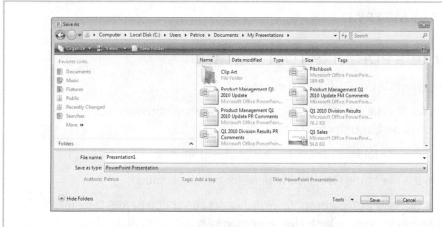

Figure 2.10 *Specify save parameters in this dialog box.*

3. In the File Name field, type a name for the presentation. The drop-down list in the File Name field includes previously saved presentations. Even if you choose one of these filenames, PowerPoint warns you so that you don't accidentally overwrite an existing presentation.

4. Choose the file format from the Save as Type drop-down list. Refer to Table 2.1 for a list of available file types. If you want to save as a PDF or XPS document, see "Saving as a PDF or XPS Document" later in this section.

5. Click the Save button to save the file.

After you save a presentation, press Ctrl+S or click the Save button to save new changes without opening the Save As dialog box. To open the Save As dialog box to make additional changes, click the File tab and select Save As.

To set and modify save options such as default formats, file locations, embedded fonts, and AutoRecovery, choose Tools, Save Options from the Save As dialog box.

Saving as a PDF or XPS Document

PowerPoint 2010 now enables you to save directly as a PDF or XPS document without requiring an add-in.

LET ME TRY IT

Saving as a PDF or XPS Document

To save as a PDF or XPS, follow these steps:

1. Click the File tab, and then click Save As from the menu to open the Save As dialog box (refer to Figure 2.10).

2. Select the folder in which to save your presentation.

3. In the File Name field, type a name for the presentation.

4. In the Save as Type drop-down list, select either PDF or XPS Document. New fields appear in the lower portion of the Save As dialog box, as shown in Figure 2.11.

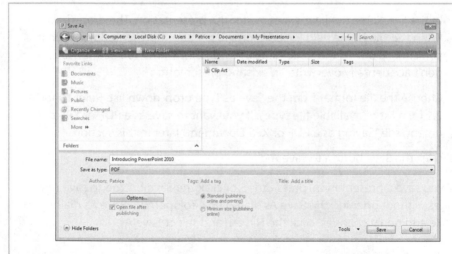

Figure 2.11   *New fields appear when you choose to save in a PDF or XPS format.*

5. Select the Open File After Publishing check box (the default) if you want to open your presentation in PDF or XPS format after saving.

6. If you want to create a document that's suitable for both online viewing and printing, select the Standard option button. If you just want people to view it online, select the Minimum Size option button.

7. Click the Options button for more options. Figure 2.12 shows the Options dialog box, which opens.

Figure 2.12 *PowerPoint offers many options for customizing PDF or XPS documents.*

8. Select any of the advanced options you want to use in this dialog box. Options include

   - **Range**—Choose whether to include all slides, the current slide only, the slides you've selected (on the Slides tab, for example), a specific range of slides, or the slides in a custom show.
   - **Publish What**—Publish slides, handouts, notes pages, or the outline view. If you select handouts, you can specify how many slides to include on each page (up to nine) and the orientation (horizontal or vertical). See Chapter 16, "Creating and Printing Presentation Materials," for more information about these options.
   - **Frame Slides**—Place a border around the slides.
   - **Include Hidden Slides**—Include slides you chose to hide on the Slide Show tab.
   - **Include Comments and Ink Markup**—Print comment pages and any ink markups you made on-screen with your presentation. This option is available only if your presentation contains comments or ink markups.

You can also include nonprinting information such as document properties, make your document ISO-compliant, or convert text to bitmaps if PowerPoint can't embed the applied fonts.

9. Click the OK button to return to the Save As dialog box.

10. Click the Save button to publish your document based on your specifications. If you chose to open your document after publishing, it opens in the appropriate application. For example, PDFs open in Adobe Reader; XPS documents require you to install Microsoft .NET Framework if you haven't already.

Changing to Another File Type

If you save your presentation in one file format and want to convert it to another, you can easily do so.

 LET ME TRY IT

Changing to Another File Type

To change your presentation's file type, follow these steps:

1. Click the File tab, and then click Save & Send to open Backstage view.

2. In the File Types section, click the Change File Type button.

3. Select one of the following file types that display on the right side of the screen (see Figure 2.13). See "Saving a Presentation" earlier in this chapter for more information about each of these file types:

    - Presentation
    - PowerPoint 97–2003 Presentation
    - OpenDocument Presentation
    - Template
    - PowerPoint Show
    - PowerPoint Picture Presentation
    - PNG Portable Network Graphics
    - JPEG File Interchange Format
    - Save as Another File Type

4. Click the Save As button to open the Save As dialog box (refer to Figure 2.10).

5. Enter a new file name for your presentation, if desired.

6. Click the Save button. PowerPoint saves your presentation in the format you specified.

Figure 2.13 *Quickly change a PowerPoint file type.*

Opening a Presentation

You can open an existing presentation in several different ways:

- Press Ctrl+O.

- Click the File tab, and click Open.

- Click the File tab, and click Recent. Select one of the presentations in the Recent Presentations list.

- Double-click the name of a PowerPoint presentation in Windows Explorer.

If you choose one of the first two methods, the Open dialog box displays, as shown in Figure 2.14.

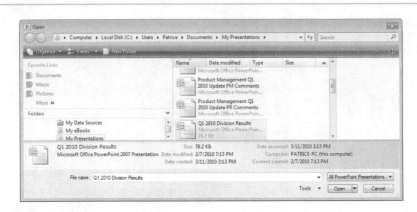

Figure 2.14 *The Open dialog box includes many additional features, including file management and search capabilities.*

LET ME TRY IT

Opening a Presentation

From the Open dialog box, follow these steps to open a file:

1. Navigate to the presentation you want to open.

2. If necessary, select the type of file you're looking for from the All PowerPoint Presentations drop-down list. PowerPoint searches for all PowerPoint presentations by default, but you can narrow this search to shows, templates, and so forth. This is useful if you have a large number of files on your computer.

3. Double-click the presentation you want to open. Alternatively, select the file, and click the Open button. PowerPoint opens the presentation.

Although opening a presentation directly is the most common action you'll take in the Open dialog box, clicking the down arrow to the right of the Open button provides several other options:

- **Open Read-Only**—Open the file as read-only. For example, if you've applied a password to the presentation, others can open it only as read-only. To change and save this file, click the **File** tab, choose **Save As** from the menu, and save with another name.

- **Open as Copy**—Open the presentation as a copy of the original. You might do this if you want to keep your original and create another presentation based on it.

- **Open in Browser**—Open a presentation in your default browser that was saved in a web page format (.HTM, .HTML, .HTX, or .ASP) from PowerPoint 2007 or earlier.

- **Open in Protected View**—Open file with restrictions to protect damage to your computer. Protected View is advisable for opening potentially dangerous files, such as those you download from an unknown source on the Internet.

- **Open and Repair**—Open and attempt to repair a corrupted presentation.

Exploring the Open Dialog Box

The Open dialog box includes several buttons that help you open and manage files.

The Organize button enables you to:

- Cut, copy, and paste files as well as undo and redo any changes you make.

- Select all files.

- Specify a layout for the Open dialog box, including the Navigation pane (the default), Details pane, and Preview pane.

- Delete and rename files.

- View and edit file properties.

The Views button enables you to view files in one of the following formats:

- **Icons**—View files and folders as icons. You have the choice of four sizes: extra large, large, medium, and small icons.

- **List**—List files and folders as small icons in columns.

- **Details**—List files and folders with small icons and information about size, type, and date last modified.

- **Tiles**—List files and folders as medium icons in columns with information about file size and type.

Renaming a Presentation

To rename a PowerPoint presentation, select it in the Open dialog box and do one of the following:

- Press F2.

Another option is to click the Organize button and select Delete from the shortcut menu. You can also delete a PowerPoint presentation in Windows Explorer. To do so, click the presentation file in Explorer, and press the Delete key.

- Right-click, and select Rename from the shortcut menu.
- Click the Organize button, and select Rename from the shortcut menu.
- Click the filename, wait a second, and then click it again.

PowerPoint converts the filename to an edit box in which you can overwrite the existing name.

Closing a Presentation

At times, you might want to close a presentation without exiting PowerPoint. This is particularly useful if you have many files open and want to save memory.

To close an open presentation, you can do one of the following:

- Click the File tab and select Close from the menu. If you haven't saved your file, PowerPoint prompts you to do so. If your presentation has been saved, PowerPoint closes it immediately.
- Click the Close [x] button in the upper-right corner of the screen to close an open presentation. Note, however, that if this is the only presentation you have open, this action also closes PowerPoint itself.
- Use the shortcut key Ctrl+W.

Deleting a Presentation

If you no longer need a PowerPoint presentation, you can delete it.

To delete a PowerPoint presentation you no longer want, select it in the Open dialog box, and press the Delete key on your keyboard. A warning dialog box appears, verifying that you want to delete the file and send it to the Recycle Bin. Click Yes to confirm the deletion.

Editing and Formatting Presentations

This chapter shows you how to create a custom presentation by modifying its themes and backgrounds.

3

Customizing Themes and Backgrounds

PowerPoint offers numerous tools to help you create presentations quickly and easily. There are times, however, when you need to go beyond these existing designs to create a truly unique presentation. Fortunately, PowerPoint makes it easy to customize its themes and backgrounds.

In this chapter, you learn the basics of customizing a theme's components, including colors, fonts, and effects. You can also listen to theme customization tips and watch videos that show you how to apply a new theme, customize a theme's color scheme, and customize PowerPoint backgrounds.

Applying Themes

When you create a presentation, PowerPoint automatically applies a theme, a coordinated set of colors, fonts, and effects. However, you can easily change the theme originally applied to your presentation in a matter of seconds.

See Chapter 2, "Creating a Basic Presentation," for a reminder about the components of a theme.

 SHOW ME Media 3.1—Applying a New Theme
Access this video file through your registered Web Edition at
my.safaribooksonline.com/9780132182553/media.

 LET ME TRY IT

Applying a New Theme

To apply a new theme to your presentation, follow these steps:

1. Click the Design tab to display potential themes in the Themes group (see Figure 3.1). This group box displays several potential themes, including your presentation's current theme to the far left.

Click to view more themes

Figure 3.1   *Select a theme or change fonts, colors, and graphic effects in the Themes*

2. If none of these themes suits your needs, click the down arrow on the right side of the Themes box to display a gallery of additional themes, as shown in Figure 3.2.

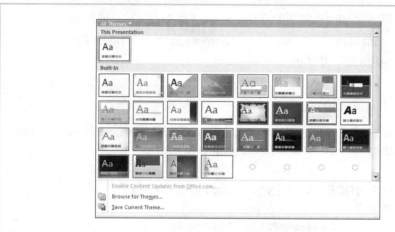

Figure 3.2   *Choose a theme that best matches your presentation.*

3. Pause your mouse over each theme to preview it in your presentation.

4. Select the theme you want to use. PowerPoint applies this new theme to your presentation.

To download additional themes from the web, go to Microsoft Office Online. Choose Search Office Online from the Themes gallery or go directly to http:/ /office.microsoft.com.

Applying Multiple Themes to a Single Presentation

PowerPoint enables you to use more than one theme in a presentation. Although it's easy to do this, you should carefully consider whether it's a good idea. Too many contrasting styles and designs can make your presentation confusing and difficult to follow. Even if you decide to apply multiple themes, your best bet is to keep them reasonably similar.

Multiple themes might be appropriate if you want to use one theme for your title slide and another for the rest of your presentation. Or if your presentation is divided into several distinct sections, you might want to use a separate theme for each. For example, let's say that you're giving a summary presentation about three divisions of a large corporation.

To apply a different theme to a group of slides, select the slides whose theme you want to change (on the Slides tab or Outline tab on the left side of the PowerPoint screen or in Slide Sorter view). On the Design tab, select the new theme in the Themes group. PowerPoint applies the new theme only to the selected slides. The unselected slides retain the original theme.

Alternatively, right-click the theme in the Themes group, and select Apply to Selected Slides from the menu.

Customizing Themes

If PowerPoint's built-in themes don't suit your needs, you can customize the fonts, colors, and effects in a theme and create your own theme.

 TELL ME MORE   Media 3.2—Customizing Themes
Access this audio recording through your registered Web Edition at
my.safaribooksonline.com/9780132182553/media.

Customizing Theme Color Schemes

Every PowerPoint theme includes a color scheme, a set of 12 coordinated colors used in the following parts of your presentation:

- Text and background (two light and two dark)
- Accents (six colors for graphs, charts, and other objects)
- Hyperlinks
- Followed hyperlinks

 SHOW ME   Media 3.3—Customizing Theme Color Schemes
Access this video file through your registered Web Edition at
my.safaribooksonline.com/9780132182553/media.

LET ME TRY IT

Applying a New Slide Color Scheme

If you don't like the colors in a particular theme, you can apply another color scheme.

To apply a new scheme, follow these steps:

1. Click the Colors button on the Design tab. A gallery of color schemes displays, as shown in Figure 3.3.

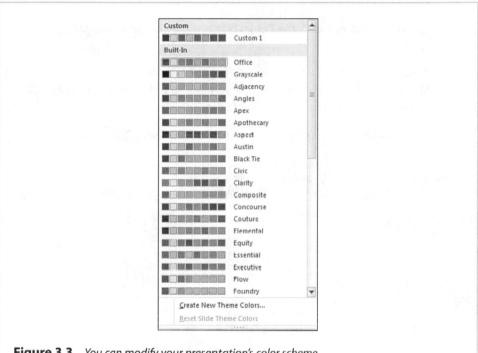

Figure 3.3   *You can modify your presentation's color scheme.*

2. Pause your mouse over each scheme to preview it on your presentation.

3. Click the scheme you prefer to apply it to your presentation.

LET ME TRY IT

Applying Multiple Color Schemes to a Single Presentation

PowerPoint also enables you to apply multiple color schemes within a single presentation. As with applying multiple themes, be sure that you have a good reason
to do this before applying many different colors to your presentation. To apply multiple color schemes to your presentation, follow these steps:

1. Select the slides to which you want to apply a separate color scheme. You
    can do this on the Slides tab or Outline tab on the left side of your screen
    or in Slide Sorter view.

2. On the Design tab, click the Colors button. The theme colors gallery dis-
    plays.

3. In the gallery, right-click the new color scheme, and choose Apply to Selected
    Slides. PowerPoint applies the color scheme to only the selected slides. The
    unselected slides retain the original color scheme.

To return to a single color scheme, select that scheme from the gallery.

Although the capability to apply multiple color schemes to your presentation
adds flexibility and creativity, be sure not to overdo it. Consider carefully before
applying more than one color scheme to verify that your presentation is still
consistent and readable.

 LET ME TRY IT

Creating a Custom Color Scheme

Occasionally, you might want to customize the individual colors in a color scheme.
For example, you might like a particular scheme but want to modify one of the
text/background colors. Or you might want to use colors that match your company's logo or other design elements.

To create a custom color scheme, follow these steps:

1. On the Design tab, click the Colors button to open the colors gallery.

2. In the gallery, select Create New Theme Colors to open the Create New
    Theme Colors dialog box. Figure 3.4 shows this dialog box.

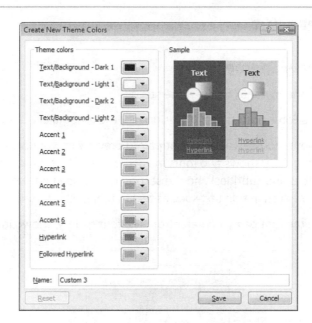

Figure 3.4 *Change the color of certain areas of your presentation to customize it.*

3. In the dialog box, select theme colors for text, backgrounds, accents, and hyperlinks from the drop-down lists. The Sample box previews your selections.

4. Enter a name for your new color scheme.

5. When you're happy with your choices, click the Save button. Your new color scheme now displays as a custom color scheme, available for selection from the gallery.

To edit custom color schemes, right-click the appropriate color scheme in the gallery, and select Edit from the shortcut menu. Make your changes in the Edit Theme Colors dialog box, and click Save.

To delete a custom color scheme, right-click the appropriate color scheme in the gallery, and select Delete from the shortcut menu. Click Yes to confirm the deletion. The custom scheme no longer displays in the gallery.

Customizing Theme Fonts

Although each theme comes with coordinating fonts, you can apply new fonts to your presentation—or create your own.

LET ME TRY IT

Applying New Theme Fonts

To apply new theme fonts, follow these steps:

1. Click the Fonts button on the Design tab. The font gallery displays.

2. Pause your mouse over each font pair to preview on your presentation. The font gallery shows two fonts in each pair. The first is for headings (both titles and subtitles) and the second is for body text, which includes all text other than title text such as text in tables, charts, and so on.

3. Choose the font pair you prefer from the font gallery, shown in Figure 3.5.

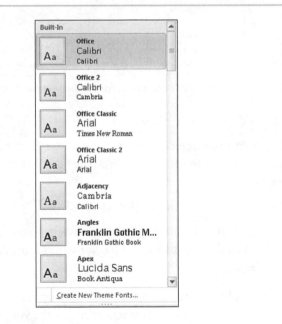

Figure 3.5 *Select the fonts you want to use in your presentation.*

 LET ME TRY IT

Creating New Theme Fonts

To create new theme fonts, follow these steps:

1. On the Design tab, click the Fonts button.

2. In the font gallery, click Create New Theme Fonts to open the Create New Theme Fonts dialog box. Figure 3.6 illustrates this dialog box. If you enable multiple language support, this dialog box might contain additional options.

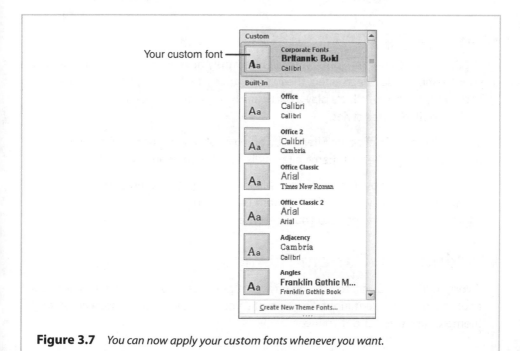

Figure 3.6   *Select your own heading and body text fonts.*

3. Select a new Heading Font and a new Body Font from the drop-down lists. The Sample box previews your selections.

4. Enter a name for your custom font pair.

5. Click the Save button. Your new custom font pair now displays in the font gallery (see Figure 3.7).

Figure 3.7   *You can now apply your custom fonts whenever you want.*

Be sure that any new fonts you apply are readable on your slides. Theme fonts are designed to be easy to read with all theme color schemes.

 **LET ME TRY IT**

Editing Custom Fonts

To edit custom fonts, follow these steps:

1. Right-click the custom font pair you want to edit in the font gallery, and choose Edit from the shortcut menu. The Edit Theme Fonts dialog box displays, which is nearly identical to the Create New Theme Fonts dialog box.

2. Make your changes in the Edit Theme Fonts dialog box.

3. Click the Save button.

To delete custom fonts, right-click the custom font pair in the font gallery, and choose Delete from the shortcut menu. Click Yes when prompted to confirm. Your custom fonts no longer display in the font gallery.

Customizing Theme Effects

In addition to colors and fonts, you can also apply new effects that coordinate with your theme. These effects affect the look of tables, text, charts, diagrams, shapes, and pictures. Theme effects play a particularly important role with objects to which you've applied shape styles.

On the Design tab, click the Effects button to apply a new theme effect to your presentation. A gallery of theme effects displays, as shown in Figure 3.8.

Pause your mouse over each effect to preview it on your presentation. Note that changes display only if your slide content is affected by theme effects. Click the effect you prefer to apply it to your presentation.

Working with Custom Themes

If you modify the fonts, colors, and effects of a theme, you might want to save it to apply to future presentations. For example, you might want to create a custom theme to use throughout your company.

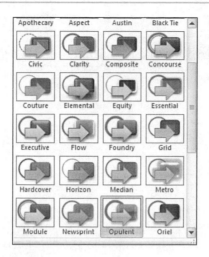

Figure 3.8   *Select a new theme effect to apply to your presentation.*

 LET ME TRY IT

Creating and Saving a Custom Theme

To create a custom theme, follow these steps:

1. Make any theme changes such as changes to your theme's colors, fonts, and effects.

2. On the Design tab, click the down arrow to the right of the Themes box.

3. Select Save Current Theme from the gallery. The Save Current Theme dialog box opens, as shown in Figure 3.9.

4. Enter a file name for your new theme.

5. Click the Save button to save your theme as an Office Theme file type (*.thmx) stored in the Document Themes folder.

Your theme is now available to select from the gallery.

In addition to creating custom themes, you can also create custom layouts. See Chapter 19, "Customizing PowerPoint," for more information.

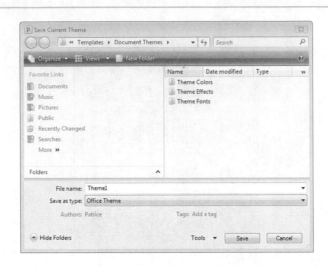

Figure 3.9 *Save your custom theme for later reuse.*

Applying and Customizing Backgrounds

You can further customize your theme by applying, removing, and modifying its background. In addition to specific color backgrounds, you can also add special background effects such as shading, patterns, textures, and pictures to your presentation.

 SHOW ME   Media 3.4—Applying and Customizing Backgrounds
Access this video file through your registered Web Edition at
my.safaribooksonline.com/9780132182553/media.

Applying a Background Style

Applying a new background style is an easy way to change the appearance of your presentation.

 LET ME TRY IT

Applying a New Background Style

To apply a background style to your presentation, follow these steps:

1. On the Design tab, click the Background Styles button. A gallery displays with 12 possible background styles designed to work with your presentation theme (see Figure 3.10).

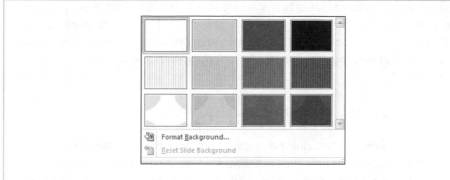

Figure 3.10   *For added effect, apply a background to jazz up your presentation.*

2. Pause over each style to preview it on your open slide.

3. Click your preferred style to apply it automatically to your presentation.

Customizing a Background

If none of the background styles suits your needs, you can customize a background style. To do so, select Format Background in the gallery to open the Format Background dialog box, as shown in Figure 3.11.

Figure 3.11   *Advanced options enable you to further customize your background.*

The Format Background dialog box is nearly identical to the Format Shape dialog box. Select your background preferences in this dialog box, and click the Apply to All button. The new background displays on your presentation slides, overriding the theme's background. See Chapter 10, "Working with Shapes," for more information.

Omitting Background Graphics

If you want to omit the background graphics included with the template you applied to your presentation, click the Hide Background Graphics check box on the Design tab. For example, clicking this check box on a presentation whose theme or template includes pictures or shapes removes these objects but retains the original colors.

Resetting a Background

If you customize your background and decide you prefer the original, you can easily reset it. To reset the background to the theme default, click the Background Styles button on the Design tab and select Reset Slide Background.

This chapter shows you how to use text and text
effects to enhance your presentation.

4

Working with Text

Adding and formatting text is a straightforward process in PowerPoint. If the standard formatting isn't enough, however, PowerPoint also offers sophisticated text formatting and customization. In addition, it automates many formatting tasks if you're in a hurry or have limited design skills.

In this chapter, you learn how to add and format text, text boxes, bullets, numbered lists, and WordArt, and spell check the text in your presentation. You can also listen to advice on the best way to format text for maximum impact and watch videos that show you how to insert a text box, create and format WordArt, and run a spelling check.

Adding Text to a Text or Title Placeholder

In PowerPoint, the most common place to add text is in a text placeholder or title placeholder that's part of a PowerPoint slide layout. See Chapter 2, "Creating a Basic Presentation," for more information about adding slide layouts that contain placeholders.

Figure 4.1 shows a sample of each type of placeholder.

You can also add text in a text box, table, WordArt object, chart, shape, or SmartArt graphic.

To move or resize a placeholder, see "Moving and Resizing a Text Box" later in this chapter.

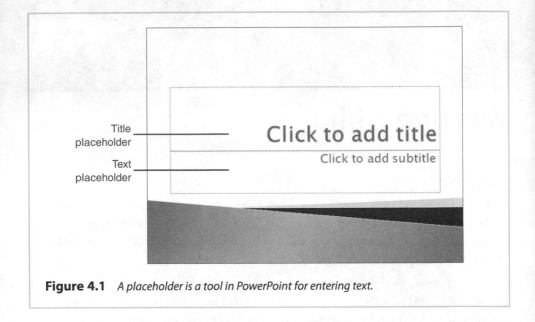

Figure 4.1   *A placeholder is a tool in PowerPoint for entering text.*

Using Text Boxes

Use a text box when you need to add text to a slide outside its original text place-holders or when you need to frame special text. Text boxes are also useful for wrapping text around an object.

SHOW ME   Media 4.1—Inserting a Text Box
Access this video file through your registered Web Edition at
my.safaribooksonline.com/9780132182553/media.

Inserting a Text Box

To insert a text box, on the Insert tab, click the Text Box button; then click where you want to place the text box on the slide, and start typing.

Figure 4.2 shows a text box.

Moving and Resizing a Text Box

If your text box isn't exactly right when you first create it, you can

- Position the mouse over one of the text box handles to resize it. The mouse pointer displays as an arrow when you resize.

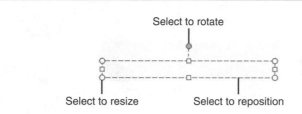

Figure 4.2 *A text box calls attention to something you want to say and lets you place the text exactly where you want it.*

- Position the mouse over the text box outline, and drag it to a new location. The mouse pointer displays as a crosshair when you reposition.

- Position the mouse over the rotation handle (small green circle at the top of the text box) to rotate the box. The mouse pointer displays as an open circle when you rotate.

You can also move and resize text and title placeholders and WordArt objects using these techniques.

Formatting a Text Box

You can format text in a text box as you would any other text, including formatting the font, font size, color, and style. See "Formatting Text," later in this chapter.

Additionally, the Text Box tab on the Format Shape dialog box offers other formatting options. To view these options, right-click a text box, and select Format Shape from the menu that displays. The Format Shape dialog box opens, as shown in Figure 4.3.

The Text Box tab of this dialog box offers a variety of formatting choices:

- **Vertical Alignment**—Align your text in the text box. Options include Top, Middle, Bottom, Top Centered, Middle Centered, and Bottom Centered. The Centered options move the text to the horizontal center of the text box, whereas the other options do not. This is different from justification: A right-justified block of text moves to the center when you choose a Centered option, but the text remains right-justified.

- **Text Direction**—Set the direction of the text. Options include Horizontal, Rotate All Text 90°, Rotate All Text 270°, and Stacked. If you select Stacked, the Order of Lines option displays. Choices include Right-to-left or Left-to-right.

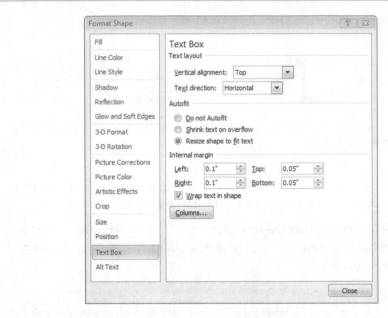

Figure 4.3   *You can make several text box customizations.*

- **Autofit**—Set the autofit options of the text box. You can choose not to autofit, to shrink overflow text so that it fits in the text box, or to resize the text box to fit the text exactly. For example, if you have one word inside a text box, it reduces the text box to a size that precisely surrounds that word.

- **Internal Margin**—Determine how much open space—or internal margin—to display in the text box. You can select fractions of inches in the Left, Right, Top, and Bottom fields.

- **Wrap Text in Shape**—Choose this option when you place text within the internal margins of a text box. If you don't, the text displays straight across the box, rather than neatly inside it.

- **Columns**—Open the Columns dialog box, in which you can set the number of columns and their spacing.

You can also apply formatting to the text inside a text box. See "Formatting Text" next in this chapter for more information.

Formatting Text

PowerPoint's themes and templates include colors, fonts, and other formatting parameters designed to work well and look good together. In this way, PowerPoint frees you to focus on your message. For maximum flexibility, however, PowerPoint offers numerous options for text formatting and customization.

 TELL ME MORE   Media 4.2—Formatting Text
Access this audio recording through your registered Web Edition at
my.safaribooksonline.com/9780132182553/media.

You can format text in several ways:

- Use the options available in the Font and Paragraph groups on the Home tab.

- Use the Font and Paragraph dialog boxes to make a number of changes in one place and to set defaults. Open these dialog boxes by clicking the dialog box launcher (down arrow) in the lower-right corner of the Font and Paragraph groups.

- Apply text formatting individually by right-clicking the target text and using options on the Mini Toolbar.

Enhancing Presentation Text

The following are some changes you might consider to enhance the presentation of your slides:

> If you type more text into a placeholder than it can show at once, PowerPoint uses its AutoFit feature to shrink the text to fit. AutoFit shrinks text only so much, though, to prevent it from becoming hard to read.

- **Enlarge or reduce font size**—If you have too little text on a slide, you can increase the font size to fill the page. You can also shrink the text in a placeholder so that it can hold more text. Be sure, however, that the font size is still appropriate for the presentation. Verify that all text is still readable on the slide, and if you're going to do an onscreen presentation, that it isn't too small to be seen by viewers at the back of a room.

- **Replace one font with another**—You might have a particular font you prefer to use in presentations. Be careful, however, not to be too creative with unusual fonts. You want to be sure that everyone can read your presentation clearly.

- **Add boldface, italics, or color**—Use these to emphasize a point with a certain word or words.

- **Add text effects**—Apply text effects such as shadow, reflection, glow, bevel, 3-D rotation, and warping.

Using the Formatting Tools on the Home Tab

The Home tab (see Figure 4.4) includes an extensive collection of text formatting tools.

Figure 4.4   *The Home tab includes buttons for commonly used text effects.*

Table 4.1 lists the formatting options in the Font group on the Home tab.

Table 4.1   Font Group Buttons

Name	Description
Font	Apply a font to the selected text.
Font Size	Set the selected text's size. Choose any common size from 8 to 96 points, or type any size in the edit box.
Increase Font Size	Increase the selected text's size by a few points.
Decrease Font Size	Decrease the selected text's size by a few points.
Clear All Formatting	Clear all formatting from selected text.
Bold	Bold the selected text.
Italic	Italicize the selected text.
Underline	Underline the selected text.
Text Shadow	Apply a shadow to the selected text.
Strikethrough	Draw a line through selected text.
Character Spacing	Adjust spacing between characters.
Change Case	Change the case of the selected text. Options include Sentence case, lowercase, UPPERCASE, Capitalize Each Word, and tOGGLE cASE.
Font Color	Apply the color you choose from the drop-down list to selected text.

To apply one of these formatting elements, select the text you want to format and click the appropriate button. Clicking the Bold, Italic, Underline, Text Shadow, or Strikethrough button a second time acts as a toggle and removes the formatting.

With the Font drop-down list, you can preview what each font actually looks like.

Remember that an unusual use of case might be difficult to read, particularly uppercase and toggle case. With text, go for readability and clarity.

Table 4.2 lists the formatting options in the Paragraph group on the Home tab.

Table 4.2   Paragraph Group Buttons

Name	Description
Bullets	Apply bullets to the selected text.
Numbering	Apply automatic numbering to the selected text.
Decrease List Level	Decrease the indent level of the selected text.
Increase List Level	Increase the indent level of the selected text.
Line Spacing	Determine number of spaces between lines, such as single or double spacing.
Align Text Left	Align text to the object's left margin.
Center	Center text within the object.
Align Text Right	Align text to the object's right margin.
Justify	Space words and letters within words so that text touches both margins in the object.
Columns	Set the number of columns to apply to the selected text.
Text Direction	Specify directional formatting, including horizontal, rotated, and stacked text options.
Align Text	Align text to the top, middle, or bottom of the text box, with an option to center as well.
Convert to SmartArt Graphic	Convert text to a SmartArt diagram.

Formatting Text with Options in the Font Dialog Box

The Font dialog box offers some advanced formatting options not available on the Home tab.

 LET ME TRY IT

Formatting Text with the Font Dialog Box

To format selected text with the options in the Font dialog box, follow these steps:

1. On the Home tab, click the dialog box launcher (down arrow) in the lower-right corner of the Font group. The Font dialog box displays, as shown in Figure 4.5.

2. In the Latin Text Font list, choose the font you want to use. Scroll down the list to see the available fonts.

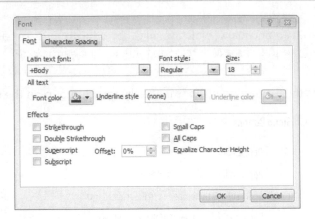

Figure 4.5   *Make font changes quickly with the Font dialog box.*

3. In the Font Style list, choose whether the font should be regular (neither bold nor italic), bold, italic, or bold and italic.

4. In the Size list, choose a preset size from 8 to 96 points, or enter a specific point size in the box.

5. Choose a color from the palette that is displayed by the Font Color drop-down list. For additional color choices, click More Colors from the palette to open the Colors dialog box. See Chapter 10, "Working with Shapes," for more information about the Colors dialog box.

6. If you want to underline text, select an Underline Style and Underline Color from the drop-down lists.

7. Apply any other effects you want by selecting the check box next to any of the following:

    • **Strikethrough**—Place a horizontal line through the selected text.
    • **Double Strikethrough**—Place two horizontal lines through the selected text.
    • **Superscript**—Raise the text above the baseline and reduces the font size. Set the Offset to 30%, which you can adjust.
    • **Subscript**—Lower the text below the baseline and reduces the font size. Set the Offset to 25%, which you can adjust.

    Offset refers to the percentage the text displays above or below the baseline, which is the invisible line on which the characters sit. For example, because subscript text is below the baseline, its offset will be a negative number.

    • **Small Caps**—Format the text in small caps.
    • **All Caps**—Capitalize the selected text.

- **Equalize Character Height**—Make all letters the same height. For additional character spacing options, select the Character Spacing tab in the Font dialog box.

8. Click the OK button to close the dialog box and apply the font formatting.

Formatting Text with Options in the Paragraph Dialog Box

The Paragraph dialog box offers some advanced formatting options not available directly on the Home tab. To open this dialog box, select the text you want to format and click the down arrow in the lower-right corner of the Paragraph group on the Home tab. The Paragraph dialog box appears, as shown in Figure 4.6.

In this dialog box, you can

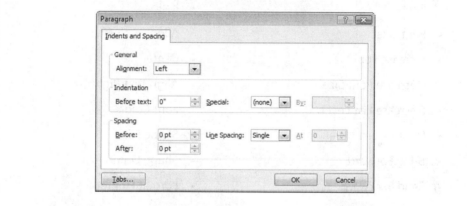

Figure 4.6   *Set alignment, indentation, and spacing in the Paragraph dialog box.*

- Set alignment, including right-aligned, left-aligned, centered, justified, and distributed text.

- Specify indentation requirements such as hanging or first-line indentation.

- Set line spacing. When a slide looks crowded or too sparse, the *line spacing,* or the amount of space between lines of text, might be at fault. Adjust line spacing until the text looks right.

- Establish tab stop parameters by clicking the Tabs button and setting the tab stop position.

Formatting Text with the Mini Toolbar

To access the Mini Toolbar, right-click the text you want to format. The Mini Toolbar appears (see Figure 4.7) just below a menu that includes options for Font, Paragraph, Bullets, and Numbering.

Figure 4.7   *The Mini Toolbar enables you to quickly access common text formatting options.*

The Mini Toolbar contains selected text formatting buttons, most of which you should be familiar with from the Font and Paragraph groups on the Home tab. These include the following:

- Font
- Font Size
- Increase Font Size
- Decrease Font Size
- Decrease List Level
- Increase List Level
- Bring Forward
- Send Backward
- Bold
- Italic
- Align Text Left
- Center
- Align Text Right
- Font Color
- Shape Fill
- Shape Outline
- Format Painter

Using Bullets

Creating a bulleted list is a common PowerPoint task, but one you should choose judiciously. A PowerPoint presentation that's just a series of slides with bullet lists isn't nearly as effective as one that uses a combination of graphic and visual elements for emphasis. You can add a bulleted list to any slide that contains text and within a table.

Consider using a list-style SmartArt graphic instead of a bullet list for greater visual impact. See Chapter 11, "Working with SmartArt," for more information about SmartArt options.

To format text as a bulleted list, select the text, and on the Home tab, click the Bullets button in the Paragraph group. PowerPoint uses the theme's default bullet style, but you can change to another bullet style if you want.

POINT-COUNTERPOINT   Media 4.3—Using Text and Bullets: Is Less Really More?

Access this audio recording through your registered Web Edition at **my.safaribooksonline.com/9780132182553/media.**

LET ME TRY IT

Changing the Bullet Style of Selected Text

To change the bullet style of selected text, follow these steps:

1. On the Home tab, click the down arrow to the right of the Bullets button.

2. Select Bullets and Numbering in the gallery that displays. The Bullets and Numbering dialog box opens, as shown in Figure 4.8.

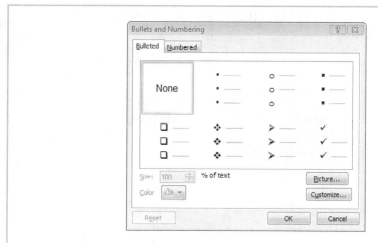

Figure 4.8   *You can choose from many different bullet types.*

3. On the Bulleted tab, select one of the seven bullet styles that appear. Choosing None removes the bulleted list.

4. Set Size as a percentage of the text. The default varies but is typically 75% or 100%. Lower the number to reduce the size; increase the number to enlarge the size.

5. Choose a color from the Color drop-down list. For additional color choices, click More Colors to open the Colors dialog box. See Chapter 10, "Working with Shapes," for more information about the Colors dialog box.

6. Click the OK button to apply the bullet style.

To change the bullets in your entire presentation, do so on the master slide. See Chapter 19, "Customizing PowerPoint," for more information.

Applying Picture Bullets

If none of the seven default bullet styles suits your needs, you can also use picture bullets or character bullets, which display a small graphic as the bullet point.

 LET ME TRY IT

Applying Picture Bullets to a List

To apply a picture bullet to a selected list, follow these steps:

1. On the Home tab, click the down arrow to the right of the Bullets button.

2. Select Bullets and Numbering in the gallery to open the Bullets and Numbering dialog box.

3. Click the Picture button to open the Picture Bullet dialog box (see Figure 4.9).

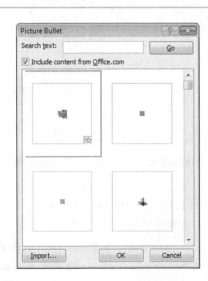

Figure 4.9 *A picture bullet can enhance a creative presentation.*

4. Select a bullet from the available options. Alternatively, enter a keyword in the Search Text field and click the Go button to locate matching bullets.

5. Click the OK button to apply the picture bullet.

> To import your own picture bullets (such as a portion of a logo or an image you already use on a website or other company literature), click the Import button to open the Add Clips to Organizer dialog box. It's best if your bullet is small— between 10 and 20 pixels square. PowerPoint shrinks larger images to fit, but the larger the image, the less desirable the result.

Applying Character Bullets

You can choose a character bullet for your bulleted list if you want something a little different. A character bullet uses one of the symbols in the Symbols dialog box as a bullet point in your presentation.

 LET ME TRY IT

Applying Character Bullets to a List

To apply character bullets to a selected list, follow these steps:

1. On the Home tab, click the down arrow to the right of the Bullets button.

2. Select Bullets and Numbering in the gallery to open the Bullets and Numbering dialog box.

3. Click the Customize button to open the Symbol dialog box, as shown in Figure 4.10.

4. Select a font from the Font drop-down list (Wingdings, Webdings, or ZDingbats are good options), and choose the bullet you want from the display area.

5. Click the OK button to apply the character bullet.

To speed up the process, you can view and choose from character bullets you've recently applied to a bullet list from the Recently Used Symbols section.

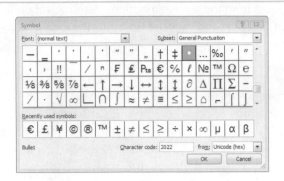

Figure 4.10 *Use a font such as Wingdings for character bullets.*

Using Numbered Lists

For a sequence of items, creating a numbered list is a good alternative to a bulleted list. For example, a series of procedural steps would work well in a numbered list. You can create numbered lists with actual numbers, Roman numerals, or letters of the alphabet.

To format text as a numbered list, select the text, and on the Home tab, click the Numbering button. PowerPoint applies the default numbering to your text.

 **LET ME TRY IT**

Changing the Numbering Style of Selected Text

If the default numbered list formatting doesn't suit your needs, you can choose an alternative. To change the numbering style of selected text, follow these steps:

1. On the Home tab, click the down arrow to the right of the Numbering button.

2. Select Bullets and Numbering in the gallery that displays. The Bullets and Numbering dialog box opens.

3. On the Numbered tab, as shown in Figure 4.11, select one of the seven number styles that display. Choosing None removes the numbered list.

4. Set Size as a percentage of the text. The default varies but is typically 75% or 100%. Lower the number to reduce the size; increase the number to enlarge the size.

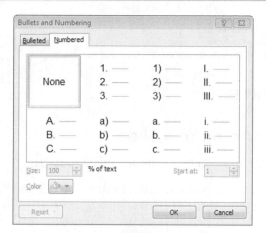

Figure 4.11   *A numbered list can put a series of items in order.*

5. Choose a color from the Color drop-down list. For additional color choices, click More Colors to open the Colors dialog box. See Chapter 10, "Working with Shapes," for more information about the Colors dialog box.

6. If you want to start numbering at something other than 1 (or lettering at something other than *a*), select a starting value in the Start At field.

7. Click the OK button to apply the numbering.

Using WordArt

WordArt lets you create special text effects such as shadowed, rotated, stretched, or multicolored text. PowerPoint treats WordArt as both an object and text, so you can apply object formatting such as fills and 3-D, and apply text formatting. You can also check the spelling in your WordArt text.

SHOW ME   Media 4.4—Using WordArt
Access this video file through your registered Web Edition at
my.safaribooksonline.com/9780132182553/media.

Be careful not to overuse WordArt in your presentation, or it can become cluttered and confusing. Use WordArt only for emphasis.

Inserting WordArt

Inserting WordArt is a simple, three-step process.

 **LET ME TRY IT**

Inserting WordArt on Your Slide

To insert a WordArt image in your slide, follow these steps:

1. On the Insert tab, click the WordArt button. The WordArt Gallery displays, as shown in Figure 4.12.

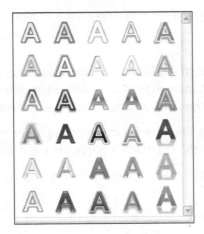

Figure 4.12   *Preview WordArt styles before you choose one.*

2. Click the WordArt style you prefer. A text box displays on your slide.

3. Replace the placeholder text with text that you want to format using WordArt.

> To move or resize a WordArt object, see "Moving and Resizing a Text Box" earlier in this chapter.

Formatting WordArt

If you want to change your initial WordArt selection, you can select a different style or customize it. Many WordArt formatting options are similar to those for shapes.

See Chapter 10 for more information about these options.

To format WordArt, select a WordArt object and click the Drawing Tools—Format tab. Figure 4.13 shows the WordArt Styles group, where you can do the following:

- Click the down arrow to the right of the WordArt Styles that displays in the group. The WordArt gallery opens, where you can apply a new WordArt style to selected text or all text in the shape. You can also click the Clear WordArt option to remove WordArt formatting.

- Click the down arrow to the right of the Text Fill button to choose another theme color, remove the fill color, or apply gradients and textures.

- Click the down arrow to the right of the Text Outline button to choose an outline color, remove the outline, or specify a weight or dash type.

- Click the down arrow to the right of the Text Effects button to apply special effects such as shadows, reflections, glows, bevels, 3-D rotation, and transforms (unusual text formations).

Figure 4.13 *Format your WordArt for additional emphasis.*

If you click the Text Fill, Text Outline, or Text Effects button directly, you apply the default formatting. You must select the down arrow to the right of these buttons to view all available options.

You can also apply the formatting options in the WordArt Styles group to other text, not just WordArt.

Proofing Your Text

Creating a quality, error-free, and easy-to-read presentation is a natural objective when you use PowerPoint. Fortunately, PowerPoint offers a spelling checker and a built-in thesaurus for finding just the right word. Keep in mind that, although an automated tool can help you catch errors, it isn't foolproof and doesn't take the place of thorough proofreading by a person.

You'll find PowerPoint's proofing tools on the Review tab. See Chapter 8, "Reviewing Presentations," for more information about the other tools on the Review tab.

Setting Spelling Check Options

To set options for spelling, click the File tab, select Options and go to the Proofing tab on the PowerPoint Options dialog box, as shown in Figure 4.14.

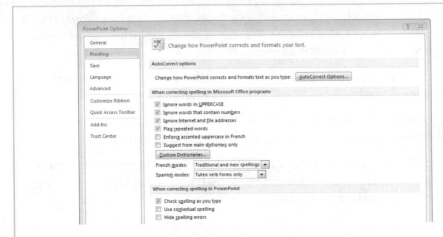

Figure 4.14   *You can set several spell-checking options.*

You can choose any of the following spelling options:

- **Ignore Words in UPPERCASE**—Don't check spelling of any word that is all uppercase.
- **Ignore Words That Contain Numbers**—Don't check spelling of any word that includes a number.
- **Ignore Internet and File Addresses**—Don't flag Internet addresses, such as www.microsoft.com, as spelling errors.
- **Flag Repeated Words**—Highlight duplicate words, such as "the the."
- **Suggest from Main Dictionary Only**—Suggest only alternative spellings from your designated main dictionary. Click the Custom Dictionaries link to select from the dictionary list.
- **Check Spelling as You Type**—Place a red squiggly line under each suspected spelling error as you type it.
- **Use Contextual Spelling**—Check spelling in context with surrounding text.
- **Hide Spelling Errors**—Don't display red underlining for suspected spelling errors.

Options for AutoCorrect formatting and languages such as French and Spanish are also available. See Chapter 19, "Customizing PowerPoint," for more information.

Checking Your Spelling

After you set the spelling options you want, you can spell check your presentation.

If you set the option to have PowerPoint check spelling as you type, you know immediately when you've possibly misspelled a word. PowerPoint places a red squiggly line under all suspected misspellings, as Figure 4.15 shows. You can either fix the error yourself or right-click to see some suggested alternatives from which to choose.

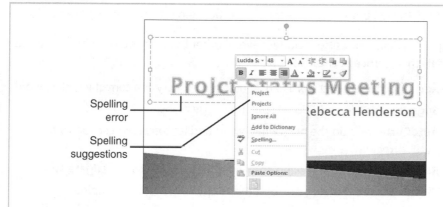

Figure 4.15 *When you right-click a spelling error, PowerPoint suggests some possible alternative spellings.*

You can also spell check your entire presentation at once.

 SHOW ME   Media 4.5—Running a Spelling Check
Access this video file through your registered Web Edition at
my.safaribooksonline.com/9780132182553/media.

 LET ME TRY IT

Running a Spelling Check

To run a spelling check, follow these steps:

1. On the Review tab, click the Spelling button. Alternatively, press F7. When PowerPoint encounters an error, it displays the Spelling dialog box.

2. Review the word in the Not in Dictionary field that the spelling checker suspects is misspelled.

3. If the word is correct, click the Ignore button (to ignore this instance of the word) or the Ignore All button (to ignore all instances of the word).

4. If the word is misspelled and the suggestion in the Change To field is correct, click the Change button (to change the individual misspelled word) or the Change All button (to change all instances of this misspelled word).

5. If the word is misspelled and the suggestion in the Change To field is not correct, enter the correct spelling in the Change To field and click either the Change button or Change All button.

6. Continue steps 3 through 6 until you finish checking the spelling. PowerPoint displays a dialog box that informs you the process is complete.

7. Click the OK button to close the dialog box and return to your presentation.

The Spelling dialog box also includes several other buttons you can choose during the spell-check process. These include

- **Add**—Add the suspect word to the custom dictionary as a correctly spelled word.
- **Suggest**—Provide additional spelling suggestions.
- **AutoCorrect**—Add the misspelled word and its corrected version to the AutoCorrect list.
- **Resume**—Continue checking spelling after you stop to investigate an error.
- **Close**—Close the dialog box before the spelling check is complete.
- **Options**—Open the PowerPoint Options dialog box to the Proofing tab, where you can specify spelling options.

Looking Up a Synonym in the Thesaurus

If you ever have trouble coming up with just the right word, PowerPoint can help you with its thesaurus.

 LET ME TRY IT

Looking Up a Synonym

To find a synonym in the thesaurus, follow these steps:

1. Select the word you want to look up. If you can't think of the exact word, type a word that's close to it.

2. On the Review tab, click the Thesaurus button. The Research task pane opens.

3. Pause the mouse over the word you want to use. A down arrow displays to the right of this word.

4. Click the down arrow and select Insert from the shortcut menu that displays. PowerPoint places the new word in your presentation.

A quick way to find a synonym is to right-click the word in question and choose Synonym from the menu. A list of possible synonyms displays.

This chapter shows you how to format and rearrange objects on your PowerPoint slides and how to organize entire presentations.

Formatting and Organizing Objects, Slides, and Presentations

After you create a presentation, you most likely will want to modify its appearance. Fortunately, it's easy to modify slides, objects, and entire presentations in PowerPoint.

In this chapter, you learn about common formatting techniques such as cut, copy, and paste, and more sophisticated formatting options that enable you to create a truly custom presentation. You can also listen to advice on how to approach object formatting and watch videos that show you how to apply paste options, arrange objects, and use the Slide Sorter view.

Formatting Objects

In PowerPoint, an *object* refers to any of the components you include on your slides, such as shapes, pictures, text boxes, placeholders, WordArt, and so forth.

PowerPoint offers numerous ways to manage and format your objects, including several automatic formatting options. Your biggest challenge is to choose the right formatting effects among so many varied options.

Manipulating Objects

You can easily cut, copy, paste, move, and resize PowerPoint objects.

Cutting an Object

To cut a selected object, click the Cut button in the Clipboard group on the Home tab or press Ctrl+X. To cut more than one object, hold down the Shift key while selecting objects, or drag a selection box around all the objects with the mouse.

If you cut something by mistake, click the Undo button to retrieve it.

Copying an Object

To copy a selected object, click the Copy button on the Home tab or press Ctrl+C.

> To copy the attributes of one object and apply them to another object, use the Format Painter button on the Home tab. For example, if you select an object with 3-D effects, click the Format Pointer button, and then select another object so that new object gets the same 3-D effects.

LET ME TRY IT

Pasting an Object

To paste a cut or copied object, follow these steps:

1. Click the down arrow below the Paste button to open the Paste Options box, as shown in Figure 5.1, where you can preview the appearance of the pasted object on your slide. If you don't want to preview, click the Paste button on the Home tab or press Ctrl+V and skip to Step 4.

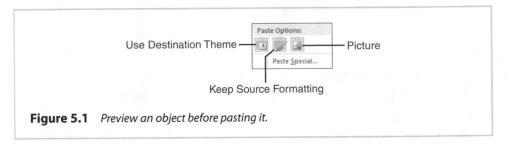

Figure 5.1   *Preview an object before pasting it.*

2. Pause your mouse over each option button to preview what the pasted object would look like on your slide before actually pasting it into your presentation. Depending on what you paste and the context in which you paste it, any of the following option buttons could display in the Paste Options box:

    • **Keep Source Formatting**—Format the object as it was formatted in the location from which you copied it.

    • **Use Destination Theme**—Apply the current theme formatting to the object. This is the default when you paste the object directly.

    • **Picture**—Convert the pasted item to a picture. To select a specific picture format, click the Paste Special link in the Paste Options box and choose a format from the Paste Special dialog box.

- **Keep Text Only**—Remove all formatting from pasted text. This displays only when you paste text without having a text placeholder open first. PowerPoint creates a placeholder for the text as it pastes it.

3. Click a button in the Paste Options box to paste using the selected paste option.

> PowerPoint's Clipboard can store 24 different items. To see what the Clipboard contains, click the down arrow to the right of the Clipboard group on the Home tab to open the Clipboard task pane. You can also select which item to paste on this pane.

4. After you paste an object, the Paste Options button displays to its lower-right side. Click the Paste Options button to view additional formatting buttons, similar to what you viewed when clicking the down arrow below the Paste button on the Home tab. You can also apply any of these options after pasting.

> If the Paste Options button doesn't display below a pasted object, verify that this feature is active. To do so, click the File tab, select Options, and go to the Advanced tab on the PowerPoint Options dialog box. Select the Show Paste Options Buttons check box and click OK.

 SHOW ME   Media 5.1—Pasting an Object
Access this video file through your registered Web Edition at
my.safaribooksonline.com/9780132182553/media.

Moving an Object

To move an object, select it and drag to a new location.

Resizing an Object

When you select an object, resizing handles display around its edges. Figure 5.2 illustrates these handles.

Resizing Handles

Drag the handles with the mouse to make the object smaller, larger, or a different shape. Notice that depending on which sizing handle you select—a corner or interior handle—you can either enlarge the entire object or change its shape. To resize the object proportionately so that it keeps its shape, press the Shift key and drag a corner handle.

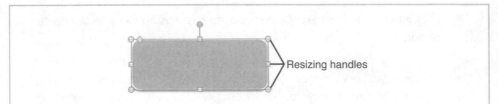

Figure 5.2   *Resizing handles make it easier to adjust the size and shape of your object.*

Arranging Objects

If your presentation includes multiple objects, you might need to order, group, align, or rotate them to achieve your desired effect. Using the tools available when you click the Arrange button on the Home tab, you can maintain complete control over the appearance of your presentation objects.

These tools are also available on the contextual Drawing Tools—Format tab that displays when you select an object.

Setting Object Order

When you place two or more objects on a slide, you might want part of one to display on top of part of another. This is called *layering* the objects. You can do this for pure visual effect or to indicate that the overlapping objects have a relationship to each other. PowerPoint lets you control each object's layering, so if two objects are layered and you want the one below to display on top, you can change it.

 LET ME TRY IT

Arranging an Object's Layer Order

To specify an object's layer order in relation to the other objects on a slide, follow these steps:

1. Select the object whose order you want to arrange. If the object you want to select is hidden from view, press the Tab key to cycle through all objects to find the one you want.

2. On the Home tab, click the Arrange button to view the following options:

    • **Bring to Front**—Bring the selected object to the front layer of the stack, placing all other objects behind it.

- **Send to Back**—Send the selected object to the back layer of the stack so that all other objects display above it.
- **Bring Forward**—Bring the selected object one layer closer to the front. This is most useful when more than two objects are layered.
- **Send Backward**—Send the selected object one layer to the back. This is also most useful when more than two objects are layered.

You can also access these layering options if you select an object, right-click, and choose from the submenu options that display.

3. Click the order option you prefer from the menu. PowerPoint applies it to your selected object.

Figure 5.3 shows two sets of layered objects.

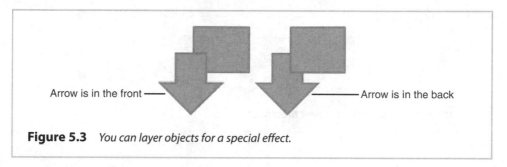

Arrow is in the front —— ———— Arrow is in the back

Figure 5.3　*You can layer objects for a special effect.*

Grouping Objects

It's difficult to move several objects on your slide and keep them positioned in pro-portion to each other. Fortunately, you can group two or more objects so that Pow-erPoint treats them as one object. For example, if you combine WordArt with a clip art image to create a logo, you can group these objects so that they stay together when you move them. A grouped set of objects moves in unison, always remaining in the same relative positions. When you format grouped objects, the formatting applies to all the objects. For example, let's say you have two grouped objects that were originally different colors. If you now recolor them, the new color applies to both objects, not just one. To make individual changes, you have to ungroup the objects.

LET ME TRY IT

Grouping Multiple Objects

To group multiple objects on a slide, follow these steps:

1. Select the objects you want to group by pressing the Shift key and clicking individual objects.

2. On the Home tab, click the Arrange button.

3. Select the Group option on the menu that displays.

The object handles now treat the objects as one, as shown in Figure 5.4.

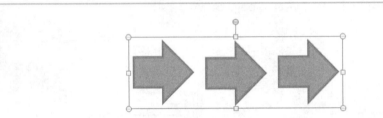

Figure 5.4 *Group objects to treat them as one.*

If you don't like the way you grouped objects and want to remove this grouping, click the Arrange button and select Ungroup from the menu. To revert back to the grouping, click the Arrange button and select Regroup.

 LET ME TRY IT

Aligning Objects

To align and distribute objects relative to each other or to the slide, follow these steps:

1. Select the objects you want to align by pressing the Shift key and clicking individual objects.

2. On the Home tab, click the Arrange button, and choose Align. A submenu displays.

3. If you want to align or distribute relative to the slide itself, select Align to Slide. If you want to align or distribute relative to the objects, select Align

Selected Objects. For example, let's say that you select several objects and want to align them to the left. If you choose Align to Slide, all the objects move to the leftmost edge of the slide. If you choose Align Selected Objects, they align to the left side of the leftmost object.

4. Choose from one of the following menu options:

- **Align Left**—Move the objects horizontally to the left.
- **Align Center**—Move the objects horizontally to the center.
- **Align Right**—Move the objects horizontally to the right.
- **Align Top**—Move the objects vertically to the top.
- **Align Middle**—Move the objects vertically to their midpoint.
- **Align Bottom**—Move the objects vertically to the bottom.
- **Distribute Horizontally**—Move the objects horizontally, spaced evenly.
- **Distribute Vertically**—Move the objects vertically, spaced evenly.

PowerPoint aligns your objects based on the direction you specify.

Alternatively, you can also select an object and use the arrow keys to nudge the object in the direction of the arrow.

Snapping to a Grid or Shape

When you align or move objects, they snap to an invisible grid that guides their positioning. This helps you align and position objects more precisely, creating a more polished and professional look. If you want to use other objects as a positioning guide, you can snap to shapes. To choose these options, on the Home tab, click the Arrange button and click Align and then Grid Settings to open the Grid and Guides dialog box (see Figure 5.5).

Figure 5.5   *Snap objects to a grid or another object.*

In this dialog box, you can

- Choose to snap objects to either a grid or other objects.
- Indicate the spacing of your grid in inches (from 1/24th of an inch to two inches).
- Select the Display Grid on Screen check box to activate the grid. You see horizontal and vertical dotted lines on your screen in the spacing width you specified, which helps you position your objects. Although the grid displays on the screen, it doesn't display in print or during a slideshow.
- Use adjustable drawing guides by selecting the Display Drawing Guides on Screen check box. This places one adjustable vertical line and one adjustable horizontal line on your screen, which you can drag to position where you want them. These, too, are invisible in print or during a slide show.
- Display smart guides when shapes are aligned. These dashed line guides display only when you move an object on a slide that contains multiple objects.

To set these options as your default, click the Set as Default button. Click OK to close the Grid and Guides dialog box.

To remove the gridlines, on the Home tab, click the Arrange button and select Align, View Gridlines to remove the check mark next to it.

Rotating and Flipping Objects

To rotate or flip a single object in a group, you need to ungroup it first and regroup the objects when you finish.

Many times when you add a shape or clip art image, it ends up facing the wrong direction. For example, you might add a callout to draw attention to specific text, but the callout is pointing the wrong way.

 LET ME TRY IT

Rotating an Object

To quickly rotate an object, follow these steps:

1. Select the object you want to rotate.
2. Place the mouse pointer over the green rotation handle that displays at the top of the object, as shown in Figure 5.6.

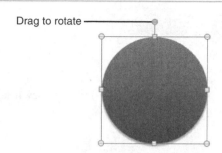

Drag to rotate ————

Figure 5.6 *Use the rotation handle to quickly rotate an object.*

3. Drag this handle to rotate the object. Pressing the Ctrl key while rotating changes the rotation angle 15 degrees at a time.

You can also select rotation options by clicking the Arrange button on the Home tab and selecting Rotate from the menu. Then, select one of the following options from the submenu:

- **Rotate Right 90°**—Move the object clockwise 90°.

- **Rotate Left 90°**—Move the object counterclockwise 90°.

- **Flip Vertical**—Turn the object vertically.

- **Flip Horizontal**—Turn the object horizontally.

- **More Rotation Options**—Open the Format Shape dialog box where you can specify size and position options.

Using the Selection and Visibility Task Pane

Using the Selection and Visibility task pane, you can reorder slide objects and specify their visibility. Choosing to hide a specific object is temporary. This action doesn't delete it from the slide, and you can choose to make it visible again at any time.

To open this pane, go to the Home tab, click the Arrange button, and select Selection Pane from the menu. Figure 5.7 shows the Selection and Visibility task pane.

Using the Format Dialog Box

You can use the Format dialog box to apply numerous formatting changes all in one place. Depending on the object you format, this dialog box is labeled either Format Shape or Format Picture. The Format dialog box duplicates some of the functions available on the Drawing Tools—Format tab, but also has some special features of its own.

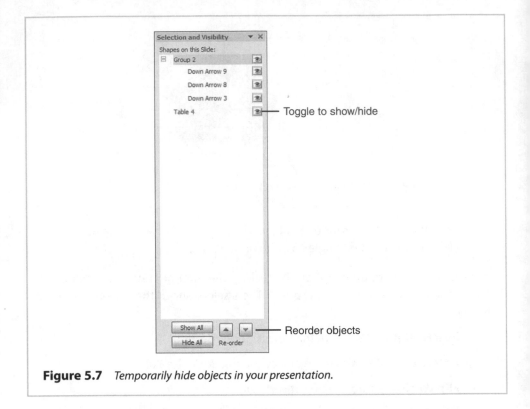

Figure 5.7 *Temporarily hide objects in your presentation.*

To open the Format Shape dialog box, right-click a shape and choose Format Shape from the menu that displays. Figure 5.8 shows the Format Shape dialog box.

Only the tabs and fields relevant to the selected shape are available for you to use. For example, some options apply only to pictures and others only to shapes or text boxes.

The options available in this dialog box include the following:

- **Fill**—Apply a variety of fill options, depending on the type of fill you select, including the capability to modify transparency, customize gradient presets, and change the scale and alignment of picture and texture fills.

- **Line Color**—Apply a gradient line and adjust presets.

- **Line Style**—Apply compound line styles and line joins.

- **Shadow**—Adjust the blur, distance, and angle of shadow presets.

- **Reflection**—Apply a preset reflection; enables you to modify transparency, size, distance, and blur.

Figure 5.8 *The Format Shape dialog box enables you to make many changes in one place.*

- **Glow and Soft Edges**—Apply a preset glow or soft edge; enables you to modify colors, size, and transparency.

- **3-D Format**—Apply 3-D formatting options, such as bevel, extrusion, contour, and surface formatting.

- **3-D Rotation**—Rotate the x, y, or z axis; set object positioning; and scale chart 3-D settings.

- **Picture Corrections**—Sharpen or soften a picture. Also modify brightness and contrast.

- **Picture Color**—Modify color saturation and tone.

- **Artistic Effects**—Apply an artistic effect to a picture such as Watercolor Sponge, Chalk Sketch, or Crisscross Etching.

- **Crop**—Specify exact cropping parameters including height and width. You can crop a picture if it contains things you don't need to show in your presentation. For example, you can crop a portrait to show just the person's face. You can also crop a picture with the mouse, which many people find easier. To do so, select the picture, and on the Drawing Tools—Format tab, click the Crop button.

- **Size**—Specify the exact height and width of an object, rather than resizing it with the mouse. This is useful if you want to create several objects of the same size and need greater precision than you can achieve by resizing with the mouse. You can also specify an exact rotation percentage, rather than rotate using menu options.

- **Position**—Enter the exact horizontal and vertical positions for the object. For example, to place an object so that its upper-left corner is exactly 1 inch left of the slide's center, enter -1 in the Horizontal field and 0 in the Vertical field, and choose Center in both of the From fields. Or to move an object that's 2.75 inches from the slide's left edge 1 inch to the left, enter 1.75 in the Horizontal field, and make sure that the From field contains Top Left Corner.

- **Text Box**—Establish text layout, AutoFit, and internal margin settings for text boxes.

- **Alt Text**—Apply alternative text to assist users with accessibility issues.

Using AutoFit

Sometimes you might have slightly too much text to fit into a placeholder. AutoFit can often help by shrinking the text size until it all fits. It works as you type: As soon as your text spills outside the placeholder, AutoFit starts shrinking it. When it does, the AutoFit Options button displays next to the placeholder. Figure 5.9 shows an example.

Figure 5.9 *Make your text more readable with AutoFit.*

AutoFit shrinks text until it's so tiny that your audience can't read it. When any text on your slide is smaller than 20 points, consider reformatting rather than reducing font size.

When you click the AutoFit Options button, a menu of formatting options displays:

- **AutoFit Text to Placeholder**—Shrink the text in the placeholder until it fits.

- **Stop Fitting Text to This Placeholder**—Restore the text to its original size.

- **Control AutoCorrect Options**—Open the AutoCorrect dialog box to the AutoFormat as You Type tab, which you use to turn AutoFit on or off. Use the AutoFit Title Text to Placeholder check box to enable or disable AutoFit in title placeholders. Use the AutoFit Body Text to Placeholder check box to enable or disable AutoFit in text placeholders. Click OK to keep your changes.

See Chapter 19, "Customizing PowerPoint," for more information about AutoCorrect.

Organizing Slides

In addition to organizing and formatting slide objects, you can also organize slides. Although you can organize slides using many PowerPoint views, the Slide Sorter view offers the most options.

See Chapter 1, "Introducing PowerPoint 2010," to learn more about PowerPoint views.

You can organize and rearrange slides in three different locations in PowerPoint:

- Outline tab in Normal view

- Slides tab in Normal view

- Slide Sorter view

If you want to do a major reorganization of a presentation that contains numerous slides, consider printing handouts with either six or nine slides per page first so that you can more easily analyze your entire presentation before making changes.

Select the icon of the slide you want to move, and drag it to a new location. Which method is best? The Outline tab is useful if you want to read the content of your slides as you reorganize. The Slides tab is a good choice if you know exactly what you want to move and want to do it quickly. If you have major reorganization to do on your presentation, you might want to use Slide Sorter view because it provides more flexibility and the capability to view the contents of your slides as you rearrange them.

Using the Slide Sorter View

To open Slide Sorter view, click the Slide Sorter button on the lower-right corner of the PowerPoint window, or click the Slide Sorter button on the View tab. Figure 5.10 displays Slide Sorter view.

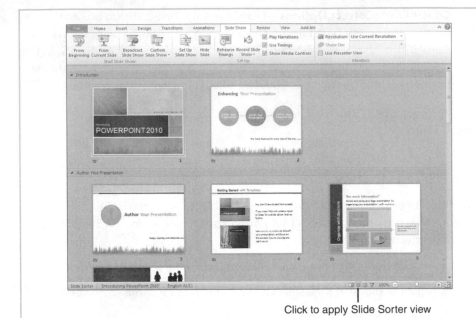

Click to apply Slide Sorter view

Figure 5.10 *Analyze and organize slides in Slide Sorter view.*

SHOW ME   Media 5.2—Using the Slide Sorter View
Access this video file through your registered Web Edition at
my.safaribooksonline.com/9780132182553/media.

In this view, you see smaller versions of your slides in several rows and columns. By viewing the basic content of each slide, you can more easily rearrange their order.

To move a slide in the Slide Sorter, select it and drag it to a new location.

To view a particular slide in more detail, double-click it.

To delete a slide in Slide Sorter view, select it and press the Delete key. To select multiple slides to delete, press Ctrl, select the slides, and then press the Delete key.

Copying and Moving Slides from One Presentation to Another

Using the Slide Sorter view, you can copy or move slides from one presentation to another. To do this, open both the source and destination presentations in Slide Sorter view. Click the Arrange All button on the View tab. PowerPoint displays both presentations in different window panes in Slide Sorter view, as shown in Figure 5.11.

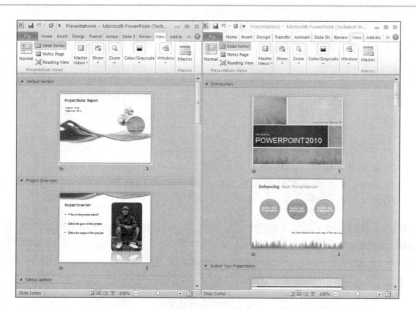

Figure 5.11 *By splitting panes between two presentations, you can copy or move slides between them.*

To copy a slide, select it and then drag it to the desired location in the other presentation. PowerPoint places the slide in the destination presentation, but it also remains in the source.

To move a slide, select it, press Ctrl+X, position the mouse in the new destination location, and press Ctrl+V. The slide is removed from the source presentation and inserted in the destination presentation. To move or copy more than one slide at a time, press Ctrl as you drag slides from the source presentation.

If each presentation uses a different template or theme, the slide changes to the formatting of the new presentation, and the Paste Options button displays. If you want to retain the formatting of the source presentation, click the down arrow to the right of the Paste Options button and choose Keep Source Formatting. To go back to the formatting of the target presentation, choose Use Destination Theme.

Although you can combine multiple themes in a single presentation, think carefully before doing so. Combining can make your presentation confusing.

To remove the dual-window view, click the Close button in the upper-right corner of the presentation you no longer want to view, and then click the Maximize button in the upper-right corner of the presentation you want to keep active.

If more than one presentation is open at a time and each is in a maximized window, you can press Ctrl+F6 to cycle through them. This helps when you want the full-screen view and want to copy/move from one presentation to the next without having to use the Window menu.

Deleting Slides

If you no longer need a slide or make a mistake and want to start again, you can delete it. You can delete slides in Normal view on either the Slides tab or the Outline tab or in Slide Sorter view.

To do so, select the slide or slides you want to delete and press the Delete key. To delete multiple consecutive slides, press the Shift key, and select the slides. To delete multiple nonconsecutive slides, hold the Ctrl key, and select the slides.

If the Slides and Outline tabs don't display, click the Normal button in the lower-right corner of the PowerPoint window to restore them.

This chapter introduces you to several ways to use tables in your PowerPoint presentation.

6

Working with Tables

Tables offer a great option for presenting and structuring related data on a PowerPoint slide in ways that are easy to read and aesthetically pleasing.

In this chapter, you explore several table creation and formatting options. You can also listen to tips on ways to make the most of your PowerPoint tables and watch videos that show you how to insert a table from the content palette, insert a table you can format as an Excel spreadsheet, and customize PowerPoint tables.

Understanding Tables

A *table* is an object that conveys related information in columns and rows. If you've created tables in other applications, such as Word, you know how valuable they are for communicating information. Tables are also efficient and flexible. For example, rather than creating three separate bullet list slides, each listing the five most important features of your three main products, you can summarize all this information in a table on a single slide. Alternatively, you can present information on individual slides and then summarize everything in a table at the end of the presentation.

 TELL ME MORE　Media 6.1—Understanding Tables
Access this audio recording through your registered Web Edition at
my.safaribooksonline.com/9780132182553/media.

You can include a table in a PowerPoint presentation in several ways:

- **Insert a table from the content palette**—PowerPoint's basic table insertion feature places a table into a slide, based on the number of rows and columns you specify. You can then format, customize, and add data to the table.

- **Draw a table**—When you need to create a complex table, one that the basic table feature can't make, you can draw it right on your slide. It takes longer to draw your own table, though.

- **Insert an Excel table**—Insert a table that takes advantage of the table formatting and calculation options available only in Excel.

Inserting a Table

One of the easiest ways to insert a table in a PowerPoint presentation is to start with a slide layout that includes the content palette.

 SHOW ME   Media 6.2—Inserting a Table
Access this video file through your registered Web Edition at
my.safaribooksonline.com/9780132182553/media.

Inserting a New Slide with a Table

To add a new slide that contains a table, follow these steps:

1. On the Home tab, click the down arrow below the New Slide button. A gallery of slide layouts displays.

2. Select one of the layouts that includes a content palette, such as the Title and Content, Two Content, Comparison, or Content with Caption layout from the gallery. A new slide displays.

3. On the content palette, click the Insert Table button to open the Insert Table dialog box, illustrated in Figure 6.1.

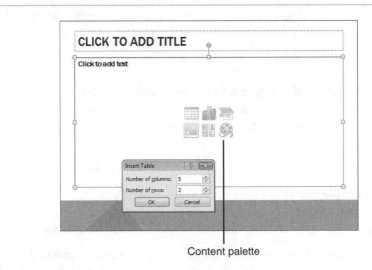

Content palette

Figure 6.1   *Choose the number of rows and columns you want to include.*

You can also open the Insert Table dialog box by clicking the Table button on the Insert tab. This option works best if you want to insert a table on a blank slide.

4. Choose the number of columns and rows to display, and click the OK button. A blank table displays in your slide, as shown in Figure 6.2.

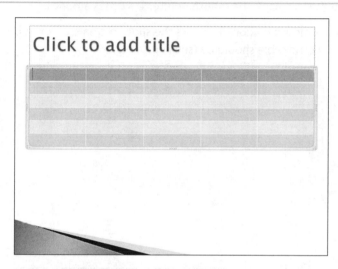

Figure 6.2   *Enter the title and table text to complete your table.*

5. Click the title placeholder to remove the placeholder text, and enter a title for the slide.

6. Next, add the text you want in each cell of the table, clicking inside the table and then either tabbing to the cell or clicking in the cell.

You can format this text as you would any other text. For example, you might want to make the first row or column bold, or add other special formatting.

Drawing Custom Tables

If the default table options don't give you what you need, create a custom table. Drawing your own table lets you make columns and rows of varying widths, for example. For some people, drawing a table is faster than customizing a table created from a table placeholder.

Drawing a Table

To draw a table, follow these steps:

1. On the Insert tab, click the Table button and select Draw Table from the menu that displays. The mouse pointer becomes a pencil.

2. Drag the mouse diagonally across the slide to create a box about the size you think the table should be (see Figure 6.3).

Figure 6.3   *Draw your own tables for total control.*

3. On the Table Tools—Design tab, click the Draw Table button in the Draw Borders group. The mouse pointer becomes a pencil again.

4. Select the type of lines you want to draw from the Pen Style, Pen Weight, and Pen Color drop-down buttons.

5. Use the pen to draw lines inside the box to make columns and rows.

If you make a mistake or want to imitate the Merge Cell feature, select the line you want to delete, and then on the Table Tools—Design tab, click the Eraser button. Use this eraser to remove the lines between rows and cells as necessary.

> To make it easier to create rows and columns, on the View tab, click Gridlines.

Inserting Excel Spreadsheets

If you want to take advantage of Excel's formatting and calculation features in your table, you can insert an Excel table in your PowerPoint presentation. You can insert an Excel table on any PowerPoint slide, but this works best on blank slides or slides with the Title Only layout.

 SHOW ME   Media 6.3—Inserting an Excel Spreadsheet
Access this video file through your registered Web Edition at
my.safaribooksonline.com/9780132182553/media.

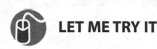 **LET ME TRY IT**

Inserting an Excel Spreadsheet

To insert a table you can format as an Excel spreadsheet, follow these steps:

1. On the Insert tab, click the Table button, and choose Excel Spreadsheet. An Excel table displays on your slide.

2. Using the table handles, resize your table to fit your slide.

3. Enter your table data as you would in an Excel spreadsheet. The ribbon now includes many Excel options including the Formulas and Data tabs. Figure 6.4 shows a sample Excel table.

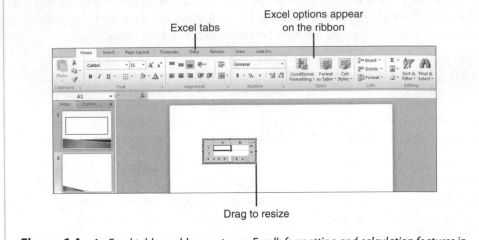

Figure 6.4 *An Excel table enables you to use Excel's formatting and calculation features in PowerPoint.*

4. Click anywhere outside the Excel table to return to the normal PowerPoint interface.

Formatting a Table

When you click in a table cell, a contextual tab displays, called the Table Tools tab. This tab includes two subtabs: Design and Layout. These tabs are contextual in that they display only in context with a table. If you're not working on a table, they don't display on the ribbon.

The Table Tools tab doesn't display when you click a table formatted as an Excel spreadsheet. Instead, double-click the Excel table to display Excel Ribbon tabs you can use for formatting.

SHOW ME Media 6.4—Formatting a Table
Access this video file through your registered Web Edition at
my.safaribooksonline.com/9780132182553/media.

Figure 6.5 illustrates the Table Tools—Design tab. Figure 6.6 illustrates the Table Tools—Layout tab. Combined, they contain the majority of the tools you need to format tables.

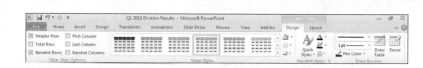

Figure 6.5 *Choose formatting options for your table, including styles and borders.*

Figure 6.6 *Manipulate table rows and columns, and set alignment.*

PowerPoint lets you format tables in a number of ways, including

- Applying different border styles, widths, and colors
- Inserting and deleting rows and columns
- Merging and splitting cells
- Applying table effects, including gradients, textures, background, and 3-D effects
- Aligning cell text to the top, bottom, or center

Setting Table Style Options

The Table Style Options group on the Table Tools—Design tab offers the following options for formatting the rows and columns in your table:

- **Header Row**—Apply a different color to the top row in a table and make its text bold.
- **Total Row**—Apply a different color to the bottom row in a table and make its text bold.
- **Banded Rows**—Highlight every other row in a table, using alternating colors, for easier viewing.
- **First Column**—Bold the text in the first column.
- **Last Column**—Bold the text in the last column.
- **Banded Columns**—Highlight every other column in a table, using alternating colors, for easier viewing.

Figure 6.7 shows a table with a header row and a total row.

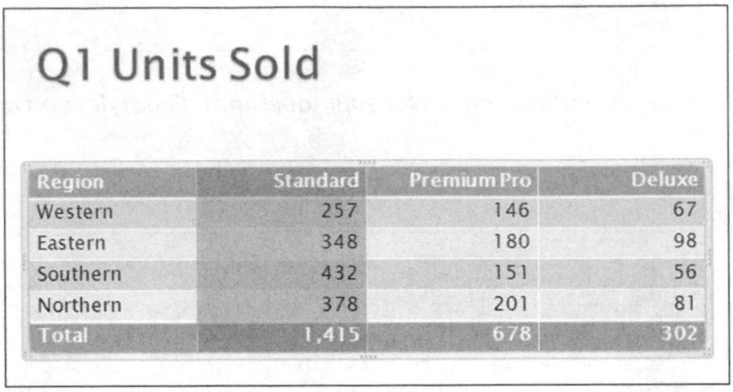

Q1 Units Sold			
Region	Standard	Premium Pro	Deluxe
Western	257	146	67
Eastern	348	180	98
Southern	432	151	56
Northern	378	201	81
Total	1,415	678	302

Figure 6.7　*Applying row and column formatting makes your table easier to read and understand.*

Applying a Table Style

The Table Styles group on the Table Tools—Design tab displays six suggested table style options. To view other options, click the down arrow on the right side of this group, as illustrated in Figure 6.8. If you want to remove formatting, click Clear Table.

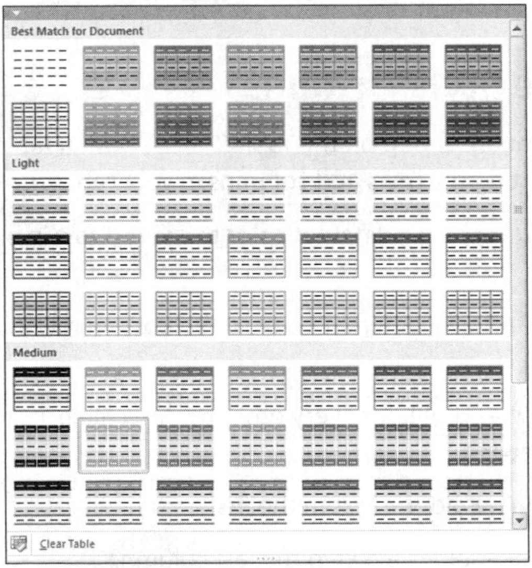

Figure 6.8　*Apply any of a variety of formatting options to your table, or clear all formatting.*

Creating a Border

Use borders to draw attention to your table or even to specific information in your table. New tables get a black, solid line border by default, but you can change this. To format the border, select the table and use the Table Tools tab to change the border style, width, and color and to set where borders display.

Setting Border Style

To set the border style, click the Pen Style drop-down list on the Table Tools— Design tab, which is located in the Draw Borders group. Choose the border style you prefer from the list, which includes the option to apply no border, a solid line, or a variety of dashed line styles, shown in Figure 6.9.

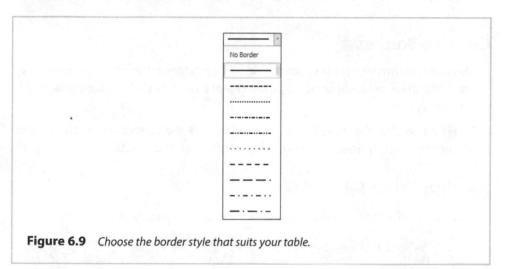

Figure 6.9   *Choose the border style that suits your table.*

Setting Border Width

To set the border width, on the Table Tools—Format tab, click the Pen Weight drop-down list and choose the width you prefer. Options include point sizes from 1/4 point (a thin line) to 6 points (a thick line), as shown in Figure 6.10.

Setting Border Colors

To set the border color, click the Pen Color button. The gallery that displays offers several possible colors, based on the presentation's theme colors. For more color choices, click More Border Colors to open the Colors dialog box. See Chapter 10, "Working with Shapes," for more information about the Colors dialog box.

Figure 6.10   *Use a thick border to create more emphasis, and a thin border to create less.*

Creating Borders

You can specify which parts of your table contain borders: the whole table or only specific outside or inside areas. Applying creative borders such as diagonals is another option.

To set borders, on the Table Tools—Design tab, click the down arrow to the right of the Borders button. Select the border you prefer from the available options.

Setting Table Fill Color

You can change the color that fills one or more cells in your table.

> Be sure that your table text is still readable if you change a cell's fill color. For example, if your text is black, don't fill cells with dark blue.

  LET ME TRY IT

Changing Table Fill Color

To change table fill color, follow these steps:

1. Select the cells whose fill color you want to change.

2. On the Table Tools—Design tab, click the down arrow next to the Shading button.

3. From the palette that displays, you can

- Choose from the colors that display on the palette. You can choose from the colors that complement your theme or from a variety of standard colors.
- Click More Fill Colors to display the Colors dialog box. You can either choose from a large number of colors in this dialog box or create a custom color.
- Apply pictures, gradients, textures, and table backgrounds. See Chapter 10 for more information about these options.

To remove a fill you no longer want, select No Fill from the palette.

Applying Table Effects

The Table Tools—Design tab also offers the option to apply formatting effects such as bevel, shadow, and reflection to your table. Click the down arrow next to the Effects button to view available formatting effects. You can also select table text and choose any of the formatting options in the WordArt Styles group.

🅖 *See Chapter 4, "Working with Text," for more information.*

Working with Columns and Rows

It never fails: As soon as you create a table and format it just so, you find that you need to add or remove information.

To insert a row into your table, click in the row above or below where you want to insert the row. Then, from the Table Tools—Layout tab, choose Insert Above or Insert Below, as appropriate. PowerPoint inserts the row, as shown in Figure 6.11.

New row

Region	Standard	Premium Pro	Deluxe
Western	257	146	67
Eastern	348	180	98
Southern	432	151	56
Northern	378	201	81
Total	1,415	678	302

Figure 6.11 *Add rows if you didn't create enough during the initial table creation.*

When you add or delete rows and columns, your table might no longer fit well on the slide. You then need to resize the table by dragging a corner. Be careful, however, that you don't hide existing text by making the cells too small during resizing.

If you want to insert multiple rows, select that number of rows before selecting the Insert command. For example, if you select two rows and then choose Insert Above in the Table Tools—Layout tab, PowerPoint inserts two rows above the selected rows.

To add a new column to your table, click in the column to the left or right of where you want to insert the column. Then choose Insert Left or Insert Right from the Table Tools—Layout tab.

Merging and Splitting Cells

One way PowerPoint makes tables flexible is by enabling you to *merge* and *split* table cells. For example, if you want a table to have a title centered at the top, you can merge all the cells across the top row. Or if you need to show two separate bits of information in one location, split one cell into two.

To merge cells, select the cells you want to merge, and on the Table Tools—Layout tab, click the Merge Cells button. Figure 6.12 illustrates five cells that were merged into one.

Merged row

Eco Choice Division			
Region	Standard	Premium Pro	Deluxe
Western	257	146	67
Eastern	348	180	98
Southern	432	151	56
Northern	378	201	81
Total	1,415	678	302

Figure 6.12   *Merged and split cells have a variety of applications within a table.*

If you already have text in each of the cells you merge, each cell text becomes a line of text in the new single cell.

To split a cell, select the cell you want to split, and on the Table Tools—Layout tab, click the Split Cells button. The Split Cells dialog box displays, where you can specify the number of rows and columns you want to insert in this particular cell.

Specifying Other Layout Options

The Table Tools—Layout tab offers other formatting options to explore.

In the Cell Size group, you can set cell size options, such as the following:

- **Table Row Height**—Apply the specified height to table rows you select.

- **Table Column Width**—Apply the specified width to the table columns you select.

- **Distribute Rows**—Resize the rows you select so that they're the same width.

- **Distribute Columns**—Resize the columns you select so that they're the same height.

In the Alignment group, you can specify alignment, text direction, margins, and table size:

- **Align Text Left**—Align selected text to the left.

- **Center**—Center selected text.

- **Align Text Right**—Align selected text to the right.

- **Align Top**—Align text to the top of the cell.

- **Center Vertically**—Align text to the vertical center of the cell.

- **Align Bottom**—Align text to the bottom of the cell.

- **Text Direction**—Set text direction as horizontal, rotated 270 degrees, rotated 90 degrees, or stacked.

- **Cell Margins**—Set text margins in a normal, narrow, or wide format, changing how far your text is from the cell's edges. You can also remove all margins.

In the Table Size group, specify the exact height and width of the table. Optionally, you can also lock the aspect ratio as you make changes (to prevent the table from getting formatted out of perspective).

In the Arrange group, perform advanced multiple-object formatting, such as bringing objects to the front or sending them to the back.

Adding Bulleted and Numbered Lists Within Tables

To create a bulleted list within a table cell, select the cell, and on the Home tab, click the Bullets button.

To create a numbered list within a table cell, select the cell, and on the Home tab, click the Numbering button.

For more bullet and numbering options, select the text you want to format; then click the down arrow next to the Bullets or Numbering button and choose Bullets and Numbering to open the Bullets and Numbering dialog box. This dialog box gives you more control over your lists by letting you choose a color for numbers and bullets, change numbering to alphabetical or outline, use picture bullets, and more.

Deleting Tables and Table Contents

If you no longer need your table or want to start over creating a table, you can delete an existing table in your PowerPoint presentation. You can also delete rows, columns, or selected table text.

To delete an entire table, on the Table Tools—Layout tab, click the Delete button, and then click Delete Table from the menu that displays.

Another way to delete a table is to click the outside border of the table to select the entire table and then press the Delete key.

To delete rows or columns, select the rows or columns you want to delete, and then on the Table Tools—Layout tab, click the Delete button. Select either Delete Rows or Delete Columns from the menu that displays. PowerPoint deletes the selected content.

To delete text in a cell, select the text (not just the cell) and press the Delete key.

This chapter shows you how to create an outline that provides a great start to your presentation.

7

Outlining Presentations

A solid, well-organized outline helps you achieve the goals of your presentation. Fortunately, PowerPoint offers several features that simplify the outlining process. You can use the Outline tab to view and manage your outline and insert outlines you create in Microsoft Word or other applications.

In this chapter, you learn how to develop and modify presentation outlines. You can also listen to tips on how to create an effective outline and watch videos that show you how to modify your outline and insert an outline from another application.

Creating an Effective Presentation Outline

Before you actually create a presentation, you need to determine its purpose, organize your ideas, and establish the flow of what you're going to say. In other words, you need to create an outline, or storyboard.

 TELL ME MORE Media 7.1—Creating an Effective Presentation Outline

Access this audio recording through your registered Web Edition at **my.safaribooksonline.com/9780132182553/media.**

There are many ways to outline a presentation: on paper, in another application such as Microsoft Word, or directly in PowerPoint. Which one is best depends on the type of presentation you're delivering, its length and complexity, and—most important—your personal preferences.

As you create your outline, keep several things in mind:

- Start your presentation with a title slide that introduces your topic and its presenter.

- Think of several main points to cover and design your presentation around those points.

- Try not to cover more than one main topic or concept in an individual slide.

- Remember that a PowerPoint outline is usually designed to accompany a verbal presentation. It's important to separate what you want your audience to see versus what you want them to hear during your presentation.

- Plan a balance of text and graphics in your outline. The best presentations contain both.

- When you use bulleted lists, be sure to maintain consistency. For example, a single bullet on a slide doesn't make sense; a list should contain at least two bullets. Too many bullets on one slide and too few on another might not work well.

- Consider using a summary slide to summarize the points you made during your presentation and conclude it.

Using the Outline Tab

No matter which method you use to create your outline, you might want to use PowerPoint's Outline tab to organize this information at some point. In Normal view, the outline displays in a pane on the left side of the window and shares the interface with the slide itself and related notes.

You can change the size of any pane in PowerPoint by dragging its border to a new location. To do this, move the mouse over the border and, when the cursor changes to a double-headed arrow, click and drag.

To view the Outline tab, click the Normal view button in the lower-right corner of the PowerPoint window. On the left side of the window, click the Outline tab to view your presentation's outline. Figure 7.1 shows the Outline tab.

Each slide is numbered and followed by a slide icon and the title text. The body text is listed under each slide. This body text includes bulleted and indented lists and other text information. The title text is also referred to as the *outline heading*, and each individual point in the body text is referred to as a *subheading*. Clip art, tables, charts, and other objects don't display in the outline.

Adding new outline information is simple. Enter the content, and press the Enter key to move to the next point. To delete a point you no longer need, select it and press the Delete key.

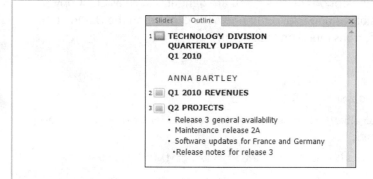

Figure 7.1   *The Outline tab offers a flexible approach to creating an outline.*

Modifying Your Outline

When you right-click the content of any slide on the Outline tab, a contextual menu displays, as shown in Figure 7.2.

Figure 7.2   *Right-click to view this menu of options from the Outline tab.*

SHOW ME   Media 7.2—Modifying Your Outline
Access this video file through your registered Web Edition at
my.safaribooksonline.com/9780132182553/media.

Although some of the options on this menu are generic—such as Cut, Copy, and Paste—most focus on editing and formatting slide content on the Outline tab. Table 7.1 lists the options found on this menu.

Table 7.1   Outline Menu Options

Menu Option	Description
Collapse	Hide all body text for the selected slides. Select Collapse All to hide all body text in the entire outline.
Expand	Display all body text for the selected slides. Select Expand All to display all body text in the entire outline.
New Slide	Insert a new slide after the selected slide.
Delete Slide	Delete the selected slides.
Promote	Change the selected text's outline level to the previous level, applying that level's style and formatting. For example, promoting text at outline level two moves it to level one.
Demote	Change the selected text's outline level to the next level, applying that level's style and formatting. For example, demoting text at outline level three moves it to level four. Demoting a slide title moves the text of the selected slide to the previous slide.
Move Up	Move the selected text so that it displays before the previous item in the outline.
Move Down	Move the selected text so that it displays after the next item in the outline.
Hyperlink	Add a hyperlink to the selected text.
Show Text Formatting	Show the actual presentation font formatting on the Outline tab.

Most of these menu options work best for slides that contain a lot of text, such as bulleted lists. If your slides emphasize other types of content, such as graphics and charts, you'll find it to be more convenient to rearrange content directly on your slides.

Promoting and Demoting Outline Points

You can demote outline headings and promote and demote subheadings to reorganize and rearrange your presentation. Promoting a first-level subheading makes it a heading (slide title) in a new slide. Promoting a secondary-level subheading (such as indented text or lower-level bullet) moves it up to the next level. On the other hand, promoting indented text outdents it.

For example, if you right-click the text of a second-level bullet in the outline (see Figure 7.3) and select Promote from the menu, the bullet becomes a first-level bullet (see Figure 7.4).

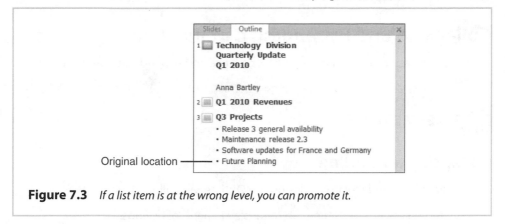

Original location ————

Figure 7.3   *If a list item is at the wrong level, you can promote it.*

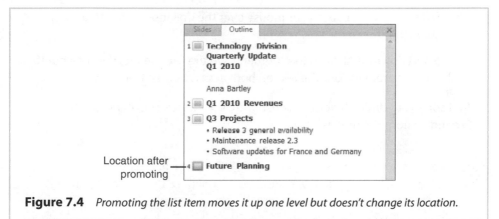

Location after ————
promoting

Figure 7.4   *Promoting the list item moves it up one level but doesn't change its location.*

If you promote a first-level bullet, it becomes a slide title, and PowerPoint inserts a new slide into the presentation.

Demoting works in much the same way as promoting. Demoting a slide title makes it a first-level item and adds the slide's contents to the end of the previous slide. Demoting other text indents the text to the next outline level.

When you demote a slide, the text content remains and carries over to the previous slide, but any graphics or notes are deleted. To keep the notes and graphics, copy them to their destination using the Clipboard, and then demote the slide.

Moving Outline Points Up and Down

You can also move each outline item up or down in the outline. To move an item up, right-click it and select Move Up from the menu. If you want to move an item down the outline, as you might expect, select Move Down from the menu.

Collapsing and Expanding Outline Points

To make it easier to read a long outline, collapse and expand slides and their body text.

 LET ME TRY IT

Collapsing an Outline

To collapse the body text of slides on the Outline tab, follow these steps:

1. Right-click in the Outline tab to display a menu of options.

2. From the menu, pause your mouse over the Collapse option to display a submenu.

3. Select Collapse All from the submenu. On the Outline tab, the slide numbers and titles remain, but the related body text is hidden from view.

To display your outline's detail again, right-click and select Expand and then Expand All from the menus.

To collapse the body text of an individual slide, right-click it and select Collapse from the menu. Right-click again, and select Expand to display the hidden text. If you want to collapse and expand more than one slide, but not all slides, press Shift, choose the consecutive slides, and then select Collapse or Expand. The slides you select must be consecutive.

Collapsing and expanding your outline makes it easier to print. You can print an entire outline in detail, only certain sections in detail, or only a collapsed summary outline.

G *See Chapter 16, "Creating and Printing Presentation Materials," for more information about printing outlines.*

Showing Slide Formatting

By default, the Outline tab displays each heading and subheading in the same font, bolding the headings for emphasis. If you want the outline to display using the actual fonts and formatting of the presentation, right-click slide content and select Show Formatting from the menu.

Each item's specific font and attributes—such as size, bold, italics, underlining, and shadow—now display in the Outline tab. The text's color is always black, though, regardless of its actual color.

Inserting an Outline from Another Application

If you create an outline in another application, such as Microsoft Word, you can insert this file directly into PowerPoint, which can work with outlines in many different formats, such as the following:

- Word documents (.doc)
- Rich Text Format (.rtf)
- Text files (.txt)
- Excel worksheets (.xls)
- HTML (.htm)

You can insert an outline into a blank presentation or into a presentation that already includes slide content. In the latter case, PowerPoint inserts the outline after the current slide.

 SHOW ME   Media 7.3—Inserting an Outline from Another Application
Access this video file through your registered Web Edition at
my.safaribooksonline.com/9780132182553/media.

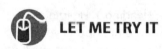 **LET ME TRY IT**

Inserting an Outline from Another Application

To insert an outline from another application, follow these steps:

Be sure the file you want to insert is closed. If it's open in another application, PowerPoint gives you an error message.

1. On the Home tab, click the down arrow below the New Slide button.
2. At the bottom of the gallery, click Slides from the Outline. Figure 7.5 shows the Insert Outline dialog box, which displays.

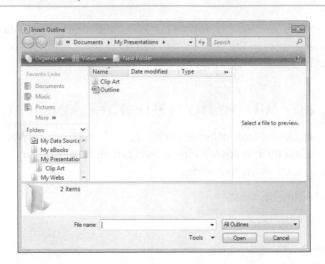

Figure 7.5   *Insert an outline you created in another application.*

The Insert Outline dialog box offers many of the same advanced options found in the Open dialog box. See Chapter 2, "Creating a Basic Presentation," for more information about these features.

3. Navigate to the file you want to import, and click the Insert button. PowerPoint creates new slides and inserts the outline content onto these slides.

For example, if you create an outline in Word, you can use Heading 1, Heading 2, and Heading 3 styles to format your document. When PowerPoint imports your outline, each Heading 1 becomes a slide title, each Heading 2 becomes first-level text, and each Heading 3 becomes second-level text. Other text isn't included in your outline. Figure 7.6 shows a PowerPoint slide with three heading levels inserted from a Word outline.

If your outline doesn't insert as you anticipated, review your source document for any possible formatting problems. Or use the Outline tab to revise your inserted content. Another option is to simply cut and paste your content onto your PowerPoint slides.

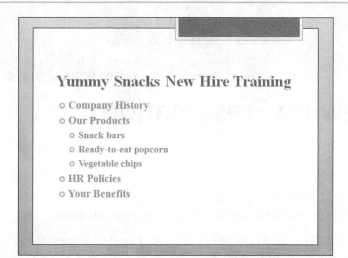

Figure 7.6   *Outline in Word, and then export your outline to PowerPoint.*

This chapter shows you how to review and compare
PowerPoint presentations.

8

Reviewing Presentations

Providing and incorporating feedback on PowerPoint presentations is an important part of the presentation design process in many organizations.

In this chapter, you learn how to use the tools found on PowerPoint's Review tab. You can also listen to tips on establishing a successful presentation review process and watch videos that show you how to add and manage comments and compare presentations.

Understanding PowerPoint Reviewing Tools

If you're a longtime PowerPoint user, you're probably familiar with PowerPoint's reviewing tools, such as adding and reviewing comments. PowerPoint 2010 also introduces the capability to compare two presentations and provides new ways to collaborate, such as co-authoring with SharePoint or Windows Live.

This chapter focuses specifically on the reviewing tools you find on the Review tab.

ⓒ *See Chapter 17, "Sharing and Collaborating on Presentations," for more information about the many ways you can collaborate on the presentation review process.*

In addition to enabling you to manage comments and compare presentations, the Review tab also offers numerous proofing and language tools. See Chapter 4, "Working with Text," for more information about these tools.

 TELL ME MORE   Media 8.1—Understanding PowerPoint
Reviewing Tools
Access this audio recording through your registered Web Edition at
my.safaribooksonline.com/9780132182553/media.

Working with Comments

Using comments—the electronic version of Post-it Notes—is key to a successful presentation review. The Comments group on the Review tab offers six buttons that provide all the features you need to review and comment on a PowerPoint presentation (see Figure 8.1).

Figure 8.1   *Use the buttons on the Review tab to add and review presentation comments.*

These buttons include

- **Show Markup**—Toggle the display of comments and changes on and off.
- **New Comment**—Insert a comment box on a slide.
- **Edit Comment**—Edit a selected comment.
- **Delete**—Delete a selected comment, all comments on the current slide, or all comments in the current presentation.
- **Previous**—Move to the previous comment in a presentation.
- **Next**—Move to the next comment in a presentation.

 SHOW ME   Media 8.2—Working with Comments
Access this video file through your registered Web Edition at
my.safaribooksonline.com/9780132182553/media.

Adding Comments to Slides

The best way to communicate your suggested changes to a presentation's author is to add a comment. You must use Normal view to add comments; Slide Sorter view doesn't support this feature.

 **LET ME TRY IT**

Adding a Comment

To add a comment to a slide, follow these steps:

1. Select the slide element to which you want to add a comment, such as a text box, chart, or graphic. If you want to comment on the slide as a whole, don't select anything.

2. On the Review tab, click the New Comment button. A yellow box displays with your name in the upper-left corner and today's date in the upper-right corner.

3. Enter your comments in the yellow box, which expands to fit the length of your comment.

4. Optionally, move your comment from its default location by selecting it and dragging it with the mouse. PowerPoint places all general comments in the upper-left corner of the slide. If you add more than one general comment, they display on top of the initial comment, covering most of it. If your comment relates to a specific slide element, the box displays next to that element.

5. When you finish entering your comment, click outside the comment box. PowerPoint hides the box but retains the comment marker that includes your initials plus the comment number.

Figure 8.2 illustrates a sample comment box for a comment that relates to the entire slide. Figure 8.3 illustrates a comment that relates to a specific slide element.

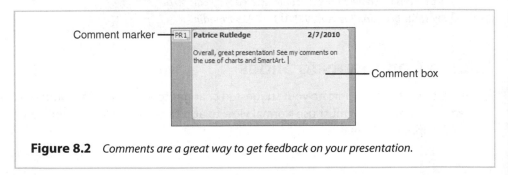

Figure 8.2 *Comments are a great way to get feedback on your presentation.*

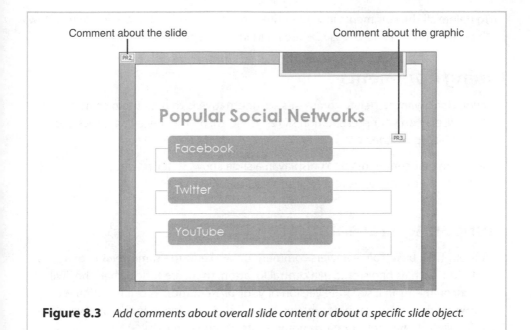

Comment about the slide

Comment about the graphic

Figure 8.3   *Add comments about overall slide content or about a specific slide object.*

Editing Comments

To modify the contents of a selected comment, click the Edit Comment button. Make the appropriate changes, and click outside the comment box to close it.

Reviewing Comments

Use the Next and Previous buttons on the Review tab to move from comment to comment, evaluating each one as you progress and making any needed presentation changes. If comments don't display in your presentation, click the Show Markup button. When you reach the end of a presentation, clicking the Next button brings you back to the presentation's first comment.

Deleting Comments

After you read a comment and make any required presentation changes, you'll probably want to delete that comment. To do so, select it and click the Delete button on the Review tab.

To delete all comments on the current slide, click the down arrow below the Delete button, and choose Delete All Markup on the Current Slide from the menu.

To delete all the comments in your entire presentation, click the down arrow below the Delete button and choose Delete All Markup in This Presentation.

Hiding Comments

If you don't want to delete comments, an alternative is to hide them so that they don't display on your presentation slides. To do so, on the Review tab, click the Show Markup button.

Be aware that comments don't display in a slide show, so it isn't necessary to hide or delete them before presenting a show.

Comparing Presentations

Although it's best if all reviewers comment on and edit the same version of a presentation, such as one stored in a central location, there are times when they will enter comments in a separate version of your presentation. It can be a time-consuming process to determine what changes a reviewer made in this new version, particularly if your presentation contains lots of slides.

 SHOW ME   Media 8.3—Comparing Presentations
Access this video file through your registered Web Edition at
my.safaribooksonline.com/9780132182553/media.

Fortunately, the new Compare group on the Review tab (see Figure 8.4) offers several options for comparing presentations and accepting or rejecting potential changes.

Until you click the Compare button and select another presentation to compare, none of the other buttons in this group is available.

 **LET ME TRY IT**

Comparing Two Presentations

To compare an open PowerPoint presentation with another presentation, follow these steps:

1. On the Review tab, click the Compare button. Figure 8.4 shows the Choose File to Merge with Current Presentation dialog box, which opens.

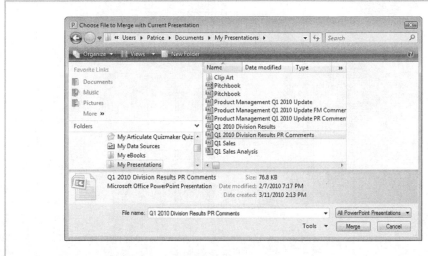

Figure 8.4 *Select a presentation to compare.*

2. Navigate to the presentation you want to compare, and click the Merge button. PowerPoint merges the two presentations and enables you to review, accept, and reject changes.

3. Manage your changes in one of the following ways:
   - Use the Revisions task pane.
   - Use the Next and Previous buttons in the Compare group.
   - Click the Accept button to accept all changes.

Which option is best for you depends on your personal preferences and the number of suggested changes. The rest of this section covers the many ways you can view, edit, accept, and reject changes in a compared presentation.

Working with the Reviewing Pane

When you click the Compare button, the Revisions task pane opens with the Details tab selected by default (see Figure 8.5).

On this tab, you can view the following:

- Slide changes, such as comments or text replacements
- Presentation changes, such as the application of a new theme

Figure 8.5   *Quickly see presentation differences on the Revisions task pane.*

On the Slides tab, shown in Figure 8.6, you can view slide changes by reviewer.

To accept all the changes for a specific reviewer, select the check box to the left of that person's name. You can also click the down arrow to the right of each slide to do the following:

- Accept changes by this reviewer (for this slide).
- Reject changes by this reviewer (for this slide).
- Preview any animations added to the comparison presentation.

To close the Revisions task pane, click the Close button (x) in the upper-right corner. Alternatively, on the Review tab, click the Reviewing Pane button, which serves as a toggle for this pane.

Viewing Revisions

You can also view and manage changes with buttons on the Review tab. Click the Next button in the Compare group to view each suggested change sequentially. PowerPoint highlights the change, letting you know what the suggested change is and who suggested it (see Figure 8.7).

Figure 8.6 *Click the down arrow in the Revisions task pane for more slide review options.*

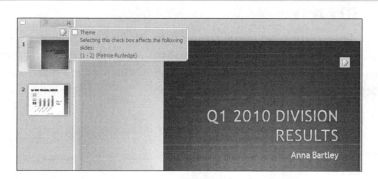

Figure 8.7 *Accept, review, or preview changes by reviewer.*

To accept the change, select the check box that precedes the change information. Continue to click the Next button until you finish cycling through all the changes. To go back, click the Previous button to return to the Previous change.

Accepting Changes

If you want to accept an active change, click the Accept button. For more options, click the down arrow below the Accept button. A menu displays, enabling you to

- Accept the current change (the same as clicking the Accept button).

- Accept all changes to the current slide.

- Accept all changes to the current presentation.

Remember that you can also accept changes on the Reviewing pane or by clicking the check box to the left of any change that displays on a slide.

Rejecting Changes

After you accept a change, the Reject button on the Review tab is now available. If you want to reject the active change, click the upper part of the Reject button. For more options, click the down arrow below the Reject button. A menu displays, enabling you to

- Reject the current change (the same as clicking the Reject button).

- Reject all changes to the current slide.

- Reject all changes to the current presentation.

Ending the Review

When you finish comparing presentations, click the End Review button. PowerPoint opens a dialog box confirming that you want to proceed. All your accepted changes are applied to your original presentation; changes you didn't accept are discarded. Note that you can't undo this action.

Working with Images, Illustrations, and Media

This chapter shows you how to add pizzazz to your presentations using images such as illustrations, photographs, and screenshots.

9

Working with Images

PowerPoint offers several ways to enliven your presentations with images, including inserting your own pictures, selecting an image from Microsoft's vast clip gallery, inserting a photo album, and—new to Office 2010—the ability to take and insert screenshots.

In this chapter, you learn how to insert, modify, and enhance images in your presentations. You can also listen to tips on making the most of your PowerPoint images and watch videos that show you how to insert clip art, create a presentation from a photo album, and modify images.

Understanding PowerPoint Images

You can insert a variety of images into your PowerPoint presentations, including both illustrations and photographs. You do this by inserting a *picture* from your own computer or network or by inserting *clip art* from PowerPoint's clip art library.

PowerPoint works with two basic types of images. *Bitmap* images are composed of pixels: tiny dots of color. A single image might contain hundreds of thousands of pixels. Bitmap images are the most common type of images on the web. Photos from digital cameras are also bitmaps. Common bitmap file formats include .bmp, .gif, .jpg, .png, and .tif.

Vector images, on the other hand, are composed of points, lines, and curves. Because you can easily resize and change the color of vector images, they are popular for producing logos and other images that need to be repurposed. Common vector file formats include .eps, .wmf, and .svg.

 TELL ME MORE   Media 9.1—Understanding PowerPoint Images
Access this audio recording through your registered Web Edition at
my.safaribooksonline.com/9780132182553/media.

Table 9.1 lists the most common image formats you can use in PowerPoint.

Table 9.1 Image Formats

File Extension	Format
.emf	Enhanced Metafile
.wmf	Windows Metafile
.jpg, .jpeg, .jfif, .jpe	JPEG File Interchange Format
.png	Portable Network Graphics
.bmp, .dib, .rle, .bmz	Windows Bitmap
.gif, .gfa	Graphics Interchange Format
.emz	Compressed Windows Enhanced Metafile
.wmz	Compressed Windows Metafile
.pcz	Compressed Macintosh PICT
.tif, .tiff	Tag/Tagged Image File Format
.wpg	WordPerfect Graphics
.cdr	CorelDraw
.cgm	Computer Graphics Metafile
.eps	Encapsulated PostScript
.pct, .pict	Macintosh PICT
.pcd	Kodak Photo CD

Inserting Pictures

To insert a picture on a slide, click the Insert tab and click the Picture button. The Insert Picture dialog box opens (see Figure 9.1), which is similar to the Open dialog box.

Ⓖ See Chapter 2, "Creating a Basic Presentation," for more information about the advanced features of the Open dialog box that are shared with the Insert Picture dialog box.

Another way to insert a picture on a slide is to use the content palette. To do so, on the Home tab, click the down arrow below the New Slide button, and select one of the slide layouts that includes the content palette. On your new slide, click the Insert Picture from File button on the palette to open the Insert Picture dialog box.

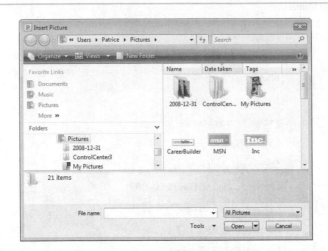

Figure 9.1   *Find and insert a picture from this dialog box.*

Select the picture you want, and click the Insert button to insert it on your slide. If you plan to make updates to this picture and would rather link to it instead, click the down arrow to the right of the Insert button and choose to either link directly to the file or insert it *and* link to it.

You can resize and reposition your picture and modify it in other ways. See "Modifying Images" later in this chapter for more information.

Inserting Clip Art

Microsoft Office offers thousands of clip art images that you can use to illustrate your presentations. Microsoft's website includes even more images. After you insert clip art into your presentation, you can reformat, recolor, and redesign it to suit your needs.

 SHOW ME   Media 9.2—Inserting Clip Art
Access this video file through your registered Web Edition at
my.safaribooksonline.com/9780132182553/media.

 **LET ME TRY IT**

Inserting Clip Art

To insert a clip art image into your PowerPoint presentation, follow these steps:

1. On the Insert tab, click the Clip Art button. The Clip Art task pane opens, as shown in Figure 9.2.

Figure 9.2 *Search for clip art by keyword.*

Another way to insert clip art on a slide is to use the content palette. To do so, on the Home tab, click the New Slide button, and select one of the slide layouts that includes the content palette. On your new slide, click the Clip Art button on the palette to open the Clip Art task pane.

2. Enter a keyword or keywords in the Search For text box. For example, you can search for images with computers, people, and so forth.

3. Specify the type of media files for which you want to search. Options include all media types, illustrations, and photographs. You can also search for audio and video clips in this task pane. See Chapter 13, "Working with Audio and Video," for more information.

4. If you want to search Office.com for additional content, select the Include Office.com Content check box. The Office.com site (http://office.microsoft. com) contains an extensive clip art collection from numerous sources.

5. Click the Go button to display matching results.

6. Drag your selected picture from the task pane to the slide.

> Optionally, click the down arrow to the right of an image to view a menu of options. From here, you can copy or delete the image, edit the image's keywords, or preview the image's properties.

You can resize and reposition your clip art image and modify it in other ways. See "Modifying Images" later in this chapter for more information.

Inserting Screenshots

Rather than using an external application to take screenshots, PowerPoint 2010 offers its own screen capture tool.

 LET ME TRY IT

Inserting Screenshots

To take a screenshot and insert it into your presentation, follow these steps:

1. Open the application from which you want to take a screenshot. For example, you might want to capture something from another Office application or from an external website.

2. Return to your PowerPoint presentation.

3. On the Insert tab, click the Screenshot button. A list of available windows appears, as shown in Figure 9.3.

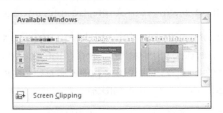

Figure 9.3   *Insert a screenshot of an open window or clip a section of a screen.*

4. If you want to take a screenshot of the entire window and insert it into your PowerPoint presentation, select that window from the list.

5. If you want to select a specific area for your screenshot, select the Screen Clipping option on the menu.

6. If you're taking a screenshot, select the area you want to include in your presentation using your mouse pointer (which now appears as a crosshair).

PowerPoint inserts the screenshot into your presentation. You can resize, reposition, and modify this image as you like. See "Modifying Images" later in this chapter for more information.

Working with Photo Albums

With its Photo Album feature, PowerPoint enables you to automatically create a presentation composed of a series of images available on your computer or on an external site. For example, you can create a travel presentation consisting of a series of photos taken on a trip.

 SHOW ME   Media 9.3—Creating a Presentation from a Photo Album
Access this video file through your registered Web Edition at
my.safaribooksonline.com/9780132182553/media.

 **LET ME TRY IT**

Creating a Presentation from a Photo Album

To create a presentation based on a photo album, follow these steps:

1. On the Insert tab, click the Photo Album button, and select New Photo Album from the menu. The Photo Album dialog box opens, as shown in Figure 9.4.

2. Click the File/Disk button to open the Insert New Pictures dialog box.

3. Navigate to the folder that contains the images you want to include in your album. To select all images, press Ctrl+A. Alternatively, press the Ctrl button on your keyboard and select individual images.

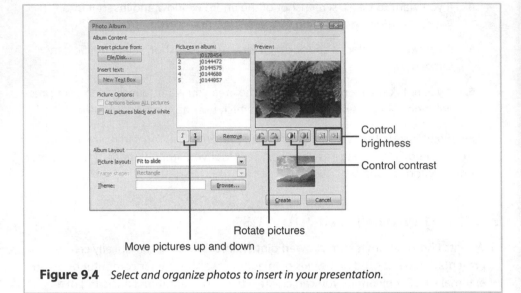

Move pictures up and down

Rotate pictures

Control brightness

Control contrast

Figure 9.4   *Select and organize photos to insert in your presentation.*

4. Click the Insert button to return to the Photo Album dialog box. PowerPoint lists the selected images in the Pictures in Album section.

5. Modify your photo album to suit your needs. For example, you can

   - Insert a text box slide by clicking the New Text Box button. When you return to your presentation, you can enter text on this slide.

   - Choose to display captions below all pictures or convert all pictures to black and white.

   - Change the order of your images by clicking the Up and Down buttons (designated by arrows).

   - Select an image and click the Remove button to delete it from the album.

   - Adjust the appearance of an image using the Rotate, Brightness, and Contrast buttons (the small buttons below the image).

   - Select a layout from the Picture Layout drop-down list, such as 1, 2, or 4 picture per page, with or without a title.

   - Apply a Frame Shape such as a rectangle (the default), rounded rectangle, simple frame, or soft edge rectangle.

   - Browse for a theme to apply to your presentation.

   When you finish setting up your photo album, click the Create button.

PowerPoint inserts the images into your presentation. You can resize, reposition, and modify the images as you like. See "Modifying Images" later in this chapter for more information.

To edit your photo album, go to the Insert tab, click the Photo Album button, and select Edit Photo Album from the menu. The Edit Photo Album dialog box opens, which is nearly identical to the original Photo Album dialog box you used to create your album. Make any changes, and click the Update button.

Modifying Images

After you insert a clip art image or picture into a PowerPoint presentation, you can modify it to suit your needs. PowerPoint 2010 includes many new image-editing features that can eliminate the need to edit your images in an external application.

The Picture Tools—Format tab appears whenever you select an image. Using this contextual tab, you can make both minor and major adjustments to an image, such as changing its color or adjusting its contrast. Although the buttons on this tab use the term "picture," most of these features also apply to clip art and screenshot images in your presentation.

 SHOW ME Media 9.4—Modifying Images
Access this video file through your registered Web Edition at
my.safaribooksonline.com/9780132182553/media.

Many of the options on the Picture Tools—Format tab include a link to the Format Picture dialog box where you can customize an image even further. You can also access this dialog box by right-clicking an image and selecting Format Picture from the menu that appears. See Chapter 5, "Formatting and Organizing Objects, Slides, and Presentations," for more information about this dialog box.

Adjusting Images

The Adjust group on the Picture Tools—Format tab enables you to remove background images, correct images, adjust color settings, and apply artistic effects. Be aware that not all these options are available, depending on the format of the image you want to modify.

Removing an Image Background

To remove the background of a selected image, click the Remove Background button on the Picture Tools—Format tab. The Background Removal tab appears, as shown in Figure 9.5.

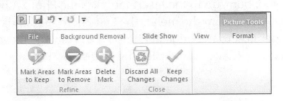

Figure 9.5   *Specify background areas to remove.*

This tab offers the following options:

- **Mark Areas to Keep**—Designate the areas to keep with a Pencil tool.

- **Mark Areas to Remove**—Designate the areas to remove with a Pencil tool.

- **Delete Mark**—Remove the background areas you marked to remove.

- **Discard All Changes**—Restore the image to its original state.

- **Keep Changes**—Save changes and closes the Background Removal tab.

It takes some time to learn to use this powerful tool effectively. If you don't like the end result, click the Undo button in the upper-left corner of the PowerPoint screen to restore your image's background.

 LET ME TRY IT

Applying Picture Corrections

To brighten and sharpen a selected image, follow these steps:

1. Select the picture you want to correct.

2. On the Picture Tools—Format tab, click the Corrections button.

3. From the gallery that appears, select an option in either the Sharpen and Soften section or the Brightness and Contrast section.

4. Pause your mouse over each style to preview what it looks like when applied to your picture.

5. When you find a style you like, click the style to apply it.

For additional picture correction options, click the Picture Corrections Options link at the bottom of the gallery. The Format Picture dialog box opens, where you can make additional modifications.

Adjusting Picture Colors

To change and adjust a selected image's colors, click the Colors button on the Picture Tools—Format tab. In the gallery that appears, as shown in Figure 9.6, you can

- Modify your image's color by specifying its purity based on a percentage (Color Saturation), specifying how light or dark the color is (Color Tone), or changing to a new color (Recolor).

- Click the More Variations link to open the Colors palette. You can choose a color from the palette or click the More Colors link to open the Colors dialog box. See Chapter 10, "Working with Shapes," for more information about this dialog box.

- Click the Set Transparent Color link to click a pixel in the selected image, thereby making all pixels of the same color transparent.

- Click the Picture Color Options link to open the Format Picture dialog box.

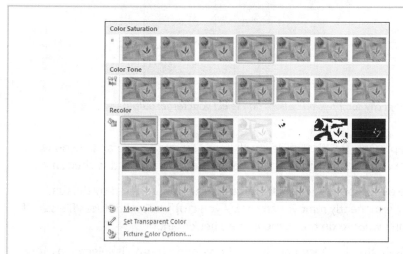

Figure 9.6   *Specify an exact color for your image.*

Applying Artistic Effects

To apply artistic effects to a selected image, such as a paint brush effect or a pencil sketch effect, click the Artistic Effects button on the Picture Tools—Format tab. In the gallery that appears, select your desired effect. To apply additional effects in the Format Picture dialog box, click the Artistic Effects Options link.

LET ME TRY IT

Compressing Pictures

Compressing pictures enables you to reduce the file size of your presentation, which makes it easier to manage and run on the web.

To compress a selected picture, follow these steps:

1. Click the Compress Pictures button on the Picture Tools—Format tab (a small button in the Adjust group). The Compress Pictures dialog box opens, as shown in Figure 9.7.

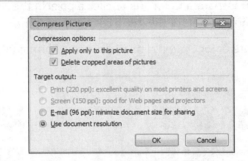

Figure 9.7 *Specify compression options and select your target output.*

2. The Apply Only to This Picture check box is selected by default. If you want to compress all the pictures in your presentation, remove this check mark.

3. The Delete Cropped Areas of Pictures check box is selected by default, which permanently removes any areas you cropped and reduces file size. If you don't want to do this, remove this check mark.

4. By default, the Use Document Resolution option button is selected as your Target Output. Optionally, you can switch to a resolution suited to Print, Screen, or E-mail. Depending on your image format, all these options might not be available.

5. Click the OK button to compress your picture.

Changing to a Different Picture

If you decide that you want to insert a different picture, but retain all the formatting you've applied to an existing presentation picture, on the Picture Tools—Format tab, click the Change Picture button (a small button in the Adjust group).

The Insert Picture dialog box opens, where you can select a new picture. PowerPoint inserts the new picture and keeps all existing formatting.

Resetting a Picture

If you've made a lot of changes to a picture and then decide you want to go back to the original, on the Picture Tools—Format tab, click the Reset Picture button (a small button in the Adjust group). PowerPoint restores your picture to its original appearance. If you want to reset picture formatting *and* size (from compression, for example), click the down arrow to the right of the Reset Picture button and select Reset Picture & Size from the menu.

Working with Picture Styles

The Picture Styles group on the Picture Tools—Format tab enables you to apply one of many preselected styles to your images. You can also add a border, apply special effects, and modify your layout.

Applying a Picture Style

To apply a picture style, select one of the styles in the Picture Styles group, or click the down arrow to the right of the group to open a gallery of additional options, as shown in Figure 9.8.

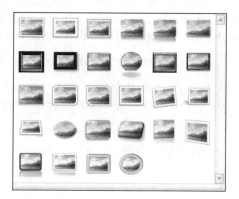

Figure 9.8 *Choose to apply a rotated white border or a soft-edge oval shape to your image.*

This gallery displays additional picture styles such as Reflected Bevel Black, Rotated White, and Soft Edge Oval. Pause your mouse over each style to preview what it looks like when applied to your picture. When you find a style you like, click it to apply.

Applying Picture Borders

To add a border to a selected image, on the Picture Tools—Format tab, click the Picture Border button. The Picture Border palette appears, as shown in Figure 9.9.

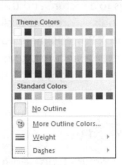

Figure 9.9   *Specify the type of picture border to apply the Picture Border palette.*

Choose from the following options:

- Apply one of the theme or standard colors. The theme colors are compatible with your slide's color scheme.

- Select No Outline to hide the existing border.

- Select More Outline Colors to open the Colors dialog box, in which you can select from many other colors or create a custom color. See Chapter 10, "Working with Shapes," for more information about this dialog box.

- Select Weight to specify the border weight—from 3/4 point to 6 points.

- Select Dashes to specify a dash style, such as square dot, dash dot, or long dash. Unless you create a thick outline, dashes probably won't be visible.

> For more options, select More Lines from the Weight or Dashes menu to open the Format Picture dialog box.

Applying Picture Effects

You can add shadow, glow, bevel, and 3-D effects to pictures by using the tools on the Picture Effects palette. To apply picture effects to a selected picture, on the Picture Tools—Format tab, click the Picture Effects button. The Picture Effects menu appears. Each menu choice leads to a gallery of additional options.

Depending on the shape you select, not all options are available. To preview a potential effect on your presentation, pause the mouse over it in the gallery.

Choose from the following options on the Picture Effects menu:

- **Preset**—Apply one of 12 ready-made effects designed to work well with your picture.

- **Shadow**—Apply an outer, inner, or perspective shadow to the shape. Select No Shadow to remove the shadow.

- **Reflection**—Apply one of several reflection variations, such as a half or full reflection. Selecting No Reflection removes the shape effect.

- **Glow**—Apply one of several glow variations in different colors and sizes. Select No Glow to remove the glow effect. Select More Glow Colors to open the Colors palette, where you can select another color.

- **Soft Edges**—Apply a soft edge, ranging in width from 1 to 50 points. Select No Soft Edges to remove the effect.

- **Bevel**—Apply one of several bevel options, such as a circle or divot. Select No Bevel to remove the effect.

- **3-D Rotation**—Apply a parallel, perspective, or oblique rotation to the selected shape. Remove the effect by selecting No Rotation.

For more choices, select the Options link at the bottom of each gallery to open the Format Picture dialog box. The exact wording of the Options link varies based on the name of the gallery, such as Shadow Options or 3-D Rotation Options.

Converting Images to SmartArt Graphics

If you want to convert an image, or a series of images, to a SmartArt Graphic, select the images, and on the Picture Tools—Format tab, click the Picture Layout button. From the gallery that appears, select the SmartArt style you want to apply to your images.

○ *See Chapter 11, "Working with SmartArt," for more information about SmartArt graphics in PowerPoint.*

Arranging Images

Like other PowerPoint objects, you can arrange the images you insert into your presentation. The Arrange group on the Picture Tools—Format tab offers numerous options for arranging images. For example, you can align, group, and rotate images and send overlapping images backward or forward to achieve a desired effect.

⊙ *See Chapter 5, "Formatting and Organizing Objects, Slides, and Presentations," for more information about using the options in the Arrange group.*

Cropping Images

If you don't want to include an entire image in your presentation, you can crop it to your exact specifications. For example, you might want to zero in on an object in the center of an image, or remove extra content at the top of an image.

To crop a selected image, on the Picture Tools—Format tab, click the Crop button. From the menu that appears, select one of the following options:

- **Crop**—Drag the mouse to determine your cropping area. Handles surround the image enabling you to specify the exact content you want to retain.

- **Crop to Shape**—Select a shape from the gallery that appears. PowerPoint modifies the image to fit the selected shape.

- **Aspect Ratio**—Crop to a specific aspect ratio, such as a 1:1 square, 2:3 portrait, or 3:2 landscape.

- **Fill**—Resize the image to fill the entire image area, maintaining the original aspect ratio.

- **Fit**—Resize the image to fit the specified image area, maintaining the original aspect ratio.

Modifying an Image's Height and Width

To modify a selected image's height or width, on the Picture Tools—Format tab, enter a new measurement in the Shape Height or Shape Width boxes. Alternatively, use the scrolling arrows to make incremental adjustments either smaller or larger.

For more image-sizing options, click the dialog box launcher (down arrow) in the lower-right corner of the Picture Styles group to open the Format Picture dialog box. On the Size tab of this dialog box, you can specify size, rotation, scale, and more.

This chapter teaches you how to create and format shapes that add pizzazz to your presentations.

10

Working with Shapes

A *shape* is an object you can place on a slide, such as a line, arrow, rectangle, circle, square, callout, and so forth. You can quickly insert a basic shape in your presentation, but after you use PowerPoint for a little while, you'll probably want to modify the default shape formats. With practice, you can use PowerPoint's shape formatting options to help your presentations communicate your message more effectively.

In this chapter, you learn how to insert shapes into your PowerPoint presentation and then modify and enhance them. You can also listen to tips about enhancing shapes and watch videos that show you how to insert shapes, apply a shape Quick Style, and apply shape effects.

Inserting Shapes

PowerPoint includes so many shape creation and formatting options that you're unlikely to ever use them all—and probably shouldn't. These features are simple enough to meet the needs of the casual user, yet powerful enough that a sophisticated PowerPoint designer can customize them heavily.

 SHOW ME Media 10.1—Inserting Shapes
Access this video file through your registered Web Edition at
my.safaribooksonline.com/9780132182553/media.

 LET ME TRY IT

Inserting a Shape

To insert a shape on your slide, follow these steps:

1. On the Insert tab, click the Shapes button. The Shapes gallery opens, as shown in Figure 10.1.

Figure 10.1   *The Shapes gallery offers many different options.*

If you've already inserted another shape and the Drawing Tools—Format tab appears, you can access the Shapes gallery from this tab as well.

2. From the gallery, select the shape you want to insert. Gallery options include the following:

- **Recently Used Shapes**—Insert one of the shapes you've most recently used in your PowerPoint presentations. If you have a new installation of PowerPoint 2010, this option won't appear.
- **Lines**—Insert a straight line or arrow, or a special line form such as a curve, scribble, or freeform. Also includes six different connectors, which draw lines between objects. When you move an object, the connector stays attached and moves with it.

To force a connection between two objects to be the shortest distance, reroute the connector. To do this, go to the Drawing Tools—Format tab, click the Edit Shape button in the Insert Shapes group, and choose Reroute Connectors.

- **Rectangles**—Insert one of nine different rectangular shapes, including the Rounded Rectangle and Snip Single Corner Rectangle.

- **Basic Shapes**—Insert a common shape, such as
  - Polygons, such as a hexagon, a triangle, a parallelogram, and so on
  - 3-D shapes, such as a box and a cylinder
  - Fun shapes, such as a crescent moon, a smiley face, and a lighting bolt
  - Grouping and connecting shapes, such as brackets and braces
- **Block Arrows**—Insert a large block arrow, curved or bent arrow, or callout with arrows.
- **Equation Shapes**—Insert a plus, minus, multiplication, division, equal, or not equal sign.
- **Flowchart**—Insert a flowchart image such as a process, a decision, a document, an input, or a terminator.
- **Stars and Banners**—Insert a wave, a scroll, a ribbon, an explosion, or a pointed star.
- **Callouts**—Insert one of several kinds of callouts. A callout is a line with a text box connected to one end. You put the line's free end on something you want to highlight, place the text box to the side, and type descriptive text in it.
- **Action Buttons**—Insert an Action Button. Action Buttons make your presentation interactive, performing actions such as navigating among slides, running programs, and playing sounds. See Chapter 18, "Working with Hyperlinks and Action Buttons," for more information about Action Buttons.

3. On your slide, click where you want the shape to appear, and drag until the shape is the size you want. You can then format the shape as you would any other object.

Keep in mind that although PowerPoint shapes make it easy to create an attractive graphic, they aren't designed for complex graphic needs. If you need something more detailed, consider using SmartArt or inserting a Microsoft Visio graphic. See Chapter 11, "Working with SmartArt," for more information.

Inserting Lines and Arrows

You can add lines and arrows to your presentation to draw attention to something, show how things are connected, or show how one thing leads to another. For example, you might want to add a line beneath a word or phrase to draw attention to it. You might also use an arrow to point to text or an object of special importance. You can also draw simple graphics with the line, rectangle, and oval shapes.

If you use lines or arrows to emphasize text, remember that they don't move even when you add or remove text. You have to move each shape manually.

 LET ME TRY IT

Drawing a Line or Arrow

To draw a line or arrow on your slide, follow these steps:

1. On the Insert tab, click the Shapes button to open the Shapes gallery (refer to Figure 10.1).

2. Click one of the buttons in the Lines section of the Shapes gallery. The mouse pointer becomes a plus sign.

3. Click (and hold down) where you want the line to begin, and drag to where you want the line to end.

Press the Shift key as you drag the mouse to create straight horizontal or vertical lines. This lets you draw lines at angles evenly divisible by 15 (0, 15, 30, 45, and so forth), which makes it much easier to create a straight line. Press the Ctrl key as you drag the mouse to draw a line from a center point, lengthening the line in both directions as you drag.

If the line looks crooked or is the wrong length, you can adjust it. First, select the line. Then pause your mouse over one of the circles that appear at the end of the line. The mouse pointer becomes a line with an arrowhead at both ends. Click and drag the circle to lengthen the line or adjust its angle. If the line isn't in the right place, you can move it. First, select the line. Then pause your mouse over the line. The mouse pointer becomes a cross with arrowheads at all four ends. Click and drag the line to move it.

Inserting Rectangles and Ovals

By using the options in the Shape Outline palette, you can easily change the appearance of a line or arrow by adjusting its width or converting it to a dashed line. See "Specifying Shape Outlines" later in this chapter for more information.

You can draw rectangular and oval shapes directly on your presentation. Using shapes lets you emphasize important information, group information, or illustrate other ideas or concepts.

To draw a rectangle, click one of the buttons in the Rectangles section of the Shapes gallery. The mouse pointer becomes a plus sign. Click where you want the rectangle to appear, and drag to draw the rectangle.

To draw a perfect circle, press the Shift key while you draw the shape.

To draw an oval, click the Oval button in the Basic Shapes section of the Shapes gallery. The mouse pointer becomes a plus sign. Click where you want the oval to appear and drag to draw the oval.

To draw a square, press the Shift key while you draw the shape.

You can then reshape and resize these images or apply other formatting to them.

You can add text to a rectangular or oval shape. If you want to add only a word or two, select the shape and type in the text you want to enter. Or click the Text Box button on either the Insert tab or the Drawing Tools—Format tab and create a text box inside the original object. Be sure, however, that the text box fits into the object without overlapping its borders.

Modifying and Enhancing Shapes

When you create or select a shape, the contextual Drawing Tools—Format tab appears, shown in Figure 10.2.

Figure 10.2   *The Drawing Tools—Format tab offers numerous options for shape creation and formatting.*

The Insert Shapes and Shape Styles groups on the Drawing Tools—Format tab are the centerpieces of PowerPoint's suite of shape creation and formatting tools. They offer a multitude of options for modifying and enhancing presentation shapes, such as specifying a shape's fill, outline, and effects.

The Home tab also offers most, but not all, of the shape formatting features available on the Drawing Tools—Format tab.

Working with Shape Quick Styles

One way to format a shape quickly is to apply a quick style. Quick Styles offer numerous fill, shading, and border options in colors that coordinate with your chosen theme.

 LET ME TRY IT

Applying a Shape Quick Style

To apply a Quick Style to a shape, follow these steps:

1. Select the shape to which you want to apply the style.

2. On the Drawing Tools—Format tab, click the down arrow to the right of the Shape Styles box to open the Shape Styles gallery, as shown in Figure 10.3.

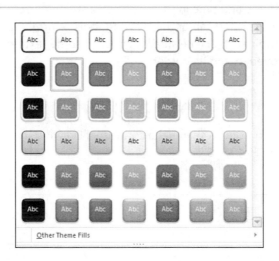

Figure 10.3 *Choose a style that coordinates with your presentation theme.*

You can also open the Shape Styles gallery by clicking the Quick Styles button on the Home tab.

3. Pause your mouse over an available style to preview the style's effect on your shape.

4. Optionally, click Other Theme Fills at the bottom of the gallery to open a palette of additional options, including several grayscale options.

As a shortcut, you can click one of the styles that display in the Shape Styles box on the tab itself without opening the gallery. The default view shows three possible styles.

5. Click a style to apply it to the selected shape.

 SHOW ME Media 10.2—Applying a Shape Quick Style
Access this audio recording through your registered Web Edition at
my.safaribooksonline.com/9780132182553/media.

Specifying Shape Fill Color

To set a shape's fill color, select it, and on the Drawing Tools—Format tab, click the down arrow to the right of the Shape Fill button. A palette displays, as shown in Figure 10.4.

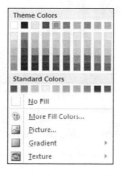

Figure 10.4 *Add colors or patterns to fill an object.*

You can do any of the following in this palette:

• Apply one of the theme, standard, or recent colors. The theme colors are compatible with your slide's color scheme.

• Click No Fill to make the object transparent. You see the slide background through the object.

- Click More Fill Colors to open the Colors dialog box, from which you can choose from many other colors or create a custom color.

- Click Picture to fill your shape with a picture you select.

- Click Gradient to apply a light or dark gradient pattern.

- Click Texture to fill the shape with one of the available texture patterns in the gallery that appears.

Using the Colors Dialog Box

Click More Fill Colors in the palette to open the Colors dialog box, as illustrated in Figure 10.5.

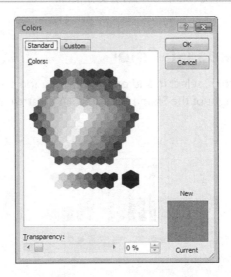

Figure 10.5 *Choose from many common colors in the Colors dialog box.*

To choose a new color, select it in the palette on the Standard tab. The color appears in the New section of the preview box to contrast with the Current color.

You can set transparency (making the color appear transparent) by dragging the Transparency scrollbar or by entering a specific transparency percentage. The higher the percentage, the more transparent the color, which enables things behind the object to show through.

Click OK to keep the color or Cancel to return to the original color.

Using a Custom Color

To add a custom color, click the Custom tab on the Colors dialog box, as shown in Figure 10.6.

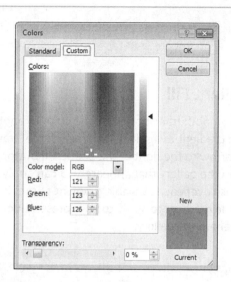

Figure 10.6 *Create a custom color to suit your exact needs.*

You can create a custom color in two ways. One way is to click and drag the crosshair in the Colors area until you find the color you want. The other way is to choose either RGB or HSL in the Color Model field and then adjust the color's level of red, green, and blue (for RGB) or hue, saturation, and luminance (for HSL). Click OK to keep the color, or click Cancel to discard it.

Red, green, and *blue* represent the amount of each of these primary colors in the color you create. The RGB color wheel used in PowerPoint is based on projected light—the kind you see with computer screen projection.

Hue represents the actual color, *saturation* represents the color's intensity, and *luminance* represents the color's brightness. In general, the lower the number, the lighter or less intense the color is.

Applying a Picture Fill

You can even fill an object with a picture. For example, you could create a shape such as a circle and fill with a logo, product image, or photo. On the Drawing

Tools—Format tab, click the down arrow to the right of the Shape Fill button, and choose Picture from the menu.

The Insert Picture dialog box opens. Find and select your picture, and click the Insert button to fill the shape with the selected picture.

Some pictures just don't look good as fills. Look at yours carefully. If it doesn't look good, press Ctrl+Z to undo it, and then apply some other fill.

Applying a Gradient Fill

A gradient creates a smooth transition from one color to another, using gentle blending. To apply a gradient to a selected shape, on the Drawing Tools—Format tab, click the down arrow to the right of the Shape Fill button, and select Gradient from the menu. From the gallery that appears, you can apply a light or dark gradient. Pause your mouse over each available gradient to preview its effect on your presentation. Click the gradient to apply to your presentation. To remove a gradient, select No Gradient in the gallery.

For more gradient options, click More Gradients in the gallery to open the Format Shape dialog box. See Chapter 5, "Formatting and Organizing Objects, Slides, and Presentations," for more information about this dialog box.

Applying a Textured Fill

To apply a texture to a selected shape, on the Drawing Tools—Format tab, click the down arrow to the right of the Shape Fill button, and choose Texture from the menu. Select your preferred texture from the gallery (see Figure 10.7), pausing your mouse over each option to preview it on your presentation.

For more options, click More Textures in the gallery to open the Format Shape dialog box.

Specifying Shape Outlines

To specify the outline of a shape—either a line or any other shape such as a circle or rectangle—select the shape and on the Drawing Tools—Format tab, click the down arrow to the right of the Shape Outline button. The Shape Outline palette appears, as shown in Figure 10.8.

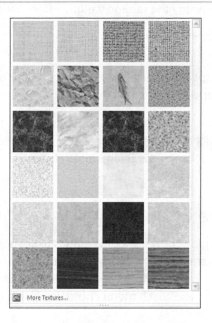

Figure 10.7   *Textures can add visual depth to a shape.*

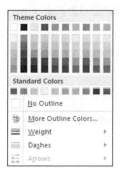

Figure 10.8   *Specify the format of a shape's outline in the Shape Outline palette.*

Choose from the following options:

- Apply one of the theme or standard colors. The theme colors are compatible with your slide's color scheme.

- Click No Outline to hide the existing line.

- Click More Outline Colors to open the Colors dialog box, in which you can select from many other colors or create a custom color.

- Click Weight to specify the outline weight—from 3/4 point to 6 points.

- Click Dashes to specify a dash style, such as square dot, dash dot, or long dash. Unless you create a thick outline, dashes probably won't be visible.

- Click Arrows to specify an arrow style. Note that this option is available only if the selected shape is a line or an arrow.

> For more options, select More Lines or More Arrows from the Weight, Dashes, or Arrows menus to open the Format Shape dialog box.

Applying Shape Effects

You can add shadow, glow, bevel, and 3-D effects to shapes by using the tools on the Shape Effects palette. To apply shape effects to a selected shape, on the Drawing Tools—Format tab, click the down arrow next to the Shape Effects button. The Shape Effects menu appears. Each menu choice leads to a gallery of additional options.

 SHOW ME   **Media 10.3—Applying Shape Effects**
Access this video file through your registered Web Edition at
my.safaribooksonline.com/9780132182553/media.

Depending on the shape you select, not all options are available. To preview a potential shape effect on your presentation, pause the mouse over it in the gallery.

Choose from the following options on the Shape Effects menu:

- **Preset**—Apply 1 of 12 ready-made effects designed to work well with your shape.

- **Shadow**—Apply an outer, inner, or perspective shadow to the shape. Select No Shadow to remove the shadow.

- **Reflection**—Apply one of several reflection variations, such as half or full reflection. Selecting No Reflection removes the shape effect.

- **Glow**—Apply one of several glow variations in different colors and sizes (see Figure 10.9). Select No Glow to remove the glow effect. Select More Glow Colors to open the Colors palette, where you can select another color. See "Using the Colors Dialog Box," earlier in this chapter for more information about colors.

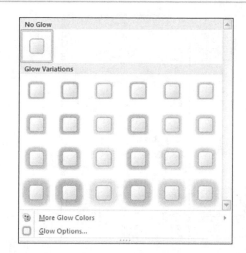

Figure 10.9   *Get dramatic with glow effects.*

- **Soft Edges**—Apply a soft edge, ranging in width from 1 to 50 points. Select No Soft Edges to remove the effect.

- **Bevel**—Apply one of several bevel options, such as a circle or divot. Select No Bevel to remove the effect.

- **3-D Rotation**—Apply a parallel, perspective, or oblique rotation to the selected shape. Remove the effect by selecting No Rotation. Figure 10.10 illustrates the 3-D Rotation gallery.

Editing Shapes

On the Drawing Tools—Format tab, click the Edit Shape button in the Insert Shapes group to open a submenu with the following choices:

> For more options, select the Options link at the bottom of each gallery to open the Format Shape dialog box. The exact wording of the Options link varies based on the name of the gallery, such as Shadow Options or 3-D Rotation Options. See Chapter 5 for more information about this dialog box.

- **Change Shape**—Change the applied shape to another shape available in the Shapes gallery.

- **Convert to Freeform**—Convert the selected shape to a freeform shape for more design flexibility.

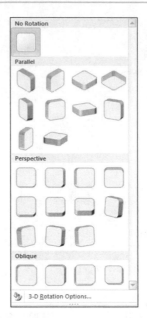

Figure 10.10   *Get creative with 3-D, but be sure that your object doesn't become too distorted.*

- **Edit Points**—Edit the points of selected shapes.

- **Reroute Connectors**—Force a connection between two objects to be the shortest distance.

Be aware that depending on the type of shape you select, not all editing options are available.

This chapter shows you how to enliven your presentation and engage your audience with SmartArt graphics.

11

Working with SmartArt

SmartArt offers a unique opportunity to present slide content, such as an organization chart or a process, in a way that makes the most of PowerPoint's many sophisticated design features.

In this chapter, you learn how to use SmartArt graphics to both inform your audience and energize your presentation. You can also listen to tips on choosing the right SmartArt layout and watch videos that show you how to insert a SmartArt graphic, use SmartArt design tools, and make the most of SmartArt formatting options.

Understanding SmartArt Graphics

SmartArt takes the power and flexibility of PowerPoint shapes one step further. SmartArt enables you to combine shapes and text to create informative lists, matrices, pyramids, and more. Then, using PowerPoint's many shape and text formatting options, you can create a custom graphic that both conveys your message and gives your presentation the "wow" factor.

 TELL ME MORE   Media 11.1—Understanding SmartArt
Access this audio recording through your registered Web Edition at
my.safaribooksonline.com/9780132182553/media.

For example, you can create a detailed organization chart with SmartArt (see Figure 11.1). Or you can create a graphic that explains a step-by-step process (see Figure 11.2).

Table 11.1 lists PowerPoint SmartArt types, each offering a variety of layouts to choose from.

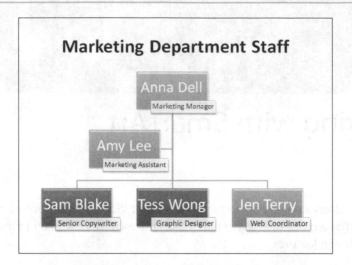

Figure 11.1   *Use one of SmartArt's many organization chart layouts.*

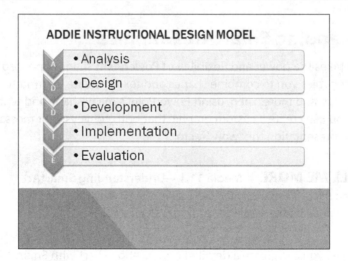

Figure 11.2   *Highlight a process in your presentation.*

Table 11.1   PowerPoint SmartArt Types

Choose This SmartArt Type	To Display
List	Nonsequential data
Process	Steps in a process or a sequential timeline
Cycle	An ongoing process
Hierarchy	Hierarchical data such as an organizational chart
Relationship	Connected data
Matrix	Parts in relation to a whole
Pyramid	Proportions from small to large
Picture	A graphical representation of data

Inserting Smart Art Graphics

The fastest way to add a SmartArt graphic to your presentation is to apply a slide layout that contains the content palette. See Chapter 2, "Creating a Basic Presentation," for more information about PowerPoint slide layouts.

 SHOW ME   Media 11.2—Inserting a SmartArt Graphic
Access this video file through your registered Web Edition at
my.safaribooksonline.com/9780132182533/media.

 LET ME TRY IT

Inserting a SmartArt Graphic

To insert a SmartArt graphic, follow these steps:

1. On the Home tab, click the down arrow below the New Slide button, and then choose an appropriate layout from the gallery that appears. For example, you could choose the Title and Content layout, the Two Content layout, or the Content with Caption layout.

2. On your new slide, click the Insert SmartArt Graphic button on the content palette, as shown in Figure 11.3. The Choose a SmartArt Graphic dialog box opens (see Figure 11.4).

Insert SmartArt

Figure 11.3 *Use the content palette as an easy starting point for inserting SmartArt.*

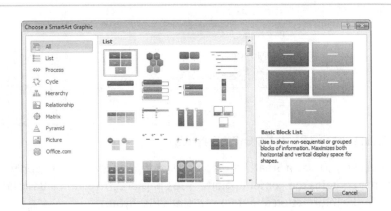

Figure 11.4 *Choose from a variety of SmartArt graphic layouts.*

3. In the Choose a SmartArt Graphic dialog box, select the button for the SmartArt layout types you want to view. Or select the All button to scroll through a list of all options. See Table 11.1 earlier in this chapter for an explanation of each graphic type.

If you're new to SmartArt, it's often difficult to determine which graphic best suits your needs. When you click each graphic icon in the Choose a SmartArt Graphic dialog box, the right side of the screen displays a detailed example of the selected SmartArt graphic and describes its use in the box below. Reviewing all your options at least once gives you a clearer idea of what's available and can provide some inspiration as well.

4. Select the icon for the graphic type you want to insert, and click the OK button. The graphic appears on your slide (see Figure 11.5).

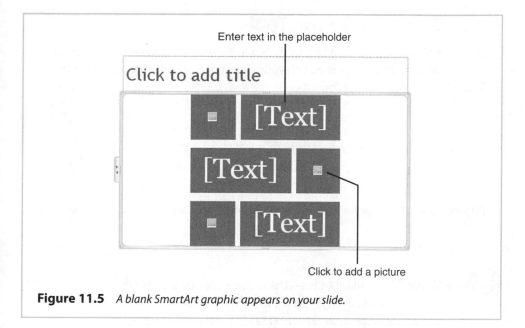

Figure 11.5   *A blank SmartArt graphic appears on your slide.*

Each SmartArt graphic includes text placeholders where you can enter the appropriate text. To enter text, click the [Text] placeholder and start typing. If you enter more text than the shape can hold, PowerPoint resizes the text. You can also enter text in the Text pane, described in the "Using the Text Pane" section later in this chapter.

If you choose a graphic that includes pictures, click the picture placeholder to open the Insert Picture dialog box.

Modifying and Formatting SmartArt Graphics

PowerPoint offers two contextual tabs that enable you to modify the design and format of your SmartArt graphics: the SmartArt Tools—Design tab and the SmartArt Tools—Format tab.

Note that these contextual tabs appear only when a graphic is selected. If they disappear, select your graphic again to view them. Also, be aware that depending on your choice of SmartArt graphic, not all options will be available on the SmartArt Tools tabs.

You can also apply animation effects to your SmartArt graphics, such as having the graphic fly in to the slide. See Chapter 14, "Working with Animation and Transitions," for more information about animating SmartArt.

Using SmartArt Design Tools

The SmartArt Tools—Design tab, as shown in Figure 11.6, enables you to create additional graphic objects, specify layout and style options, and convert your SmartArt graphic to other formats.

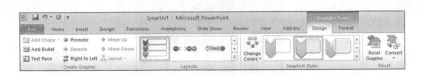

Figure 11.6   *The SmartArt Tools—Design tab is one of two SmartArt Tools contextual tabs.*

 SHOW ME   Media 11.3—Using SmartArt Design Tools
Access this video file through your registered Web Edition at
my.safaribooksonline.com/9780132182553/media.

Adding Shapes

Although SmartArt graphics already contain shapes by default, you can add more shapes if you need. For example, you could create a basic cycle graphic, which comes with five shapes, and then decide you need to add a sixth.

 LET ME TRY IT

Adding a Shape to a SmartArt Graphic

To add a shape to a SmartArt graphic, follow these steps:

1. Select the SmartArt graphic to which you want to add a shape.

2. On the SmartArt Tools—Design tab, click the down arrow to the right of the Add Shape button to display a menu of options.

3. Select from the following menu choices:
   - **Add Shape After**—Add an identical shape after a selected shape.
   - **Add Shape Before**—Add an identical shape before a selected shape.
   - **Add Shape Above**—Add an identical shape above a selected shape.
   - **Add Shape Below**—Add an identical shape below a selected shape.
   - **Add Assistant**—Add an assistant shape to an organization chart.

The options available are based on your choice of SmartArt. For example, the Add Assistant menu option is available only if your graphic is an organization chart.

If you want to place an additional shape in the default location for your graphic type (such as at the end of a list), you can click the Add Shape button directly, without viewing the menu options.

Adding Bullets

If your SmartArt graphic supports bulleted lists, you can add a text bullet by clicking the Add Bullet button on the SmartArt Tools—Design tab. You must select a specific graphic object for this button to become active.

Using the Text Pane

Although you can enter text directly on your SmartArt graphic, using the Text pane is a good idea if you have a lot of text or your graphic is more complex.

To open the Text pane, click the Text Pane button on the SmartArt Tools—Design tab. Figure 11.7 shows a sample Text pane.

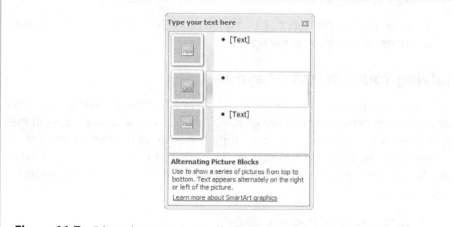

Figure 11.7   *Edit and organize text on the Text pane.*

In this pane, you can enter and revise text, use the buttons in the Create Graphic group to promote or demote objects, and edit any pictures if you selected a graphic type that includes pictures.

To close the Text pane, click the Close button (x) in the upper-right corner or click the Text Pane button on the SmartArt Tools—Design tab again, which acts as a toggle.

Organizing SmartArt Content

The Create Graphic group on the SmartArt Tools—Design tab (refer to Figure 11.3) also includes several buttons that help you organize the content in your graphic. For example, you can promote, demote, or reorder objects to customize your graphic exactly the way you want. Be aware that like other options on the SmartArt Tools—Design tab, the availability of these buttons depends on your graphic type and what object is selected.

The buttons include

- **Promote**—Move selected object up a level. You can also use this with the Text pane.

- **Demote**—Move selected object down a level. You can also use this with the Text pane.

- **Right to Left**—Change layout from the right to the left.

- **Reorder Up**—Move selected object up in a sequence.

- **Reorder Down**—Move selected object down in a sequence.

- **Layout**—Modify the layout of an organization chart, such as displaying subordinates to the left or to the right.

Modifying Your SmartArt Layout

The Layouts group on the SmartArt Tools—Design tab offers several layout options that you can apply to your SmartArt graphic. Three options appear on the tab itself, but you can click the down arrow to the right of the group to open a gallery of additional options. Pause the mouse over each option to preview it on your slide. These layouts correspond to the layouts that appear on the Choose a SmartArt Graphic dialog box.

Changing SmartArt Colors

If you don't like your graphic's default color scheme, you can quickly change it by clicking the Change Colors button on the SmartArt Tools—Design tab. Figure 11.8 shows the gallery that displays, offering color choices suited to your specific SmartArt graphic type.

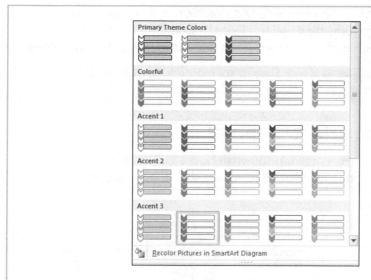

Figure 11.8 *Get colorful by changing your SmartArt colors.*

You can choose a primary theme color, select something more colorful, or opt for one of your theme's accent colors.

Applying a SmartArt Style

If you want to quickly dress up your SmartArt graphic, apply one of the many ready-made styles designed to complement your presentation's theme. To do so, select a style in the SmartArt Styles group on the SmartArt Tools—Design tab. For more options, click the down arrow to display a gallery where you can chose a style that's a good match for your document, or try out a 3-D style.

Resetting a SmartArt Graphic

If you've made a lot of changes to your SmartArt graphic and decide you don't like what you've done, on the SmartArt Tools—Design tab, click the Reset Graphic button. PowerPoint deletes all the formatting changes you've made to your graphic and restores its original format. PowerPoint doesn't delete any text you've added, however.

Converting a SmartArt Graphic

If you decide that you don't want to use a SmartArt graphic you created but would like to retain your text as a bulleted list, on the SmartArt Tools—Design tab, click the Convert button, and select Convert to Text from the menu.

Another option is to convert your SmartArt graphic to a shape so that you can take advantage of shape-formatting options. To do this, on the SmartArt Tools—Design tab, click the Convert button, and then select Convert to Shapes from the menu.

🔄 *See Chapter 10, "Working with Shapes," for more information about PowerPoint shapes.*

Formatting SmartArt Graphics

The SmartArt Tools—Format tab, as shown in Figure 11.9, offers numerous SmartArt formatting options, many of which are shared with other PowerPoint objects.

Figure 11.9   *Create a custom look with the options on the SmartArt Tools—Format tab.*

On this tab, you can

- Edit a 3-D graphic in 2-D.

- Format and change individual SmartArt shapes.

- Apply shape style, fills, outlines, and effects. See Chapter 10 for more information about shape styles.

- Apply WordArt styles, fills, outlines, and effects to SmartArt text. See Chapter 4, "Working with Text," for more information about WordArt styles.

- Arrange SmartArt objects, such as moving objects forward and backward and aligning, grouping, and rotating objects. See Chapter 5, "Formatting and Organizing Objects, Slides, and Presentations," for more information about arranging objects.

- Change the height and width of your SmartArt graphic by clicking the Size button.

 SHOW ME   **Media 11.4—Formatting SmartArt Graphics**

Access this video file through your registered Web Edition at
my.safaribooksonline.com/97801321825530/media.

Editing in 2-D

If you applied a 3-D style to your SmartArt graphic, you can temporarily return to 2-D to edit it by clicking the Edit in 2-D button on the SmartArt Tools—Format tab. When you finish editing, click this button again to return to your 3-D style.

Changing the Appearance of SmartArt Shapes

Although SmartArt graphics include default shapes, you might prefer a different shape. For example, if you select a Basic Block List, your graphic includes several basic rectangles. Your preference, however, might be rounded rectangles.

 LET ME TRY IT

Changing SmartArt Shapes

To change the appearance of the shapes in your SmartArt graphic, follow these steps:

1. Select the shape or shapes you want to change. To select multiple shapes, press the Ctrl key while clicking the shapes you want to change.

2. On the SmartArt Tools—Format tab, click the Change Shape button. A gallery of shape options appears, as shown in Figure 11.10.

3. Select the shape you prefer to change your selected shapes.

Resizing Shapes

If you want to resize selected shapes on your graphic, click either the Larger or Smaller button on the SmartArt Tools—Format tab. You can continue clicking these buttons until you reach your desired size.

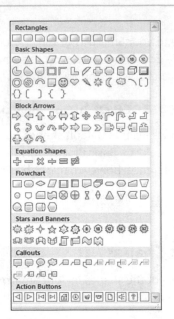

Figure 11.10   *Select a new shape in this gallery.*

This chapter shows you how to create charts in PowerPoint as well as insert charts from Microsoft Excel.

12

Working with Charts

Charts enliven your presentation with visual impact and convey routine data in a way that your audience can easily understand and analyze.

In this chapter, you learn how to insert and format eye-catching, informative charts into your PowerPoint presentations. You can also listen to tips on choosing the right chart type and formats and watch videos that show you how to create a chart in PowerPoint, insert a chart you created in Excel, and format your charts.

Understanding Charts

Charts enable you to display, analyze, and compare numerical data in a graphical format. For example, you can use a column chart to compare sales revenue by region over a period of time (see Figure 12.1). Or you can create a pie chart that illustrates the percentage of revenue each of your product lines contributes to your total company revenue (see Figure 12.2).

PowerPoint also offers a vast array of design and formatting options to make your charts as aesthetically pleasing as they are informational, giving your presentation the wow factor.

PowerPoint 2010 uses the worksheet and charting tools available in Excel 2010 to create charts. When you insert a chart, a separate Excel window opens where you enter data that PowerPoint then uses to create a chart. Note that you must have Excel installed for this feature to work properly. You can also create a chart directly in Excel and insert it into your presentation.

TELL ME MORE   Media 12.1—Understanding Charts

Access this audio recording through your registered Web Edition at
my.safaribooksonline.com/9780132182553/media.

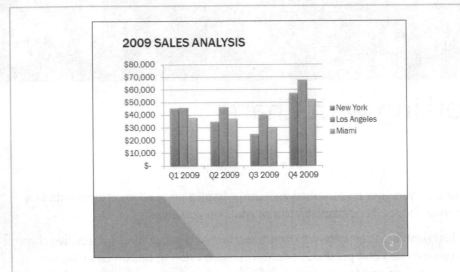

Figure 12.1　*Compare data with a column chart.*

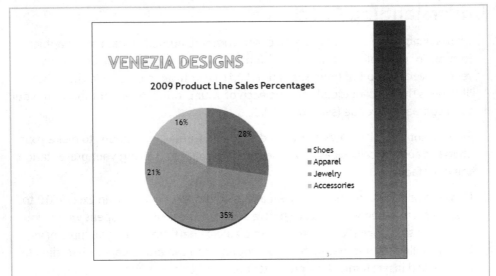

Figure 12.2　*Analyze percentages with a pie chart.*

Understanding Chart Terminology

Before creating a chart, it's a good idea to learn—or refresh your memory about—basic chart terminology. Table 12.1 lists the basic concepts you need to understand to make the most of PowerPoint chart functionality.

Table 12.1 Chart Terminology

Term	Definition
Axis	A line defining the chart area. PowerPoint charts have two axes: a vertical axis that displays data (the y-axis) and a horizontal axis that displays categories (the x-axis).
Chart area	The entire chart and all its components.
Data label	A label that provides information about a data marker.
Data points	Values that display on a chart in the form of columns, bars, or pie slices, for example. A *data marker* represents each individual data point.
Data series	A group of related data points on a chart, identified by a specific color or pattern.
Legend	A small box that describes the patterns or colors used to distinguish chart data series or categories.
Plot area	The area of the chart included inside the axes.

Understanding Chart Types

PowerPoint offers multiple chart types, each with several variations to choose from. For example, if you want to create a column chart, PowerPoint offers 19 different variations of the basic column chart, including options for creating 3-D, clustered, pyramid, and cone column charts.

The total number of chart types—more than 70 in all—can become overwhelming. To choose the right chart type, think carefully about the information you want to present and the message you want to convey with this data, and then select a chart type suited to your data. From there, choose the variation that provides the optimal visual impact and works well with your PowerPoint theme. If you don't have a lot of experience creating charts, you might need to experiment to find just the right match.

Table 12.2 lists PowerPoint chart types.

Table 12.2 PowerPoint Chart Types

Chart Type	Description
Column	Compare data in two or more vertical columns. This chart type works well if you want to compare categories or data across a specific time span.
Line	Display data across a line with markers for each value.
Pie	Display a round pie-shaped chart with percentages of a total.
Bar	Compare data in two or more horizontal bars.

Table 12.2   PowerPoint Chart Types

Chart Type	Description
Area	Display value trends in a single area.
X Y (Scatter)	Compare data with lines and markers.
Stock	Display stock data (or other scientific data) in terms of volume and open, high, low, and close value.
Surface	Display numeric data in 3-D columns and rows.
Doughnut	Display a round pie-shaped chart that can include multiple series of data.
Bubble	Display x and y values in columns with an additional value appearing as a bubble.
Radar	Compare the value of several series of data.

Inserting Charts

The fastest way to add a chart to your presentation is to apply a slide layout that contains the content palette.

⏎ *See Chapter 2, "Creating a Basic Presentation," for more information about PowerPoint slide layouts.*

 SHOW ME   Media 12.2—Inserting a Chart
Access this video file through your registered Web Edition at
my.safaribooksonline.com/9780132182553/media.

 LET ME TRY IT

Inserting a Chart

To insert a chart, follow these steps:

1. Click the down arrow below the New slide button on the Home tab, and then choose an appropriate layout from the gallery that displays. For example, you can choose the Title and Content layout, the Two Content layout, or the Content with Caption layout.

2. On your new slide, click the Insert Chart button on the content palette, as shown in Figure 12.3. The Insert Chart dialog box opens (see Figure 12.4).

Another way to insert a chart is to click the Chart button on the Insert tab.

Insert Chart button

Figure 12.3   *Click the Insert Chart button to start.*

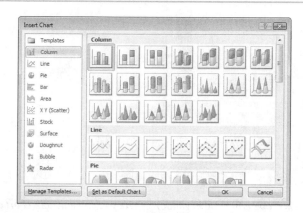

Figure 12.4   *Choose from a variety of chart types.*

3. In the Insert Chart dialog box, select the button for the chart type you want to insert. Or scroll the contents of the Insert Chart dialog box to view all options. See "Understanding Chart Types," earlier in this chapter, for an explanation of each chart type.

You can also view any chart templates you've saved by clicking the Templates button. See "Saving Your Chart as a Template," later in this chapter, for more information about creating chart templates. In the Insert Chart dialog box, you can also click the Manage Templates button to open the Charts window, where you can rename and delete your saved charts.

4. Select the icon for the specific chart type you want to insert, and click the OK button. The chart appears on your slide. In addition, Excel opens in another window with sample data in the format needed for the selected chart type (see Figure 12.5).

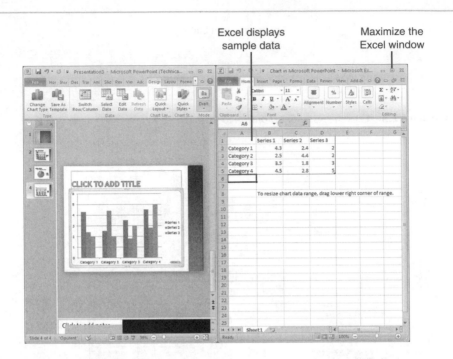

Figure 12.5   *Excel opens in another window where you can edit your chart data.*

> If you use the same chart type on a frequent basis, click the Set as Default Chart button to select this chart type by default every time you open the Insert Chart dialog box.

5. Click the Maximize button in the upper-right corner of Excel to maximize the Excel worksheet where you can enter the data for your selected chart type.

6. Replace the sample data that displays in Excel (refer to Figure 12.5) with your actual data. The format of the sample data varies based on the chart type you selected in the Insert Chart dialog box. Note that any text formatting you apply in Excel, such as bolding or cell styles, doesn't carry over to PowerPoint, but number formatting such as changing regular numbers to dollar amounts does carry over.

7. Return to the PowerPoint window to view and format your chart.

Inserting a Chart from Excel

If you want to reuse an existing chart from an Excel spreadsheet, you can quickly copy and paste it into PowerPoint.

 SHOW ME   Media 12.3—Inserting a Chart from Excel
Access this video file through your registered Web Edition at
my.safaribooksonline.com/9780132182553/media.

 LET ME TRY IT

Inserting an Excel Chart

To insert a chart from Excel, follow these steps:

1. Open the Excel worksheet that contains the chart you want to use in PowerPoint.

2. Select and copy (Ctrl+C) the chart you want to use.

3. Open your PowerPoint presentation and paste (Ctrl+V) the chart on the slide where you want to insert it.

4. Click the Paste Options button below the lower-right corner of the chart and select one of the following buttons, as shown in Figure 12.6:

   • **Use Destination Theme & Embed Workbook**—Embed the chart in your presentation and apply formatting from your presentation theme. You can modify the chart in PowerPoint, but any changes you make to the source in Excel won't be carried over.
   • **Keep Source Formatting & Embed Workbook**—Embed the chart in your presentation and retain the formatting applied in Excel. You can modify the chart in PowerPoint, but any changes you make to the source in Excel won't be carried over.

Figure 12.6   *Specify whether to embed or link to your chart and how to format it.*

- **Use Destination Theme & Link Data**—Insert the chart in your presentation (with a link to the source in Excel) and apply formatting from your presentation theme. Any changes you make to the source chart in Excel are carried over to PowerPoint.
- **Keep Source Formatting & Link Data**—Insert the chart in your presentation (with a link to the source in Excel) and retain the formatting applied in Excel. Any changes you make to the source chart in Excel are carried over to PowerPoint.
- **Picture**—Insert the chart as a picture. You can format your chart as you would any other picture in PowerPoint, but you can't change or update the chart data.

You can then format and modify your chart based on the constraints of your Paste Options selection.

Modifying and Formatting Charts

PowerPoint includes three contextual tabs that enable you to modify the design, layout, and format of your charts. These are, appropriately named, the Chart Tools—Design tab, the Chart Tools—Layout tab, and the Chart Tools—Format tab. These tabs are nearly identical to the Chart Tools tabs in Excel.

Note that these contextual tabs display only when a chart is selected. If they disappear, select your chart again to view them. Also be aware that depending on your choice of chart type, not all options are available on the Chart Tools tabs. For example, not all chart types have axes, trendlines, and so forth. In addition, some options pertain only to 3-D charts.

You can also apply animation effects to your charts, such as having each series fly in separately. See Chapter 14, "Working with Animation and Transitions," for more information about chart animations.

 SHOW ME   Media 12.4—Modifying and Formatting Charts
Access this video file through your registered Web Edition at
my.safaribooksonline.com/9780132182553/media.

Modifying Chart Design

The Chart Tools—Design tab, as shown in Figure 12.7, enables you to change your chart type, edit chart data, and apply chart layouts and styles.

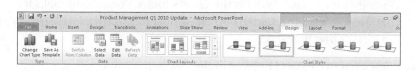

Figure 12.7   *The Chart Tools— Design tab is one of three Chart Tools contextual tabs.*

Changing the Chart Type

If you don't like the way your chart looks and would like to try a different chart type, click the Change Chart Type button on the Chart Tools—Design tab to open the Change Chart Type dialog box. This dialog box is nearly identical to the Insert Chart dialog box, covered in the "Inserting a Chart" section earlier in this chapter. Select a new chart type, and click the OK button to return to your slide.

 LET ME TRY IT

Saving Your Chart as a Template

If you make changes to your chart's design, layout, and format and would like to reuse it again, you can save it as a template.

To create a template based on your current chart, follow these steps:

1. On the Chart Tools—Design tab, click the Save as Template button. Figure 12.8 shows the Save Chart Template dialog box, which opens.

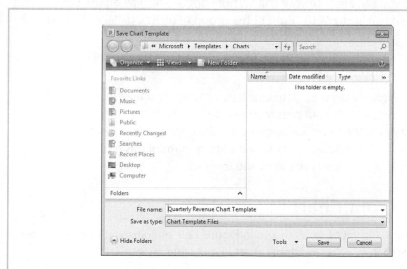

Figure 12.8   *Reuse a common chart format as a template.*

2. Verify that the default folder is the Charts folder. PowerPoint looks for chart templates in this folder when it populates the Templates section in the Insert Chart dialog box.

3. Enter a name for your template in the File Name field.

4. Click the Save button to save your template, and return to your chart.

This template now displays as a choice in the Insert Chart dialog box for future use.

Modifying Chart Data

PowerPoint enables you to edit the data in your charts at any time and refresh data from a linked Excel chart.

The Data group on the Chart Tools—Design tab includes the following buttons:

- **Switch Rows/Columns**—Reverse the x- and y-axes.
- **Select Data**—Open the Select Data Source dialog box where you can specify the chart data range and edit series and category labels.
- **Edit Data**—Open the Excel worksheet where you can edit your chart data.
- **Refresh Data**—Update a PowerPoint chart with data from a linked Excel worksheet.

Modifying Your Chart Layout

The Chart Layouts group on the Chart Tools—Design tab offers several layout options that you can apply to your chart. Three options display on the tab, but you can click the down arrow to the right of the group to open a gallery of additional options.

Applying a Chart Style

If you want to quickly dress up your chart, you can apply one of many chart styles designed to complement your presentation's theme. To do so, select one of the suggested styles in the Chart Styles group on the Chart Tools—Design tab. For more options, click the down arrow to the bottom-right of this group to display a gallery of options in a variety of colors and formats.

Modifying Your Chart's Layout

The Chart Tools—Layout tab, as shown in Figure 12.9, enables you to change your chart type, edit chart data, and apply chart layouts and styles.

Figure 12.9 *Choose from dozens of layout options on the Chart Tools—Layout tab.*

Inserting Objects

To dress up your charts even more, you can add additional objects such as pictures, shapes, and text boxes. The Insert group on the Chart Tools—Layout tab offers three buttons:

- **Pictures**—Click the Picture button to open the Insert Picture dialog box where you can choose a picture on your computer or network. See Chapter 9, "Working with Images," for more information about the Insert Picture dialog box.

- **Shapes**—Click the Shapes button to display the Shapes gallery. See Chapter 10, "Working with Shapes," for more information about inserting shapes.

- **Text boxes**—Click the Text Box button to draw a text box on your slide. See Chapter 4, "Working with Text," for more information about creating text boxes.

Modifying Chart Labels

In the Labels group on the Chart Tools—Layout tab, you can modify the following labels:

- **Chart Title**—Display your chart title as a centered overlay, above the chart, or not at all.

- **Axis Titles**—Display the primary horizontal axis title below the axis or not at all. Display the primary vertical axis title in one of three formats (rotated, vertically, or horizontally) or not at all.

- **Legend**—Display the legend at the right, top, left, or bottom; as an overlay at the right or left; or not at all.

- **Data Labels**—Display data labels in one of four ways in relation to the data point (centered, inside the end, inside the base, or outside the end) or not at all.

- **Data Table**—Display a data table with or without a legend key or not at all.

It's sometimes hard to imagine how all these label options will actually look on your chart, so you might need to experiment a bit to find the format that works best.

Select the More link at the end of each menu to open the Format Data Table dialog box where you can select from additional options.

Modifying Chart Axes

To modify the horizontal or vertical axis, click the Axes button on the Chart Tools—Layout tab and select one of the following from the menu:

- **Primary Horizontal Axis**—Display the axis from left to right with labels, from right to left with labels, without labels, or not at all.

- **Primary Vertical Axis**—Display the axis with the default order and labels, with numbers in the thousands, with numbers in the millions, with numbers in the billions, with a log scale, or not at all.

Modifying Chart Gridlines

To modify the horizontal or vertical axis, click the Axes button on the Chart Tools—Layout tab, and select one of the following from the menu:

- **Primary Horizontal Gridlines**—Display horizontal gridlines for major units, minor units, major and minor units, or not at all.

- **Primary Vertical Gridlines**—Display vertical gridlines for major units, minor units, major and minor units, or not at all.

- **Depth Gridlines**—Display depth gridlines for major units, minor units, major and minor units, or not at all.

Modify Chart Backgrounds

If you don't like the default background of your chart, you can modify it or remove it altogether. Depending on the type of chart on your slide, one or more of the following buttons might be available in the Background group on the Chart Tools—Layout tab:

- **Plot Area**—Display the chart plot area with the default fill color, or remove this fill.

- **Chart Wall**—On 3-D charts, display the chart wall with the default color fill, or remove this fill.

- **Chart Floor**—On 3-D charts, display the chart floor with the default color fill, or remove this fill.

- **3-D Rotation**—Choose from numerous rotation options in the Format Chart Area dialog box.

Analyzing Chart Data

If you want to analyze the data on your chart, you can add trendlines, other lines such as drop lines or high-low lines, up/down bars, or error bars.

Depending on the type of chart on your slide, one or more of the following buttons might be available in the Analysis group on the Chart Tools—Layout tab:

- **Trendline**—Display a linear, exponential, linear forecast, or two-period moving average trendline based on a specific series in your chart, or remove all trendlines.

- **Lines**—Display drop lines, high-low lines, or remove all lines on a line chart.

- **Up/Down Bar**—Display up/down bars, or remove all bars on a line chart.

- **Error Bars**—Display error bars using standard error, by percentage or with standard deviation, or remove all error bars.

Formatting Charts

The Chart Tools—Format tab, as shown in Figure 12.10, enables you to apply formatting to specific chart areas, such as the axes, legend, gridlines, and series.

Figure 12.10 *Apply subtle or sophisticated formatting on the Chart Tools—Format tab.*

  LET ME TRY IT

Formatting Chart Areas

To format specific chart areas, follow these steps:

1. Select the area of the chart you want to format from the Chart Area dropdown list on the Chart Tools—Format tab.

2. Select the chart area you want to format from the menu. The options that appear in the menu vary based on the chart type. For example, a pie chart doesn't have axes.

3. Click the Format Selection button to open the Format dialog box. Again, the exact name of the dialog box and its content varies based on your chart type and what you selected to format. For example, Figure 12.11 shows the Format Axis dialog box, which opens if you choose to format an axis on a bar chart.

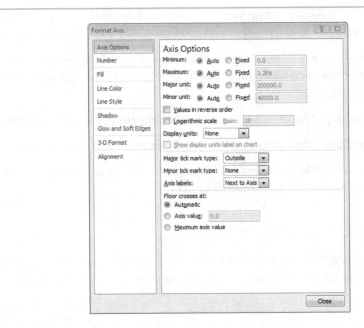

Figure 12.11   *The Format dialog box takes many forms, such as the Format Axis dialog box.*

4. Specify your formatting changes in the Format dialog box.

5. Click the Close button to apply your changes, and return to your chart.

The Chart Tools—Format tab also offers features shared with the Format tabs that appear in context when performing other tasks in PowerPoint, such as applying shape styles and WordArt styles and arranging chart elements. See Chapter 10 for more information about this tab.

13

Working with Audio and Video

The selective use of audio and video is a great way to add impact to any presentation. PowerPoint 2010 includes several familiar options for incorporating multimedia and many new video-editing features. In addition, it introduces the capability to create a video from your presentation.

In this chapter, you learn how to insert, format, and set playback options for both audio and video clips. You can also listen to tips on working with PowerPoint's many new audio and video tools and watch videos that show you how to insert a video clip from your computer, format audio and video clips, and create a video from your presentation.

Working with Audio and Video

PowerPoint offers a multitude of options when it comes to incorporating audio and video into your presentation, including several ways to insert clips and a vast array of formatting and playback options. PowerPoint also supports a wide variety of common audio and video file formats.

 TELL ME MORE   Media 13.1—Working with Audio and Video
Access this audio recording through your registered Web Edition at
my.safaribooksonline.com/9780132182553/media.

Table 13.1 lists the audio and video file formats PowerPoint supports.

In addition to inserting existing video clips into your presentation, PowerPoint 2010 now enables you to convert your presentation to a video that you can play anywhere on the web. See Chapter 17, "Sharing and Collaborating on Presentations," for more information.

Table 13.1 Audio and Video File Formats

Audio File Formats	Video File Formats
Audio Interchange File Format (.aiff), the standard audio format for Apple Macintosh computers	Advanced Systems Format (.asf), a Windows media file format for streaming media
Audio format used by Sun, Java, and Unix (.au)	Audio Video Interactive (.avi), a Windows video file format
Musical Instrument Digital Interface (.midi), an audio file format common with electronic musical instruments	Moving Picture Experts Group (.mpeg), a common movie file format
MPEG-1 Audio Layer 3 (.mp3), a common audio format for digital music	Windows Media Video (.wmv), a video file format developed by Microsoft for streaming video
Waveform Audio File Format (.wav), the standard audio format for Windows-based PCs	QuickTime video file (.mov), Apple's proprietary multimedia framework that handles both audio and video formats
Windows Media Audio (.wma), an audio format developed by Microsoft	Adobe Flash Media, multimedia format created with Adobe Flash
QuickTime Video (audio component)	

Inserting Audio Clips

PowerPoint offers three ways to insert audio clips into your presentation. You can

- Insert an audio clip stored on your computer or network.
- Insert an audio clip from Microsoft's clip collection.
- Record an audio clip and insert it.

Inserting your own audio clip and recording an audio clip are covered in this section.

⊙ See "Inserting Audio and Video Clips from the Clip Art Task Pane" later in this chapter for more information about inserting a clip from Microsoft's clip collection.

Inserting Audio Clips from Your Computer

 **LET ME TRY IT**

Inserting an Audio Clip

To insert an audio clip stored on your computer or a network location, follow these steps:

1. Navigate to the presentation slide where you want to insert your audio clip.

2. On the Insert tab, click the Audio button to open the Insert Audio dialog box, as shown in Figure 13.1.

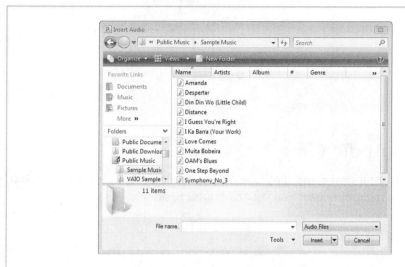

Figure 13.1 *Insert an audio clip stored on your computer.*

The Insert Audio dialog box shares many advanced options with the Open dialog box. See Chapter 2, "Creating a Basic Presentation," for more information about these options.

3. Navigate to the audio clip you want to insert, and click the Insert button. PowerPoint inserts the audio into your slide in the form of an Audio Clip icon, as shown in Figure 13.2.

4. Modify and format the audio clip as desired.

When you select an audio clip on a slide, the player control bar displays below it. The Audio Tools—Format and Audio Tools—Playback tabs also display.

See *"Formatting Audio and Video Clips"* and *"Specifying Audio and Video Playback Options"* later in this chapter for more information about these tabs.

If desired, you can reposition your audio clip elsewhere on your slide.

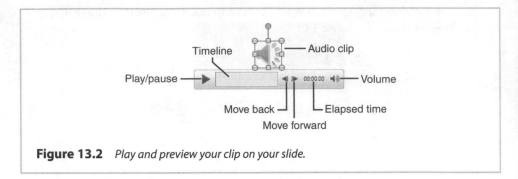

Figure 13.2   *Play and preview your clip on your slide.*

Recording Audio Clips

You can record your own audio clips to insert in your PowerPoint presentation. You need to have a microphone jack on your computer to do this.

 LET ME TRY IT

Recording an Audio Clip

To record an audio clip, follow these steps:

1. Navigate to the presentation slide where you want to insert your audio clip.

2. On the Insert tab, click the down arrow below the Audio button.

3. From the menu, select Record Audio to open the Record Sound dialog box, as shown in Figure 13.3.

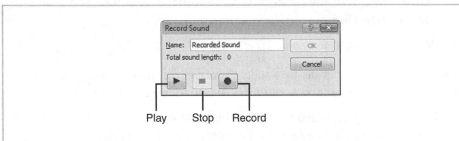

Figure 13.3   *Record a sound to play with a particular slide.*

4. Enter a description for this sound in the Name field.

5. Click the Record button to begin recording your sound.

6. Click the Stop button when you finish recording. To play back the sound, click the Play button.

7. Click the OK button to save the sound with the presentation; click Cancel to exit and start over.

An audio clip icon now displays in your presentation. You can reposition and resize it if desired. For example, you might want to place this icon in the lower-right corner of your slide to focus your audience on the slide content.

Deleting Audio Clips

To delete an audio clip from a slide, select it and press the Delete key.

Inserting Video Clips

PowerPoint offers three ways to insert video clips into your presentation:

- Insert a video clip stored on your computer or network.
- Insert a video clip hosted on an external website.
- Insert an audio clip from Microsoft's clip art collection.

Inserting your own video clip and inserting a clip from the web are covered in this section.

Ⓖ *See "Inserting Audio and Video Clips from the Clip Art Task Pane" later in this chapter for more information about inserting a clip from Microsoft's clip collection.*

To delete a video clip from a slide, select it and press the Delete key.

 **LET ME TRY IT**

Inserting a Video Clip from Your Computer

To insert a video clip from your computer or a network location, follow these steps:

1. Navigate to the presentation slide where you want to insert your video clip.

2. On the Insert tab, click the Video button to open the Insert Video dialog box, as shown in Figure 13.4.

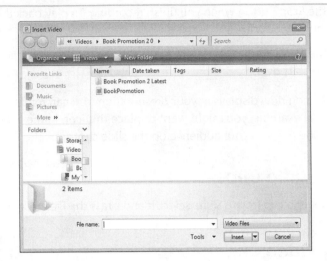

Figure 13.4   *Select your own video to insert.*

The Insert Video dialog box shares many advanced options with the Open dialog box. See Chapter 2, "Creating a Basic Presentation," for more information about these options.

   3. Navigate to the video you want to insert, and click the Insert button. PowerPoint inserts the video into your slide, as shown in Figure 13.5.

   4. Modify and format the video clip as desired.

Another way to insert audio or video clips from the clip art gallery is to use the content palette. To do so, click the down arrow below the New Slide button on the Home tab, and select one of the slide layouts that includes the content palette. On your new slide, click the Insert Media Clip button on the palette to open the Insert Video dialog box.

Select the video to display the player controls below it, including the Play/Pause button, a timeline, the Move Back and Move Forward buttons, an elapsed time counter, and a volume control. The Video Tools—Format and Video Tools—Playback tabs also display.

    🄖 *See "Formatting Audio and Video Clips" and "Specifying Audio and Video Playback Options" later in this chapter for more information about these tabs.*

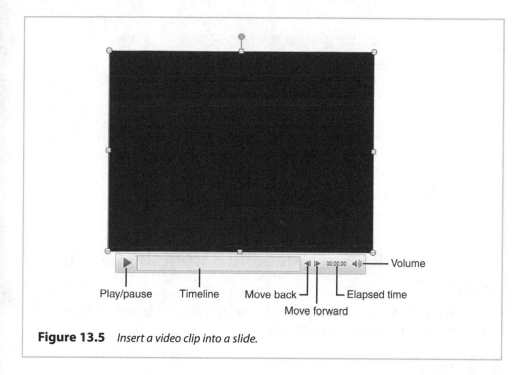

Figure 13.5   *Insert a video clip into a slide.*

SHOW ME   Media 13.2—Inserting a Video Clip from Your Computer
*Access this video file through your registered Web Edition at
my.safaribooksonline.com/9780132182553/media.*

LET ME TRY IT

Inserting Video from a Website

PowerPoint introduces the ability to insert a video clip from an external website, such as a video on your company's website or a YouTube video.

To insert a video clip from a website, follow these steps:

1.   On the Insert tab, click the down arrow below the Video button.

2.   From the menu, select Video from Web Site to open the Insert Video from Web Site dialog box, as shown in Figure 13.6.

3.   Copy the code from the website and paste it into the text box. To insert a YouTube video, for example, copy and paste the embedded code in this box.

4.   Click the Insert button to insert the video clip onto your slide.

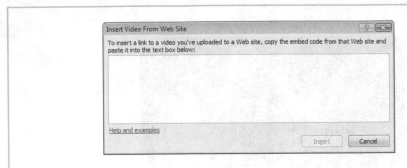

Figure 13.6   *Insert a video from a website, such as a YouTube video.*

Inserting Audio and Video Clips from the Clip Art Task Pane

Microsoft's Clip Art task pane offers more than just a vast collection of clip art; it also includes many audio and video clips.

 **LET ME TRY IT**

Inserting an Audio or Video Clip from the Clip Art Task Pane

To insert an audio or video clip from Microsoft's clip collection, follow these steps:

1. On the Insert tab, click the down arrow below the Video button and select Clip Art Video from the menu (to insert a video clip). Alternatively, click the down arrow below the Audio button, and select Clip Art Audio from the menu (to insert an audio clip). The Clip Art task pane opens, as shown in Figure 13.7.

Another way to insert audio or video clips from the clip art gallery is to use the content palette. To do so, click the down arrow below the New Slide button on the Home tab, and select one of the slide layouts that includes the content palette. On your new slide, click the Clip Art button on the palette to open the Clip Art task pane.

Figure 13.7   *Search for audio and video clips on the Clip Art task pane.*

2. By default, either Audio or Videos is selected in the Results Should Be drop-down list, based on your choice in step 1. If you want to search for something or search for multiple media file types, you can modify your selection here.

3. Optionally, enter a keyword or keywords in the Search For text box to narrow your search results.

4. If you want to search Office.com for additional content, select the Include Office.com Content checkbox. The Office.com site (http://office.microsoft.com) contains an extensive clip art collection from numerous sources.

5. Click the Go button to display matching results.

6. Click the down arrow to the right of the clip you want, and select Insert from the menu that appears.

Formatting Audio and Video Clips

The Audio Tools—Format tab and Video Tools—Format tab display when you select an audio or video clip on a PowerPoint slide. Figures 13.8 and 13.9 show these two tabs, which offer many options for formatting your media clips. With a few exceptions, these tabs are nearly identical and are also similar to the options on the Picture Tools—Format tab covered in detail in Chapter 9, "Working with Images." This chapter focuses on formatting issues unique to audio and video clips.

Figure 13.8   *Format the appearance of the Audio Clip icon.*

Figure 13.9   *Dress up your video with video styles and borders.*

 SHOW ME   **Media 13.3—Formatting Audio and Video Clips**
Access this audio recording through your registered Web Edition at
my.safaribooksonline.com/9780132182553/media.

Adjusting Audio and Video Clips

The Adjust group on the Video Tools—Format tab and the Audio Tools—Format tab enable you to remove background images from the Audio Clip icon, correct images, adjust color settings, and apply artistic effects. Be aware that not all these options are available, depending on the format of the image you want to modify.

⊙ *See "Adjusting Images," in Chapter 9 for more information.*

Specifying a Video Poster Frame

If you inserted a video clip, you can specify the appearance of the initial preview image, referred to as the *poster frame*. For example, you can display a static image from the video, a company logo, or even the photo of a speaker in the video.

To specify a poster frame for a selected video, go to the Video Tools—Format tab, and click the Poster Frame button.

Select one of the following options from the menu:

- **Current Frame**—Use the current frame as the poster frame. To activate this option, you must play your video on your slide and pause it at the specific frame you want to use.

- **Image from File**—Open the Insert Picture dialog box where you can select an image from your computer or network location.

- **Reset**—Restore the default poster frame.

Working with Audio and Video Styles

The Audio Styles group on the Audio Tools—Format tab and the Video Styles group on the Video Tools—Format tab enable you to

- Apply one of many preselected styles to your media clips, ranging from subtle to moderate to intense.

- Add a border around your clip.

- Apply special clip effects.

- Modify your video shape.

Note that for video, these effects apply to the video's preview image, and for audio, the effects apply to the Audio Clip icon.

Figure 13.10 shows an example of the rotated, gradient style applied to a video clip.

📀 See "Working with Picture Styles," in Chapter 9 for more information.

Arranging Audio and Video Clips

The Arrange group on the Video Tools—Format tab and the Audio Tools—Format tab offers numerous options for arranging media clips. For example, you can align, group, and rotate images and send overlapping clips backward or forward to achieve a desired effect.

📀 See Chapter 5, "Formatting and Organizing Objects, Slides, and Presentations," for more information about using the options in the Arrange group.

Figure 13.10   *Apply varied styles to your videos to give them a new look.*

Resizing Audio and Video Clips

If you don't want to include an entire clip image in your presentation, you can crop it to your exact specifications. For example, you might want to zero in on an object in the center of a clip or remove extra content at the top of a clip. To do so, select the clip, and click the Crop button on the Format tab. Handles surround the image, enabling you to specify the exact content you want to retain. Drag the mouse to determine your cropping area.

Alternatively, enter precise size specifications in the Height and Width boxes.

Cropping a clip refers to reducing the size of its physical image. If you want to play only a certain section of the clip's audio or video content, you need to trim it, which you can do on the Playback tab.

Specifying Audio and Video Playback Options

The Audio Tools—Playback tab and Video Tools—Playback tab appear when you select an audio or video clip on a PowerPoint slide. The Playback tab offers many options for specifying how you want to play your clips in an actual slide show. Figures 13.11 and 13.12 show these two tabs.

Figure 13.11   *Specify how you want to play an audio video.*

Figure 13.12   *On the Video Tools—Playback tab, you can trim video content and determine how to start your video.*

Playing a Clip

To play a clip directly on your slide, click the Play button on the Playback tab. Alternatively, click the Play button on the player control bar that appears below your clip. This is a good way to preview clips before actually running a show.

Adding a Bookmark

If you want to return to a specific place in one of your clips, you can bookmark it. To create a bookmark, play the selected clip, and pause at the location where you want to place the bookmark. Next, click the Add Bookmark button on the Playback tab. PowerPoint inserts a bookmark on the clip's timeline. Figure 13.13 shows a sample audio bookmark.

Bookmarks are useful if you want to start playing your clip at a certain location or want to replay a specific segment for emphasis. You can also bookmark start and stop times if you want to trim your clip.

Editing Audio and Video Clips

In the Editing group on the Playback tab, you can trim your clip by specifying exact start and stop times. You can also add fade in and fade out effects to your clip in increments of .25 a second.

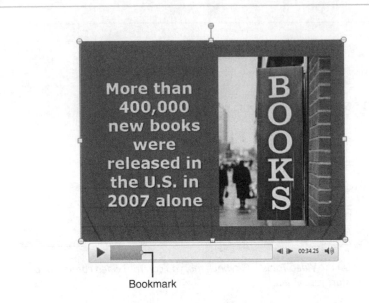

Figure 13.13   *Use a bookmark to easily return to a specific location in your clip.*

To trim a selected audio clip, click the Trim Audio button on the Audio Tools—Playback tab. The Trim Audio dialog box displays, as shown in Figure 13.14. To trim a selected video clip, click the Trim Video button on the Video Tools—Playback tab. The Trim Video dialog box displays, as shown in Figure 13.15.

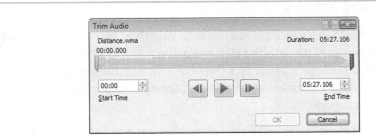

Figure 13.14   *Play only a certain section of an audio by trimming it.*

Although these dialog boxes differ in size, their fields are identical. To trim a clip, you can

- Enter times in the Start Time and End Time fields.
- Use the Play, Previous Frame, and Next Frame buttons to review your clip and determine start and end times.

Figure 13.15 *PowerPoint offers several ways you can trim your videos.*

- Use the sliders (green for start time and red for end time) to specify what to trim. This is particularly useful if you've already added bookmarks to your clip.

When you finish trimming, click the OK button to return to your slide.

Specifying Audio and Video Options

The Audio Options group and Video Options group on the Playback tab share many of the same buttons and features. These include

- **Volume**—Specify the volume level: low, medium, high, or mute.
- **Start**—Specify whether to start a clip automatically, start it with a mouse click, or play it across slides (audio only).
- **Hide During Show**—Hide the Audio Clip icon during a slide show (audio only). You should play your clip automatically if you select this option.
- **Play Full Screen**—Select this check box to play a video full screen during a slide show (video only).
- **Hide While Not Playing**—Hide the video preview image when it's not playing (video only).

- **Loop Until Stopped**—Repeat playing a clip until you manually stop it.
- **Rewind After Playing**—Return to the beginning of a clip after you play it.

Compressing Media Files for Improved Performance

To improve the playback performance of your media files and save disk space, you can compress these files.

 **LET ME TRY IT**

Compressing Media Files

To compress the media files in an open presentation, follow these steps:

1. Click the File tab, and then select Info to open Backstage view.

2. Click the Compress Media button, shown in Figure 13.16, and select from the following menu of options:

   - **Presentation Quality**—Maintain high-quality audio and video.
   - **Internet Quality**—Maintain quality suitable for streaming media on the Internet.
   - **Low Quality**—Maintain basic quality while reducing file size to that suitable for emailing a presentation.

   Be aware that the Compress Media button is available only if your presentation contains an audio or video file you can compress.

3. Review the Compress Media dialog box, which shows you the compression in progress. Depending on the number of media files in your presentation, this could take several minutes. When the compression process completes, the dialog box informs you how much space you saved, such as 1.4MB.

   To restore your presentation to its original status, select the Undo menu option.

4. Click the Close button to close the dialog box.

Remember that compressing files affects presentation quality. Be sure to preview your presentation after compression to evaluate its impact.

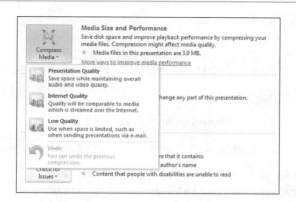

Figure 13.16 *Compress your audio and video files to improve playback performance.*

Creating Videos from PowerPoint Presentations

PowerPoint 2010 introduces the capability to create a full-fidelity video from your PowerPoint presentation. You can distribute your video on the web or mobile device, or through more traditional methods, such as on a DVD or through email.

Before creating your video, decide what format you want to use, and verify that your slide content will work with this format. For example, if you want to run your video on portable devices, using small text isn't a viable option. In addition, you need to create any timings or narration before creating your video.

G *See Chapter 15, "Presenting a Slide Show," for more information.*

PowerPoint creates videos in Window Media Video (.wmv) format. Videos include all slide content except media you inserted in a previous version of PowerPoint (insert them in PowerPoint 2010 to include them), macros, and OLE/ActiveX controls.

 SHOW ME   Media 13.4—Creating a Video from a PowerPoint **Presentation**
Access this video file through your registered Web Edition at
my.safaribooksonline.com/9780132182553/media.

LET ME TRY IT

Creating a Video from a PowerPoint Presentation

To create a video, follow these steps:

1. Open the presentation you want to save as a video.

2. Click the File tab, and select Save & Send to open Backstage view.

3. Click the Create a Video button in the File Types section. The right side of the page shows the Create a Video section, as shown in Figure 13.17.

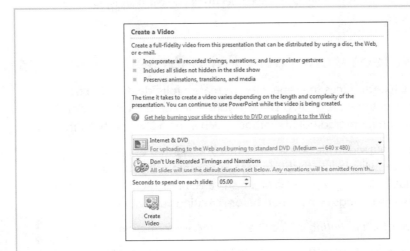

Figure 13.17   *PowerPoint 2010 enables you to create videos from your presentations.*

4. From the first drop-down list, select one of the following video formats:

   - **Computer & HD Displays**—Create a video that plays on a computer monitor, project, or high-definition display at 960 x 720 resolution. This generates a video with very high quality but generates the largest file size.

   - **Internet & DVD**—Create a video that you can upload to the web or burn to a DVD at 640 x 480 resolution. This generates a video with medium quality and a moderate file size.

   - **Portable Devices**—Creates a video that plays on a mobile device such as Microsoft Zune or a smartphone at 320 x 240 resolution. This generates a video with lower quality and the smallest file size.

5. From the second drop-down list, select one of the following options:

- **Don't Use Recorded Timings or Narrations**—Use timing specified in the Seconds to Spend on Each Slide box. The default is 5 seconds, but you can increase or decrease this as desired.

- **Use Recorded Timings and Narrations**—Use the timings, narrations, and recorded laser pointing directives you specified on the Slide Show tab. See Chapter 15 for more information. This option isn't available if you haven't recorded any timings or narrations.

If you would like to add timings and narrations, click the Record Timings and Narrations link to open the Record Slide Show dialog box. Click the Preview Timings and Narrations to preview your presentation as it would display in your video with timings and narrations.

6. Click the Create Video button to open the Save As dialog box.

7. Enter a file name for your video and click the OK button. PowerPoint starts the video creation process. The time it takes to create your video depends on the number of slides in your presentation, your slide content, and the video format you choose.

From here, you can do the following:

- Play this video on your computer, by going to its folder location and double-clicking it.

- Upload your video to your website, blog, or a video-sharing site such as YouTube.

- Burn your video to a DVD using DVD-burning software, such as Windows DVD Maker, included with many versions of Windows Vista and Windows 7.

- Save to a shared site such as SharePoint, SkyDrive, or Microsoft Office Live.

- Send to others via email, as described in Chapter 17, "Sharing and Collaborating on Presentations."

This chapter introduces you to the many ways you can add motion to your presentation through animation and transitions.

14

Working with Animation and Transitions

PowerPoint offers numerous options for animating your slide content and enlivening your presentation. You can animate the transition from one slide to another or animate how objects and text display on a slide. You can also customize these basic animations in a variety of ways.

In this chapter, you learn how to smoothly transition your slides and animate slide objects, including text, charts, SmartArt graphics, and media files. You can also listen to tips on making the most of PowerPoint animation and transition features and watch videos that show you how to set slide transitions, apply animation to objects, and customize animations on the Animation pane.

Understanding Animation and Transitions

Like most of PowerPoint's capabilities, animation can be either simple or complex. It all depends on how creative and sophisticated you want to make your presentation. Animation can definitely enliven any presentation, but as with any special effect, be careful not to overdo it. Too much animation can actually detract from your presentation. Animation also increases presentation file size.

 TELL ME MORE   **Media 14.1—Understanding Animation and Transitions**
Access this audio recording through your registered Web Edition at my.safaribooksonline.com/9780132182553/media.

PowerPoint offers two main ways to animate and add motion to your presentation, as follows:

- **Slide transitions**—Determine how to change from one slide to the next in your presentation. By default, when you move from one slide to another, the next slide immediately appears. With animation, you can make the old slide fade away to reveal the new slide or make the new slide move down from the top of the screen to cover the old slide.

- **Text and object animation**—Animate PowerPoint objects, such as text or shapes, using directional effects similar to slide transitions. For example, you can use an animation to wipe title text into your presentation. You can also specify more sophisticated animation options, such as the order and timing of multiple animation objects in one slide.

Setting Slide Transitions

Setting slide transitions is one of the most common animation effects. You can apply a slide transition to the entire presentation or just to the current slide. PowerPoint offers a variety of transition options ranging from subtle to dynamic, including the capability to fade, wipe, reveal, or even introduce a slide with a honeycomb effect. If you aren't familiar with these effects, you can try them out on your slides before applying them. Most transitions enable you to choose a direction as well. For example, you can wipe up, down, left, or right.

As with so many PowerPoint features, use restraint with slide transitions. For the most professional results, choose one transition to use for every slide in a presentation. Or if you want to highlight one or two particular slides, you can apply just the right transition to those, but don't apply custom transitions to the remaining slides. Too many different transitions can make your presentation confusing and inconsistent, detracting from your message.

 SHOW ME   Media 14.2   Setting Slide Transitions
Access this video file through your registered Web Edition at
my.safaribooksonline.com/9780132182553/media.

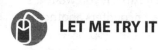 **LET ME TRY IT**

Setting Up Presentation Slide Transitions

To set up slide transitions, follow these steps:

1. Select the slides to which you want to apply the transition in either Slide Sorter view or on the Slides tab of Normal view. To select all slides, press Ctrl+A.

2. On the Transitions tab, choose one of the transitions that appears in the Transition to This Slide group.

3. For more options, click the down arrow in the lower-right corner of the group, and choose one of the transitions from the Transitions gallery. Figure 14.1 illustrates this gallery.

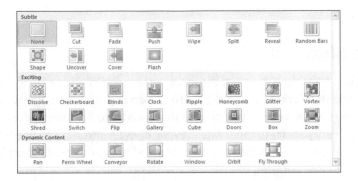

Figure 14.1   *You can specify how you want to move from one slide to another slide during a presentation.*

4. Click the Effect Options button to open a gallery of effects that determine the direction your transition moves, such as from the top or from the bottom-right. Options vary based on the transition you select, and each includes an image that illustrates the direction.

5. To add a sound effect to your transition, select a sound from the Sound drop-down list. If you want to use a sound stored on your computer, choose Other Sound from the drop-down list to open the Add Audio dialog box, select the sound to use, and click the Open button. If you want the sound to continue playing until the presentation encounters another sound file, select the Loop Until Next Sound option on the drop-down menu. See Chapter 13, "Working with Audio and Video," for more sound options.

Use sounds sparingly on slide transitions. They can unintentionally generate laughter or even annoyance in your audience.

6. Select the amount of time (in seconds) you want the transition to take introducing each slide in the Duration field.

7. Select the On Mouse Click check box to advance to the next slide when
    you click the mouse or press a key such as the spacebar, Enter, Page Up, or
    Page Down. This is selected by default.

8. If you would rather have PowerPoint automatically change to the next
    slide after a specified amount of time, select the After check box and enter
    a specific time, in minutes and seconds, in the field beside it. Any timings
    you've already added to your slide show display in this box.

9. To preview your transitions, click the Preview button on the left side of the
    Transitions tab.

10. Click the Apply to All button to apply the transitions to all slides in your pres-
    entation.

Applying Animation to Objects

You can apply basic animation to objects such as shapes, text placeholders, text
boxes, SmartArt graphics, and charts using the options available in the Animation
group on the Animations tab, as shown in Figure 14.2.

Figure 14.2   *The Animations tab offers numerous options for adding motion to your
slides.*

 SHOW ME   Media 14.3—Applying Animation to Objects
*Access this video file through your registered Web Edition at
my.safaribooksonline.com/9780132182553/media.*

 **LET ME TRY IT**

Animating Objects

To apply animations to objects, follow these steps:

1. Select the object or objects you want to animate. If you select more than
    one object, PowerPoint applies the animation to both objects at the same

time. If you want the animations to occur in sequence, you must apply animation separately.

2. On the Animations tab, select the animation you want to apply from the Animation group. Several options appear on the ribbon, but you can click the down arrow in the lower-right corner of the group and choose one of the options that appear in the gallery (see Figure 14.3).

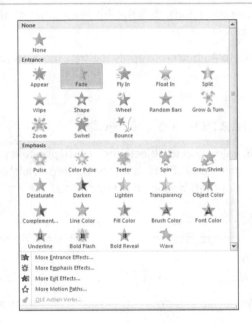

Figure 14.3   *Choose from a variety of animation effects in the gallery.*

PowerPoint offers four categories of animations:

- **Entrance**—Determine how the text or object enters the slide.
- **Emphasis**—Add emphasis to the text or object.
- **Exit**—Determine how the text or object exits the slide.
- **Motion Paths**—Set a path that the selected text or object follows.

Select More Entrance Effects, More Emphasis Effects, More Exit Effects, or More Motion Paths in the gallery to open a dialog box with additional options.

3. Click the Effect Options button to choose the direction to apply the animation. The options that appear here vary based on the animation you chose.

For example, if you choose the Fly In animation, this list includes eight options, including From Bottom or From Right. If the animation you selected doesn't offer effect options, you can't select this button.

4. Click the Trigger button to specify what triggers this animation to start. Your choices include setting triggers based on the click of a specific object on the slide or on a bookmark.

5. Click the down arrow to the right of the Start button to specify when to start the animation:

    • **On Click**—Start the animation when you click the mouse.

    • **With Previous**—Start the animation when the previous animation in the list starts.

    • **After Previous**—Start the animation after the previous animation in the list finishes.

6. Select a Delay, in seconds, between each animation. If you don't want a delay, select 00.00 in this field. Otherwise, you can specify delays in 0.25 increments.

7. Select a Duration, in seconds, to determine how long the animation should last. The smallest duration you can choose is 00.01, which introduces, and ends, your animation almost instantly. Otherwise, you can specify durations in 0.25 increments. If you choose a long duration, be aware that this creates a slow motion effect.

8. Click the Preview button to preview your animation choices.

Customizing Animations on the Animation Pane

The tools available on the Animations tab should suit most of your animation needs. However, if you want to customize your animations even more, you can do so on the Animation pane. For example, you use this task pane to set animation effects for text, charts, SmartArt graphics, and media clips.

To open the pane (see Figure 14.4), click the Animation Pane button on the Animations tab.

Be aware that if you haven't applied any animations yet, the pane will be empty and its features and buttons will be inactive.

Figure 14.4   *Further enhance your animation effects on the Animation pane.*

Each animation you applied displays in the Animation pane in the order in which you applied it. The icon that precedes it tells you what kind of animation it is and corresponds to the icons that display in the Animation group on the Animations tab. The light yellow bar that follows it indicates the duration of the animation. Pause the mouse over the animation in the list to display more information, such as the start option and effect type. If you have multiple animations in this list, the list is numbered, and the numbers also display on your slide to show where the animations are located. These numbers don't display in print or during a slide show, however.

Select an animated object in the list, and click the down arrow to its right to open a menu of additional options, described in more detail later in this section.

Click the Play button to see the animations in your current view, or click the Slide Show button to see the animations in a slide show.

Setting Additional Effects

To add additional effects to an animation listed in the pane—such as directional, sound, text, and color enhancements—click the down arrow to the right of an animation in the list and choose Effect Options from the menu that appears. A dialog box opens with the Effect tab selected (see Figure 14.5).

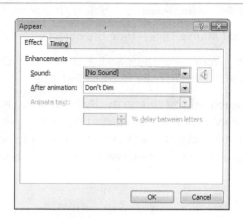

Figure 14.5 *Continue to customize your custom animation with the options in this dialog box.*

The dialog box's name and content depend on the kind of animation event you're customizing. For example, if you choose the Appear entrance effect, the Appear dialog box opens. As an example, the Effect tab on the Appear dialog box offers the following options:

- **Sound**—If you want a sound effect to accompany the effect, select a sound from the drop-down list. If you don't want to include a sound, choose No Sound, which is the default option. For even more sounds, choose Other Sound to open the Add Audio dialog box. See Chapter 13 for information about using sounds.

- **Volume**—Raise or lower the sound effect's volume level. You can also choose to mute the effect.

- **After Animation**—Specify how to end your animation, such as by displaying the object in a new color or hiding it after animation. Options include

  - **Standard Colors**—Apply a color from the default palette, which changes the object's color after the animation finishes.

  - **More Colors**—Display the Colors dialog box from which you can choose any color. The object changes to this color after the animation finishes. See Chapter 10, "Working with Shapes," for more information about the Colors dialog box.

  - **Don't Dim**—Continue to display a static image of the object after animation.

- **Hide After Animation**—Hide the object after animation.

- **Hide on Next Mouse Click**—Hide the object when you click the mouse.

- **Animate Text**—From the drop-down list, choose a method for introducing text: All at Once (the default), By Word, or By Letter.

- **% Delay Between**—If you choose the By Word or By Letter option, you can set how long PowerPoint waits after starting to display one word or letter before starting to display the next word or letter. Fifty percent means that the previous word is 50% displayed when the next word begins to display.

Setting Timings

To set exact timing effects for your custom animations, click the down arrow next to an animation in the Animation pane, and choose Timing from the menu that appears. A dialog box opens with the Timing tab selected, as shown in Figure 14.6.

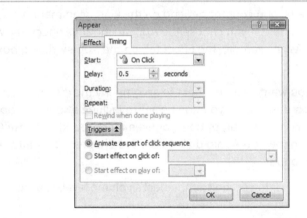

Figure 14.6   *Make additional timing modifications on the Timing tab.*

Remember that the name of this dialog box reflects the type of animation effect whose timing you want to customize. On the Timing tab, you can set the following options:

- **Start**—Specify when to start the animation:

  - **On Click**—Start the animation when you click the mouse.

  - **With Previous**—Start the animation when the previous animation in the list starts.

  - **After Previous**—Start the animation after the previous animation in the list finishes.

- **Delay**—Enter the delay in seconds.

- **Duration**—Choose a duration—from very slow to very fast.

- **Repeat**—Indicate how many times you want the animation to repeat. Options include none (which means that it plays once); two, three, four, five, or ten times; until the next mouse click; or until the next slide.

- **Rewind When Done Playing**—Click this check box if you want to return the animation to its original position when it finishes playing.

- **Triggers**—Click the Triggers button to display three more fields on this tab that let you determine what triggers this animation to start:

  - **Animate as Part of Click Sequence**—Animate as part of the click sequence in the Custom Animation list.

  - **Start Effect on Click Of**—Choose a specific animation from the drop-down list on which to trigger this animation.

  - **Start Effect on Play Of**—Animate at the start of a media file.

Animating Charts

You can add more effects to a chart to which you've applied an animation. To do so, click the down arrow next to the chart in the Animation pane, and choose Effect Options from the menu. Figure 14.7 shows the dialog box that displays. Remember that the dialog box name reflects the type of effect you've applied, such as Fly In or Fade.

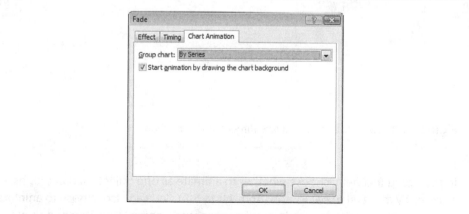

Figure 14.7 *Animating a chart is another possibility.*

Click the Chart Animation tab and, from the Group Chart drop-down list, indicate how you want to introduce the chart elements. Options include As One Object, By Series, By Category, By Element in Series, and By Element in Category.

🔄 *See Chapter 12, "Working with Charts," for more information about inserting charts in your presentation.*

If you choose any option other than As One Object, the Start Animation by Drawing the Chart Background check box activates, letting you begin the animation with a chart background and then filling it in.

Animating Text

If the object you animate includes text, such as a text placeholder or text box, you can apply special text effects to your animation. To do so, click the down arrow next to the object in the Animation pane, choose Effect Options from the menu, and click the Text Animation tab. Figure 14.8 shows this tab.

Figure 14.8   *Emphasize specific words through text animation.*

In the Group Text field, choose whether to animate as one object, all paragraphs at once, or by the level of paragraph (from 1st to 5th). You can also choose to animate text automatically after a certain number of seconds, animate an attached shape, or animate text in reverse orders.

Depending on the type of text you animate, all these options might not be available. For example, let's say that you want to animate a text box that includes several lines of text or perhaps a bulleted list. By choosing to animate by first-level paragraph, you can display each line individually rather than allow your audience to see your entire list at once.

Animating SmartArt Graphics

Animating SmartArt graphics is another animation customization you can apply. To do so, click the down arrow next to the graphic in the Animation pane, choose Effect Options from the menu, and click the SmartArt Animation tab (see Figure 14.9).

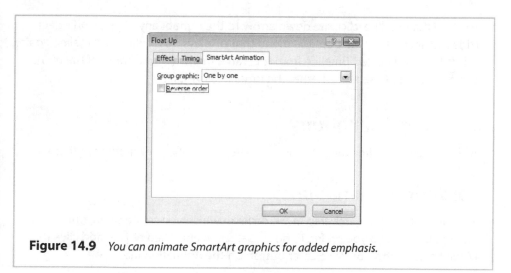

Figure 14.9 *You can animate SmartArt graphics for added emphasis.*

From the Group Graphic drop-down list, choose the way you want to introduce the graphic onto the slide. The choices depend on the kind of SmartArt graphic you animate.

Animating Audio and Video Files

You can also customize animations to media clips such as an audio or video file. For example, to customize an audio clip animation, click the down arrow next to the clip in the Animation pane, and choose Effect Options from the menu. The Play Audio dialog box opens, where you can customize audio effects, timing, and volume.

Viewing the Advanced Timeline

The Animation pane also displays the Advanced Timeline, which lets you further customize timings by dragging the timeline's scrollbar. Figure 14.10 illustrates this timeline.

Figure 14.10   *Define specific timings to give your presentation a professional polish.*

To close the timeline, click the down arrow to the right of any object, and select Hide Advanced Timeline from the menu that displays. To display the timeline again, select Show Advanced Timeline from this same menu. (The wording of the menu option changes based on whether the timeline is visible.)

Managing Animations

After you create animations, it's easy to reorder, modify, or even remove them.

Reordering Animations

Your animations are numbered in the order in which you create them, but you can change this order if you prefer. To do so, select an animated object, and click the Move Earlier button or Move Later button on the Animation tab.

You can also reorder animations on the Animation pane by using the Reorder arrow buttons at the bottom of the pane. Another option is to drag an animation to another location in the pane.

Modifying Animations

After you apply custom animations to a slide, you might decide that you want to modify them. For example, you might want to change the type of effect you applied from Fade to Float In or from Pulse to Grow/Shrink. To do so, select the object, and choose a new animation effect from the Animation group.

Removing Animations

To remove an animation from a selected object or objects, click the None button in the Animation group. Alternatively, select the animated object in the Animation pane, click the down arrow, and select Remove from the menu. To remove all animations, select the first animation in the list, press the Shift key, select the last animation in the list, click the down arrow, and select Remove. If you make a mistake and want to restore your deletions, click the Undo button on the Quick Access toolbar.

Reusing Animations with the Animation Painter

To copy an animation you added to one object and apply it to another object, you can use the Animation Painter button on the Animations tab. This button works in much the same way as the Format Painter button.

To apply the animation from a selected object to another object, click the Animation Painter button, and then select the new object. To apply animations to more than one object, double-click the Animation Painter button, and then select the new objects.

IV

Making Presentations

This chapter teaches you how to set up and deliver your slide show.

15

Presenting a Slide Show

After you create all the slides in your presentation, you'll want to plan how to present them in a slide show. Fortunately, PowerPoint makes it easy to set up, rehearse, and present a show.

In this chapter, you learn how to manage the slide show process, from setup to delivery. You can also listen to tips on how to prepare for a polished delivery, overcome the fear of public speaking, and manage the backchannel during your presentation, as well as watch videos that teach you how to set up a slide show, navigate a show, and broadcast a show.

Understanding Slide Shows

In PowerPoint, all the tools you need to manage slide shows are on the Slide Show tab, shown in Figure 15.1.

You can deliver a PowerPoint presentation in three different ways:

- **Present it live with a speaker**   This is the most common method of delivering a PowerPoint presentation—full screen in front of an audience.

- **Browse it individually through the PowerPoint browser**—This option lets someone view your presentation at any convenient time in a browser window with navigation elements such as a scrollbar.

- **Display it at a kiosk**—This method lets you create a self-running presentation. It displays full screen and loops continuously—that is, after the final slide, the presentation starts over. Timings you set determine how long each slide is visible. You might set up a kiosk show as part of a tradeshow demonstration. You can add voice narration if you want, but be sure that your show plays where the narration will be audible.

Figure 15.1 *Set up, manage, and run your slide shows from the Slide Show tab.*

This list includes the options available when you set up your show in PowerPoint's Set Up Show dialog box. You can also create a video from your presentation, save and share it as a PDF, or upload it to a website for on-demand play, options that are covered in Chapters 2, "Creating a Basic Presentation," and 13, "Working with Audio and Video."

Before you deliver a PowerPoint presentation, think through its entire visual flow. This is the time to rehearse in your mind what you want to present and how you want to present it, as well as plan for the technical aspects of your presentation.

 TELL ME MORE   Media 15.1—**Preparing for a Polished Delivery**
Access this audio file through your registered Web Edition at
my.safaribooksonline.com/9780132182553/media.

Setting Up a Show

Although you can deliver your presentation instantly by pressing F5, it usually makes sense to set it up ahead of time to specify the exact options you want to use.

 SHOW ME   Media 15.2—**Setting Up a Show**
Access this video file through your registered Web Edition at
my.safaribooksonline.com/9780132182553/media.

 LET ME TRY IT

Setting Up a Show

To set up a PowerPoint slide show, follow these steps:

1. On the Slide Show tab, click the Set Up Slide Show button. The Set Up Show dialog box opens, as shown in Figure 15.2.

2. Select a Show Type. Options include Presented by a Speaker (Full Screen), Browsed by an Individual (Window), or Browsed at a Kiosk (Full Screen).

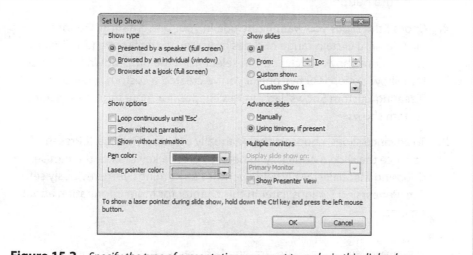

Figure 15.2 *Specify the type of presentation you want to make in this dialog box.*

3. Specify the Show Options you want to set:

- **Loop Continuously Until 'Esc'**—Play your presentation over and over until you press the Esc key. This check box is available only if you select the Presented by a Speaker or Browsed by an Individual option. A presentation loops continuously by default if browsed at a kiosk.

- **Show Without Narration**—Temporarily deactivate any accompanying narrations. For example, if you are presenting at a tradeshow, narrations might be either inaudible or distracting. See "Recording a Voice Narration" later in this chapter for more details about creating narrations.

- **Show Without Animation**—Temporarily deactivate any accompanying slide animations. For example, you might want to use animations in some situations, but not all. See Chapter 14, "Working with Animation and Transitions," for more information about animation.

- **Pen Color**—Specify the pen color to display when using the pen function during a show. This option is available only when you choose Presented by a Speaker as your show type. Click the arrow to the right of this field and either choose a default color or click More Colors to open the Colors dialog box and choose from a wider variety of colors.

- **Laser Pointer Color**—Specify whether to use a red, green, or blue laser pointer during a show. New for PowerPoint 2010, the laser pointer enables you to activate a pointer by pressing the Ctrl key and clicking the left mouse button.

4. Choose the slides you want to include in your presentation. Options include All, a certain range of slides indicated in the From and To boxes, and Custom Show, which you can select from the drop-down list. The Custom Show option is active only if you've created a custom show. See "Creating Custom Shows" later in this chapter for more information about custom shows.

5. To advance slides, choose either Manually or Using Timings, If Present. To advance the slide manually, you need to press a key or click the mouse. Choosing Manually in this field overrides any timings you previously set. See "Rehearsing Timings" later in this chapter for more information about timings.

Be sure that you chose the Using Timings, If Present option if you want to browse at a kiosk. You can't browse manually at a kiosk.

6. Select the Show Presenter View check box if you want to use two monitors to present your slide show. With this option, you can use one monitor to display just your slides and another to display speaker's notes, preview text, and the elapsed time of your presentation among other useful tools. The system verifies that you can present on multiple monitors and enables you to choose the monitor on which to present your slide show.

You can also set monitor options in the Monitors group on the Slide Show tab.

7. Click the OK button to close the Set Up Show dialog box.

Rehearsing Timings

PowerPoint can automate slide transitions, using transition timing that you set. PowerPoint shows a slide for the amount of time you choose, and then transitions to the next slide. You can also set timings by rehearsing your presentation—PowerPoint keeps track of how long you spend on each slide. After you rehearse a presentation, you can save those timings. You might not always want PowerPoint to move you from slide to slide, however. For example, it can sometimes take you more or less time to discuss a slide in person, or an audience member might interrupt your presentation with a question. Even if you don't want to automate your slide transitions, rehearsing timings can be useful because it helps you adjust your presentation to fit into an allotted amount of time.

To rehearse and set timings, go to the Slide Show tab and click the Rehearse Timings button. The presentation displays in Slide Show view, opening the Recording toolbar in the upper-left corner, as shown in Figure 15.3. This toolbar contains the following buttons: Next, Pause Recording, Slide Time, Repeat, and Elapsed Time, which enable you to control and navigate your recording as well as manage the time you spend on each slide.

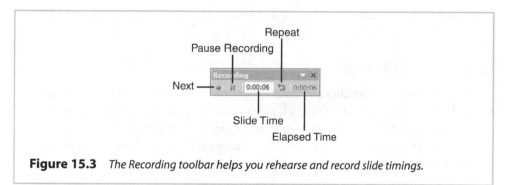

Figure 15.3   *The Recording toolbar helps you rehearse and record slide timings.*

Begin talking through your presentation, clicking the Next button in the toolbar (or clicking your mouse, or pressing any key) to advance to the next slide. If you need to stop temporarily, click the Pause Recording button. If you make a mistake and want to start over on your current slide, click the Repeat button.

The elapsed time of the current slide displays in the Slide Time box in the center of the toolbar. You can also enter a time manually in this box. The time field on the right side of the toolbar shows you the elapsed time of the entire presentation.

After you rehearse the last slide, PowerPoint asks whether you want to save the timings. If you click Yes, the presentation opens in Slide Sorter view with the timings displayed under each slide (see Figure 15.4).

Using Timings

If you want to use slide timings during a slide show, verify that the Use Timings checkbox is selected on the Slide Show tab, which is the default setting. You can also choose whether or not to use timings on the Set Up Show dialog box.

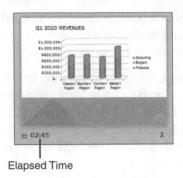

Elapsed Time

Figure 15.4   *View the elapsed time for each slide narration in Slide Sorter view.*

Deleting Timings

To delete slide timings, click the down arrow below the Record Slide Show button on the Slide Show tab and select Clear from the menu that displays. From the sub-menu, choose to clear timings on the current slide or clear timings on all slides. If you haven't set automatic timings for your presentation, the Clear menu option isn't available.

Recording Voice Narrations

You can record your own voiceover to accompany:

- A web-based presentation.
- An on-demand presentation that people can listen to at any time.
- An automated presentation, such as one you run continuously at a tradeshow booth.
- A presentation delivered by a speaker that includes special recorded commentary by a particular individual. An example of this would be a human resources representative delivering an employee orientation that includes voice narration from the CEO.

Before recording your narration, create a script and rehearse it several times until it flows smoothly and matches your presentation.

You need to have a microphone and a sound card to record a narration. And remember—the better the quality of the equipment you use, the more professional your narration will sound.

 **LET ME TRY IT**

Recording a Voice Narration

To record a voice narration, follow these steps:

1. On the Slide Show tab, click the Record Slide Show button.

> If you want to start recording from the current slide, click the down arrow below the Record Slide Show button and choose Start Recording from Current Slide.

2. In the Record Slide Show dialog box (see Figure 15.5), specify whether you want to record slide and animation timings, narrations and laser pointer, or both, and then click the Start Recording button.

Figure 15.5 *Specify what you want to record in the Record Slide Show dialog box.*

3. The presentation displays in Slide Show view, opening the Recording toolbar in the upper-left corner (refer to Figure 15.3).

4. Record your presentation as you move through the slide show, by clicking the Next button on the Recording toolbar or by pressing the Page Down button on your keyboard. The toolbar displays your elapsed time on the current slide (time indicator in the middle of the toolbar) as well as your overall elapsed time (on the right).

> To pause your recording, click the Pause button on the Recording toolbar. When you're ready to resume recording, click the Pause button again.

5. When you reach the end of the presentation, it opens in Slide Sorter view with the slide timings listed below each slide (refer to Figure 15.4).

Rerecording Narrations

If you make a mistake in recording, you can rerecord your entire narration or rerecord a specific slide. To rerecord a specific slide, click the down arrow below the Record Slide Show button and choose Start Recording from Current Slide.

Playing Narrations

To play voice narrations during a slide show, verify that the Play Narrations checkbox is selected on the Slide Show tab, which is the default setting. If you insert media clips such as sounds, and then add a voice narration, the narration takes precedence over the media clips. As a result, you'll hear only the narration. To resolve this, delete the narration if the media clips are of more importance, or include the clips in the narration you record.

Deleting Narrations

To delete slide narrations, click the down arrow below the Record Slide Show button and select Clear from the menu that displays. From the submenu that displays, you can choose to clear narration on the current slide or clear narrations on all slides.

Creating Custom Shows

At times, you might need to deliver a presentation to several audiences, but modify the presentation to suit each individual audience's needs. With custom shows, you can create a presentation once and then specify customized versions that include only the individual slides you need. This saves you from creating several nearly identical presentations.

For example, you might want to create a sales presentation that you can use with three different types of prospective clients. Let's say that the first seven slides of your show cover information about your company and its history, which remains the same for all three types of prospects. But you've also created individual slides for each of your three prospect groups that detail your successes in those industries. You can then design three custom shows—each of which includes the seven main slides, plus the specific slides that pertain only to a certain prospect type. This helps save you time and effort when you need to update information in the seven main slides; you need to do it only once.

LET ME TRY IT

Creating a Custom Show

To create a custom show, follow these steps:

1. On the Slide Show tab, click the Custom Slide Show button.

2. Select Custom Shows from the menu to open the Custom Shows dialog box, shown in Figure 15.6.

Figure 15.6 *Customizing your slide shows saves time and reduces duplication.*

3. Click the New button to open the Define Custom Show dialog box, shown in Figure 15.7.

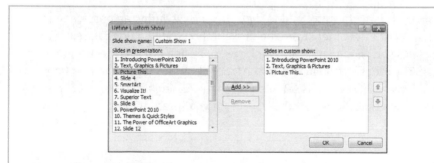

Figure 15.7 *Add a new custom show in this dialog box.*

4. Replace the default name in the Slide Show Name text box with a title for your show.

5. From the Slides in Presentation list, choose the first slide to include in your custom show.

6. Click the Add button to copy this slide to the Slides in Custom Show list.

7. Repeat steps 5 and 6 until you've copied all the slides you want to this list. If you need to remove a slide from the Slides in Custom Show list, select it and click the Remove button.

Use the up and down buttons to the right of the Slides in Custom Show list to reorder a selected slide.

8. Click the OK button to save the custom show and return to the Custom Shows dialog box. From this dialog box, you can edit, remove, or copy any selected custom show.

Copying a custom slide show is useful if you want to create several similar versions of a custom show and don't want to repeat the same steps.

9. To preview what the show will look like, click the Show button. The show previews in Slide Show view.

10. Click the Close button to close the Custom Shows dialog box.

To play a custom show, go to the Slide Show tab and click the Custom Slide Show button. Choose the show you want to play from the menu, and it begins automatically.

Occasionally, you might want to hide slides from view during an onscreen presentation but not delete them from the presentation itself. To do that, select the slide or slides you want to hide and click the Hide Slide button on the Slide Show tab. The slides remain in the presentation, but they don't display when you run your slide show. This is often easier than creating a custom show, particularly if you don't plan to repeat this version of your presentation.

Viewing Your Show

After you plan and set up your PowerPoint presentation, it's time to present it. To do this, press F5. Alternatively, click the From Beginning button or the From Current Slide button on the Slide Show tab.

 SHOW ME   Media 15.3—Viewing Your Show
Access this video file through your registered Web Edition at
my.safaribooksonline.com/9780132182553/media.

TELL ME MORE   Media 15.4—Overcoming the Fear of Public
Speaking
Access this audio file through your registered Web Edition at
my.safaribooksonline.com/9780132182553/media.

Before presenting your show live, you should preview it to test content, flow, and narration. After you determine that your show itself is flawless, you should work on perfecting your delivery, particularly if you don't deliver live presentations very often. By simulating live conditions as much as possible in your practice sessions, you'll increase your odds of delivering a perfect presentation.

When you present a show, PowerPoint uses the settings you entered in the Set Up Show dialog box. For example, you can view in a browser or full screen, depending on what you entered in this dialog box. Whether you need to advance each slide manually depends on your choices in this dialog box. How you navigate the presentation also depends on how you view it:

- **Full screen**   The presentation displays full screen if you choose the Presented by a Speaker or the Browsed at a Kiosk option in the Set Up Show dialog box. The major difference between the two is that when a speaker makes the presentation, you have numerous navigation options available because a person is in control of the presentation. When you browse at a kiosk, these navigation options aren't available because the show runs itself.

- **PowerPoint browser**—The show displays in the PowerPoint browser if you choose Browsed by an Individual in the Set Up Show dialog box. You can use the scrollbar to scroll through the presentation if it's available, or you can use the Page Up and Page Down keys to navigate manually. To switch to the full-screen view, right-click the screen and choose Full Screen.

Displaying a scrollbar can make it easier for viewers to navigate your show. Specify whether to display a scrollbar in the Set Up Show dialog box.

Navigating a Show Full Screen

When a speaker presents a PowerPoint slide show, the presentation appears full screen. If you set up your show without automatic timing, you have to manually move among the slides during the show.

TELL ME MORE   Media 15.5—Managing the Backchannel During Your Presentation

Access this audio file through your registered Web Edition at
my.safaribooksonline.com/9780132182553/media.

There are several ways to navigate your presentation full screen: using the invisible buttons in the lower-left corner of your screen, using the shortcut menu that displays when you right-click a slide, or using keyboard commands.

Navigating with Onscreen Buttons

To view PowerPoint's hidden navigation buttons, pause your mouse over the lower-left corner of your screen. The following buttons display:

- **Previous**—Return to the previous slide.

- **Pen**—Display a brief menu with pen and arrow pointer options. See "Setting Pointer Options" and "Using the Onscreen Pen to Mark Your Presentation" later in this chapter for more information.

- **Menu**—Display the complete presentation menu. See "Navigating with the Slide Show Menu" below for more information.

- **Next**—Move to the next slide.

Navigating with the Slide Show Menu

During a slide show, you can right-click anywhere on the screen to view a shortcut menu, as shown in Figure 15.8.

Figure 15.8   *PowerPoint offers many shortcuts while you're presenting.*

This menu includes the following slide show options:

- **Next**—Move to the next slide.

The capability to toggle between a black or white screen is a useful tool. For example, if you want to explain a detailed concept and want your audience to focus on what you're saying and not on the slide, you can temporarily make the screen either black or white. This is also useful during breaks for long presentations.

- **Previous**—Move to the previous slide.

- **Last Viewed**—Move to the slide last viewed.

- **Go to Slide**—Select the slide you want to view from the list of presentation slides.

- **Go to Section**—Select the section you want to view from the list of presentation sections. This option is available only if you created sections.

- **Custom Show**—Select the custom show you want to view from the list of custom shows. This option is available only if you created custom shows.

- **Screen**—Switch to a black or white screen, show or hide ink markup, and display the Windows taskbar so that you can switch to another application.

- **Pointer Options**—Activate the arrow pointer, pen, or highlighter; set the ink color; erase markings; and choose to hide or display the mouse cursor.

- **Help**—Open the Slide Show Help dialog box where you can view a list of the shortcut keystrokes you can use during a slide show. See "Navigating with Keyboard Commands" later in this chapter for more information.

- **Pause**—Pause a slide show that's running automatically.

Although the options on this menu are useful, you'll probably want to avoid using most of these features during an actual presentation because a break in your flow can be distracting. One case in which you might want to do so during a presentation would be when you have to go back to previous slides to answer questions or clarify a point and don't want to page through numerous slides to do so.

- **End Show**—End the show and return to PowerPoint.

Navigating with Keyboard Commands

Navigating your slide show with keyboard commands is a third option. Table 15.1 lists all the ways PowerPoint gives you to navigate a slide show.

Right-click anywhere on the screen and choose Help from the shortcut menu to display this list of shortcuts within your slide show.

Table 15.1   Slide Show Keyboard Commands

Slide Show Action	Method
Advance to next slide	Left-click the mouse
	Press the spacebar
	Press the letter N
	Press the right-arrow key
	Press the down-arrow key
	Press the Enter key
	Press the Page Down key
Return to previous slide	Press the Backspace key
	Press the letter PowerPoint
	Press the left-arrow key
	Press the up-arrow key
	Press the Page Up key
Go to a specific slide	Enter the number of the slide and press the Enter key
Black/unblack the screen (toggle)	Press the letter B
	Press the period key (.)
White/unwhite the screen (toggle)	Press the letter W
	Press the comma (,)
Display/hide the arrow (toggle)	Press the letter A
	Press the equal sign (=)
Stop/restart a timed show (toggle)	Press the letter S
	Press the plus sign (+)
End the show	Press the Esc key
	Press Ctrl+Break
	Press the minus ([ms])key
Erase screen drawing made with pen	Press the letter E

Table 15.1 Slide Show Keyboard Commands

Slide Show Action	Method
Advance to hidden slide	Press the letter H
Rehearse using new timing	Press the letter T
Rehearse using original timing	Press the letter O
Activate the pen	Press Ctrl+P
Activate the arrow pointer	Press Ctrl+A
Hide pointer/button	Press Ctrl+H
Automatically show/hide pointer	Press Ctrl+U

Setting Pointer Options

You can use or hide an arrow pointer during a PowerPoint presentation. The arrow pointer can help you draw the audience's attention to objects on your slides.

To activate the arrow, move the mouse. If the arrow doesn't display, right-click and choose Pointer Options, Arrow from the menu. The arrow displays as a standard mouse pointer arrow on your screen, which you can use to point to specific areas. To change the arrow to a laser pointer, press the Ctrl key and click the left mouse button.

By default, the arrow disappears after three seconds of inactivity, and reappears whenever you move the mouse. This setting is fine for most presentations, but you can choose to have the arrow always or never appear. To do so, right-click and choose Pointer Options, Arrow Options from the menu that appears. Then choose one of these three commands:

- **Automatic**—Display the arrow when you move your mouse and disappear after three seconds of inactivity (default).
- **Visible**—Always display the arrow in your presentation.
- **Hidden**—Never display the arrow in your presentation.

Figure 15.9 shows the standard arrow pointer with which most people are familiar.

Using the Onscreen Pen to Mark Your Presentation

Using the onscreen pen, you can actually mark right on your slides as you deliver a presentation. This feature works best if you have a pen tablet or a Tablet PC, but you'll also get good value from it if all you have is a mouse.

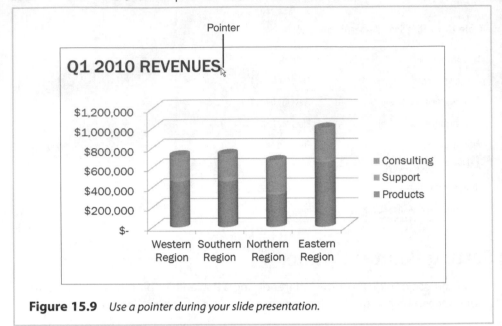

Figure 15.9   *Use a pointer during your slide presentation.*

To use the pen, right-click, choose Pointer Options, and choose the kind of ink to use (Pen or Highlighter). Your mouse cursor becomes a dot (when you choose a pen) or a colored bar (when you choose highlighter). Click and hold the mouse button, and then drag the cursor to make your mark. Figure 15.10 shows some ink markings.

You can choose your pen's color by right-clicking your slide show screen and choosing Pointer Options, Ink Color. Select your preferred color on the color palette that displays. You can also preset the pen color in the Set Up Show dialog box.

When you don't need your ink markings anymore, you can erase them. To erase a specific ink marking, right-click and choose Pointer Options, Eraser from the menu that appears. The mouse cursor looks like an eraser. Click an ink marking to erase it. To erase all your ink markings, right-click and choose Pointer Options, Erase All Ink on Slide from the menu that appears or press the letter E.

After you finish delivering your presentation, PowerPoint asks whether you want to keep your ink annotations. If you click the Keep button, the annotations become drawing objects in the presentation.

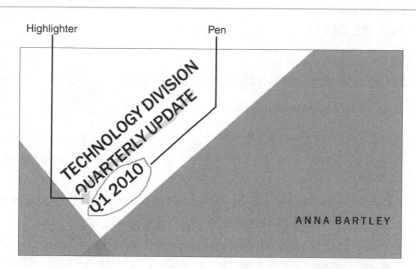

Figure 15.10   *Use a pen or the highlighter to draw attention to elements in the presentation.*

Packaging a Presentation onto a CD

Sometimes a presentation needs to run on a computer other than the one on which it was created. For example, you might travel to a meeting without your laptop computer and need to give a presentation on a supplied computer. You can save your presentation as is to a CD or e-mail it ahead—but still, you worry. Are the fonts in your presentation installed on the computer? Is this version of PowerPoint installed? Is *any* version of PowerPoint installed? Did I remember all the linked files the presentation uses?

Package for CD relieves these worries. It writes your presentation, with its fonts and linked files if you want, to a CD. It also includes the PowerPoint Viewer by default so that you always have everything you need to run your presentation. You can choose whether the presentation runs automatically when you insert the CD into a computer. You can also package more than one presentation onto a CD and choose whether they should run automatically in sequence.

The PowerPoint Viewer (PowerPointViewer.exe) lets people view a PowerPoint presentation when they don't have PowerPoint installed on their computers. You can freely distribute the Viewer without any license fee. Although the viewer is automatically included on your presentation CD if you use Package for CD, you can also download it manually from the Microsoft Download Center (www.microsoft.com/downloads).

LET ME TRY IT

Packaging a Presentation onto a CD

To package a presentation onto a CD, follow these steps:

1. Open a presentation to package.

2. Click the File tab and select Save & Send to open the Save & Send tab in Backstage view.

3. Select Package Presentation for CD in the File Types list and then click the Package for CD button on the right side of the screen.

4. In the Package for CD dialog box, as shown in Figure 15.11, enter a name that describes the presentation you're packaging in the Name the CD field.

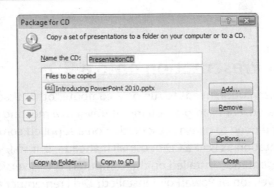

Figure 15.11   *With Package for CD, you can deliver your presentation on another computer.*

5. The current presentation's filename displays in the Files to Be Copied area. To package more presentations onto this CD, click the Add button. The Add Files dialog box opens. Select the presentations to package and click the Add button to return to the Package for CD dialog box.

6. If you are packaging more than one presentation, you can arrange the presentations in the order in which you want them to run. To move a presentation, select it and then click one of the arrow buttons on the left side of the dialog box to reposition it.

7. Click the Options button to open the Options dialog box (see Figure 15.12), where you can specify any of the following options:

- **Linked Files**—PowerPoint packages linked files by default. If you don't want to package them, click this box to remove the check mark.

- **Embedded TrueType Fonts**—If your presentation uses any fonts you're not positive are on the computer you'll use, select this check box. PowerPoint packages the fonts so that your presentation is sure to look the way you created it.

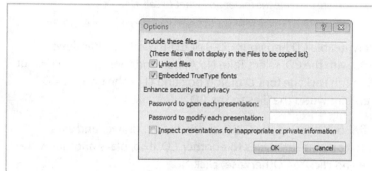

Figure 15.12 *Specify whether to package linked files and fonts.*

You can embed other TrueType fonts that you install only if they aren't restricted by license or copyright. You'll receive an error message if you try to embed a restricted font.

- **Password to Open Each Presentation and Password to Modify Each Presentation**—If you want to prevent others from opening or changing your presentations, enter passwords in these fields.

- **Inspect Presentations for Inappropriate or Private Information**—Open the Document Inspector dialog box during the packaging process, in which you can choose to inspect comments, annotations, invisible on-slide content, off-slide content, document properties, personal information, and presentation notes.

8. Click the OK button when you're done to return to the Package for CD dialog box.

9. If you want to create a folder on your hard drive that contains everything that will be on the CD, click the Copy to Folder button. The Copy to Folder dialog box opens (see Figure 15.13).

10. Type a name for the folder, choose where to add the folder, and click the OK button. PowerPoint creates the folder and copies all the files to it.

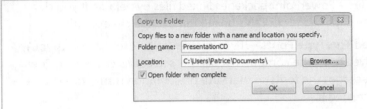

Figure 15.13   *Choose where to create the folder and what to call it.*

11.   Place a blank writeable CD into your CD-R or CD-RW drive. If Windows asks you what to do with the CD, select Take No Action and then click the OK button. Go back to the Package for CD dialog box and click the Copy to CD button. PowerPoint writes the files to the CD.

When PowerPoint finishes creating the CD, it opens the CD drawer and asks whether you want to copy the same files to another CD. If so, place another writeable CD in the drive and click Yes. Otherwise, click No.

Broadcasting a Slide Show

PowerPoint 2010 introduces the PowerPoint Broadcast Service, which enables you to share your presentation in high fidelity with anyone on the web, even if they don't have PowerPoint installed on their computer.

Using PowerPoint Broadcast Service requires either SharePoint Server 2010 with Office Web Apps installed or a Windows Live ID, which you can receive at no charge at http://home.live.com.

SHOW ME   Media 15.6—Broadcasting a Slide Show
Access this video file through your registered Web Edition at
my.safaribooksonline.com/9780132182553/media.

LET ME TRY IT

Broadcasting a Slide Show

To broadcast a slide show, follow these steps:

1.   Open the presentation you want to broadcast.

2.   On the Slide Show tab, click the Broadcast Slide Show button to open the Broadcast Slide Show dialog box, as shown in Figure 15.14.

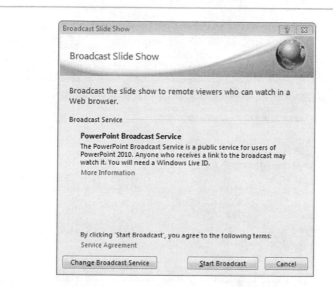

Figure 15.14 *Easily broadcast your slide show on the web.*

3. Click the Start Broadcast button to start your presentation using the PowerPoint Broadcast Service (the default). PowerPoint connects you to the Broadcast Service, which could take a few minutes.

If you don't want to use the default PowerPoint Broadcast Service, click the Change Broadcast Service button to enter the URL of a new broadcast service, for example a SharePoint URL.

4. In the dialog box that displays, enter your Windows Live e-mail address and password and click the OK button. If you chose a different service, the content of this dialog box could vary.

5. The Broadcast Slide Show dialog box displays a link you can share with remote viewers (see Figure 15.15). Click the Send in E-mail link to share using Microsoft Outlook. Alternatively, copy the link and share using another means such as instant message or web mail service.

6. Before broadcasting, review the options on the Broadcast tab, shown in Figure 15.16, where you can choose whether to start your show from the beginning or from the current slide, specify a show resolution, use presenter view with multiple monitors, or send invitations.

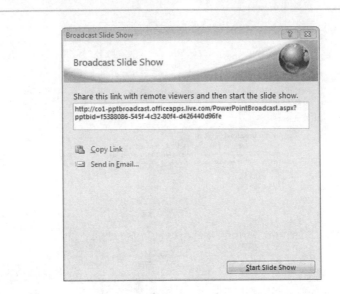

Figure 15.15 *Share this link with anyone you want to view your show.*

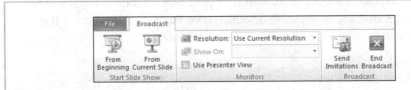

Figure 15.16 *Make any final show modifications on the Broadcast tab.*

7. When you're ready to broadcast your show, click the Start Slide Show button. PowerPoint starts your slide show on the web, where your viewers can
see it.

8. When you finish your broadcast, click the End Broadcast button to disconnect
all your remote viewers. PowerPoint opens a confirmation dialog box to confirm that you want to disconnect.

This chapter shows you how to print your
PowerPoint presentations.

16

Creating and Printing Presentation Materials

PowerPoint enables you to print more than just slides. You can also print notes to remind yourself of what you want to say while presenting, handouts to give to your audience, and outlines to help you proof your content. PowerPoint also includes numerous customization options for printing auxiliary materials.

In this chapter, you learn how to prepare, preview, and print PowerPoint presentations. You can also listen to presentation printing tips and watch videos that show you how to prepare your presentation for printing and preview what your presentation will look like on paper.

Understanding PowerPoint Printing Options

PowerPoint offers several options for printing your presentation, as follows:

- **Full page slides**—Print each slide on a single page.

- **Notes pages**—Print a single slide and its accompanying notes on one page. You create notes in the Notes pane, which is visible in Normal view. Figure 16.1 shows the Notes pane, where you can create detailed speaker's notes about your presentation. Notes are a useful way to remind yourself about what you're going to present. You can also use the Notes pane to provide additional details for your audience if you plan to distribute your presentation to them.

If you choose to print three slides per handout, PowerPoint provides lined spaces to the right of each slide where you can write notes. If you choose another number of pages, you won't have this note space.

- **Handouts**—Print from one to nine slides on a page, either horizontally or vertically. This can greatly reduce the number of pages and amount of printer toner required to print your presentation. When you print handouts, you see only the slides, not the accompanying notes.

- **Outlines**—Print your slide content without graphic formatting.

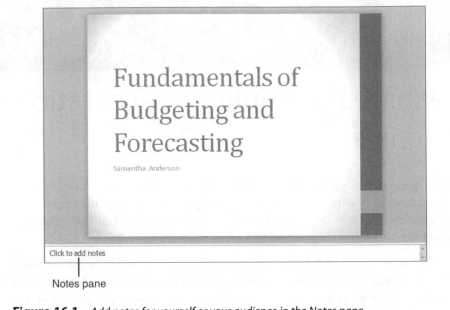

Figure 16.1 *Add notes for yourself or your audience in the Notes pane.*

 TELL ME MORE   Media 16.1—Ensuring a Smooth Printing Process
Access this audio file through your registered Web Edition at
my.safaribooksonline.com/9780132182553/media.

Consider a greener alternative to printing a copy of your presentation for each member of your audience. You can save your presentation as a PDF (Portable Document Format electronic document) using the same formatting options as a print presentation (slides, handouts, notes pages, and outlines). See Chapter 2, "Creating a Basic Presentation," for more information about creating PDFs. Alternatively, consider posting a public presentation on the web at SlideShare.net or a similar presentation-sharing site.

To avoid wasting paper, first make sure that your PowerPoint presentation is ready to print. Set page and print options, customize headers and footers, and preview your presentation as you want it appear when printed. Printing your presentation at least once is a good idea if you don't plan on distributing handouts to your audience. When you proof a hard copy version, you often notice errors that you didn't catch on the screen.

Printing PowerPoint Presentations

The Print tab in Backstage view enables you to specify print settings, preview your slides, and print your presentation. Click the File tab and select Print from the menu to open the Print tab, as shown in Figure 16.2.

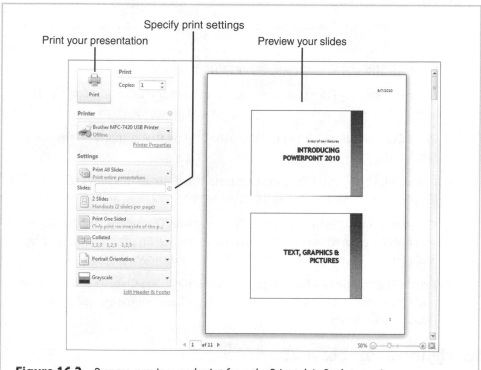

Figure 16.2 *Prepare, preview, and print from the Print tab in Backstage view.*

Preparing to Print

Before you print, apply any special print settings. The Settings section includes five boxes with drop-down lists where you can specify these options (refer to Figure 16.2). The text that displays in each box varies depending on the last selection you made.

You can customize printing defaults for the existing presentation in the PowerPoint Options dialog box. To access it, click the File tab, choose Options, and go to the Print section of the Advanced tab. See Chapter 19, "Customizing PowerPoint," for more information about these print options.

SHOW ME   Media 16.2—Preparing to Print
Access this video file through your registered Web Edition at
my.safaribooksonline.com/9780132182553/media.

Selecting Slides to Print

Click the first box in the Settings section to select the slides you want to print. Your options include

- **Print All Slides**—Print the entire presentation.

- **Print Selection**—Print slides you select on the Slide tab or in Slide Sorter view.

- **Print Current Slide**—Print only the current slide that displays on the Print tab.

- **Custom Range**—Print the slide numbers you enter in the Slides text box. For example, you could enter **1-4, 10** to print slides 1, 2, 3, 4, and 10.

- **Custom Shows**—Select a custom show to print. This option doesn't display if you haven't created at least one custom show. See Chapter 15, "Presenting a Slide Show," for more information about custom shows.

- **Print Hidden Slides**—Print slides you've hidden. See Chapter 5, "Formatting and Organizing Objects, Slides, and Presentations," for more information about hiding slides.

Specifying a Print Layout

Click the second box in the Settings section to select the print layout you want to use. Options include Full Page Slides, Notes Pages, Outline, or nine different Handout layouts (see Figure 16.3).

This menu also includes the following options:

- **Frame Slides**—Include a border around the slides.

- **Scale to Fit Paper**—Change the size of slides to fit the paper, making them either larger or smaller as appropriate.

- **High Quality**—Print your presentation at the highest quality available with your printer.

- **Print Comments and Ink Markup**—Print comment pages and any ink markups you make on-screen with your presentation. This option is available only if your presentation contains comments or ink markups.

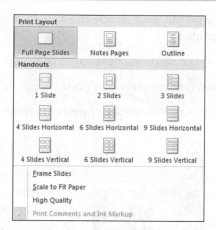

Figure 16.3 *Your print layout options include nine different handout formats.*

Printing on Both Sides of the Page

Click the third box in the Settings section to specify whether you want to print on both sides of the page. The default is to print on one side only, but you can choose to print on both sides, flipping either on the long edge or the short edge of the paper.

Collating Presentation Printouts

Click the fourth box in the Settings section to specify how you want to collate your printouts. If you choose to print more than one copy of your presentation, specify whether to collate. Collating keeps multiple copies in sequence. If you print five copies of a presentation without collating, for example, you will print five copies of page one, five copies of page two, and so on.

Specifying Print Orientation

Click the fifth box in the Settings section to specify the orientation of your printouts: portrait or landscape. This option isn't available if you select Full Page Slides as your print layout. In this case, your slides print in landscape layout by default.

Specifying Colors Options

Click the sixth box in the Settings section to specify color options for your printed presentation. You can print in color, grayscale, or pure black and white.

If you don't have a color printer, your choice affects how your presentation prints on a black-and-white printer:

- **Color**—Your printer converts your presentation's colors to shades of gray.
- **Grayscale**—PowerPoint converts your presentation to true grayscale.
- **Pure Black and White**—PowerPoint converts your presentation to pure black and white.

Depending on the colors and shapes in your slide, the color option you select might produce different results. For example, on one slide, Color and Grayscale could produce similar results; on another slide, Grayscale and Pure Black and White could look alike. You need to experiment to see which option yields the optimal look in print.

Table 16.1 illustrates how each PowerPoint object displays when printed in grayscale or black and white.

Table 16.1 Grayscale and Black-and-White Objects

Object	Grayscale	Black and White
Bitmaps	Grayscale	Grayscale
Charts	Grayscale	Grayscale
Embossing	Grayscale	None
Fill	Grayscale	White
Frames	Black	Black
Lines	Black	Black
Patterns	Grayscale	White
Shadows (object)	Grayscale	Black
Shadows (text)	Grayscale	None
Slide backgrounds	White	White
Text	Black	Black

In addition to previewing what your color presentation will look like in grayscale or black and white, on the Print tab in Backstage view, you can also preview from the View tab. To preview in grayscale, click the Grayscale button on the View tab. The Grayscale tab displays, offering additional grayscale and black-and-white options. Click the Back to Color View button to close.

To preview the same presentation in black and white, click the Pure Black and White button on the View tab. The presentation displays in black and white and the Black and White tab displays.

Customizing Headers and Footers

You can also add headers and footers to your slides, notes, and handouts when you print them. To do this, click the Edit Header & Footer link on the Print tab in Backstage view. The Header and Footer dialog box opens, as shown in Figure 16.4.

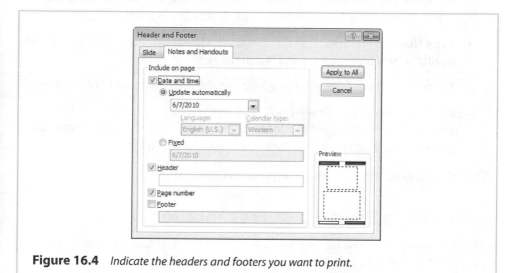

Figure 16.4 *Indicate the headers and footers you want to print.*

This dialog box includes two tabs with similar options: the Slide tab and the Notes and Handouts tab. You can add any or all of the following when you print slides, notes, handouts, or outlines:

- **Date and Time**—Select this check box, and then either enter a fixed date or choose to update the date automatically. If you choose to update automatically, pick a format from the drop-down list. Options include displaying the date only, the time only, or the date and time in up to 13 different ways. You can also choose your base language and calendar type, depending on the language you choose in the Language drop-down list. If only English is enabled, the Language list isn't active. The date and time display on the upper-right corner of the page.

The date options you can choose from the Update Automatically drop-down list depend on your choice of language/country. For example, choosing English (UK) results in date options that display a dd/mm/yy format rather than the mm/dd/yy format used in the United States.

- **Slide Number**—Print the slide number in the lower-right corner of the page. Available only on the Slide tab.

- **Header**—Print the header text you enter in the text box on the upper-left corner of the page. Available only on the Notes and Handouts tab.

- **Page Number**—Print a page number on the lower-right corner of each page. Available only on the Notes and Handouts tab.

- **Footer**—Print the footer text you enter on the lower-left corner of the page.

- **Don't Show on Title Slide**—Don't print the selected options on the title slide. Hiding your headers and footers on the first slide of your presentation gives it a more polished look. Available only on the Slide tab.

Click the Apply to All button to close the dialog box.

Previewing a PowerPoint Presentation

The right side of the Print tab previews the way your presentation displays when printed, shown in Figure 16.5.

Any changes you make to your presentation settings are reflected in this view, so you can verify before printing whether the choices you make work for you.

Below the slide, you can click the left and right arrows to scroll through the presentation. You can also use the zoom control to reduce or enlarge the size of the slides.

Alternatively, click the Print Preview button on the Quick Access toolbar (or press Ctrl+P) to open the Print tab and preview your presentation. See Chapter 19 for more information about adding this button to the toolbar if it isn't already available.

Printing Your Presentation

After you specify your print settings and preview the results, it's time to print.

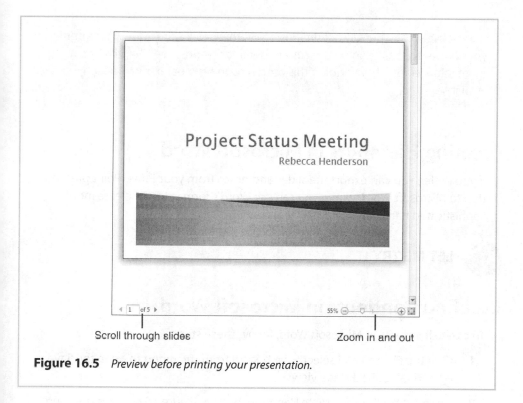

Scroll through slides   Zoom in and out

Figure 16.5 *Preview before printing your presentation.*

 LET ME TRY IT

Printing Your Presentation

To print your presentation, follow these steps:

1. On the Print tab in Backstage view (refer to Figure 16.2), select the number of Copies to print. If you want to print more than one copy, remember to specify collation options. See "Collating Presentation Printouts" earlier in this chapter for more information.

2. Select the printer to use from the Printer drop-down list. The list of options depends on what you connect to or install on your computer such as printers, fax machines, PDF creation software, and so forth.

3. Optionally, click the Printer Properties link to change the selected printer's properties and print parameters.

4. Click the Print button to print your formatted presentation to the printer you selected.

Alternatively, click the Quick Print button on the Quick Access toolbar to print your presentation based on the current default settings. See Chapter 19 for more information about adding this button to the toolbar if it isn't already available.

Creating Handouts in Microsoft Word

If you prefer, you can export the slides and notes from your PowerPoint presentation to Microsoft Word, where you can use Word's formatting to create more sophisticated handouts.

 **LET ME TRY IT**

Creating Handouts in Microsoft Word

To create handouts in Microsoft Word, follow these steps:

1. Click the File tab and select Save & Send from the menu to open the Save & Send tab in Backstage view.

2. On this tab, click the Create Handouts button. Figure 16.6 shows the Send to Microsoft Word dialog box, which opens.

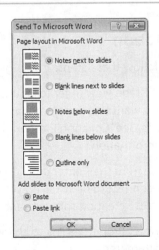

Figure 16.6   *Create handouts in Microsoft Word from your PowerPoint presentation.*

3. Choose one of the following page layout options:

    -   Notes Next to Slides

    -   Blank Lines Next to Slides

    -   Notes Below Slides

    -   Blank Lines Below Slides

    -   Outline Only

4. Specify whether you want to paste the slides into your Word document or paste as a link. If you link the slides, they update in Word whenever you make changes in PowerPoint.

5. Click the OK button to open a Microsoft Word document in the layout you specified.

This chapter introduces the many ways you can share and collaborate on your PowerPoint presentations.

17

Sharing and Collaborating on Presentations

Sharing and collaborating with colleagues is critical to developing a successful presentation in many organizations. In this chapter, you explore the many ways to work with others on your presentations. You can also listen to tips on sharing and collaborating in PowerPoint and watch videos that show you how to protect your presentation, inspect your presentation, and save your presentation to the web on SkyDrive.

Exploring Ways to Share and Collaborate in PowerPoint

PowerPoint offers a multitude of sharing and collaboration options, including several new to PowerPoint 2010. Your options include

- Sending your presentation to others via e-mail

- Saving your presentation to the web on Windows Live SkyDrive or to a corporate SharePoint site

- Publishing slides to a Slide Library hosted on SharePoint

- Co-authoring with either SharePoint or SkyDrive

- Messaging colleagues from within PowerPoint and sharing your desktop via Microsoft Office Communications Server 2007 R2

- Collaborating with Microsoft Office Live Workspace

 TELL ME MORE   Media 17.1—Exploring Ways to Share and Collaborate in PowerPoint 2010

Access this audio recording through your registered Web Edition at my.safaribooksonline.com/9780132182553/media.

Protecting Your Presentation

PowerPoint offers several options for protecting your presentation before you share it with others or post it online or in a centralized location. For example, you can apply a password, make your presentation read-only, apply a digital signature, or use Information Rights Management (IRM) to control presentation access. Whether you choose to protect your presentation depends on the group of people you work with, your need for security, and your audience. Obviously, if you post a presentation in a public location directed at a wide audience of viewers, you wouldn't want to protect with a password or otherwise limit access.

 SHOW ME   Media 17.2—Protecting Your Presentation
Access this video file through your registered Web Edition at
my.safaribooksonline.com/9780132182553/media.

On the File tab, select Info to open Backstage view. In the Permissions section, click the Protect Presentation button (see Figure 17.1), and select from the following menu options:

- **Mark as Final**—Convert your presentation to read-only. No one can edit or make changes to a final presentation.

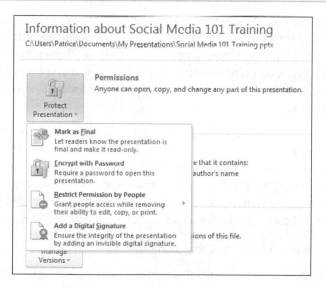

Figure 17.1   *Protecting your presentation before sharing is an optional step.*

- **Encrypt with Password**—Open the Encrypt Document dialog box (see Figure 17.2), where you can enter a password that anyone needs to open your presentation in the future. PowerPoint passwords are case-sensitive. In other words, "PASSWORD" and "password" are treated as separate passwords.

Figure 17.2   *Apply a password to your presentation if you want to control who has access to it.*

If you forget your password, you can no longer open or modify your presentation, so choose a password that's easy for you to remember, or write it down in a secure location.

- **Restrict Permission by People**—Grant access permission to your presentations and other Office documents using Information Rights Management (IRM). Using IRM, you can prevent unauthorized forwarding, copying, editing, printing, or faxing of your presentation, and specify file expiration dates for presentations you no longer want anyone to view after a certain date. IRM requires a Windows Live ID (http://home.live.com). If you don't have IRM, selecting Restricted Access from the submenu that displays enables you to sign up for it.

- **Add a Digital Signature**—Open a dialog box that enables you to add a *digital signature*, an invisible, electronic, encrypted signature stamp that's attached in a certificate to vouch for its authenticity. Adding a digital signature to your presentation plays an authentication role similar to the signing of a paper document. The average PowerPoint user won't normally set up digital certificates; this is the domain of an organization's IT department.

There are two ways to create a digital signature in PowerPoint:

- Get a digital ID from a Microsoft partner, which enables other users to verify the authenticity of your signature.

- Create your own digital ID, enabling you to verify the authenticity of your signature only on the computer you're using. Other users cannot verify the authenticity of your signature.

Preparing Your Presentation for Sharing

Before you share your presentation with others, you should consider doing several things: inspect your presentation for confidential information, validate its accessibility, and check for compatibility with previous versions.

Inspecting Your Presentation

Before sharing your presentation with others, you normally review your content and run a spell check. In addition, you should also inspect your presentation for hidden data and personal information stored in comments, notes, or document properties. A quick check can help you avoid displaying confidential or embarrassing information with others.

Because you might not be able to undo changes the Document Inspector makes to your presentation, it's a good idea to run the Inspector on a copy of your original presentation.

SHOW ME   Media 17.3—Inspecting Your Presentation
Access this video file through your registered Web Edition at
my.safaribooksonline.com/9780132182553/media.

LET ME TRY IT

Inspecting Your Presentation

To run the Document Inspector, follow these steps:

1. On the File tab, select Info to open Backstage view.

2. In the Prepare for Sharing section, click the Check for Issues button.

3. From the menu that displays, select Inspect Document. The Document Inspector dialog box displays, as shown in Figure 17.3.

Figure 17.3   *Use the Document Inspector to find and remove hidden and personal information from your presentation before sharing.*

If you don't save your presentation before running the Document Inspector, a dialog box displays, prompting you to save before continuing.

4. Select the types of content for which to search. The Document Inspector dialog box describes each content type in detail.

The Document Inspector doesn't search for objects with animation effects. If you're concerned about animation effects, you should search for these manually.

5. Click the Inspect button. The Document Inspector dialog box changes, displaying inspection results, as shown in Figure 17.4.

6. Click the Remove All button next to any items you want to remove.

7. Click the Close button to exit the dialog box.

In many cases, you inspect your presentation before sending it out for review by others and then again before finalizing to ensure that you remove all comments inserted during the review process.

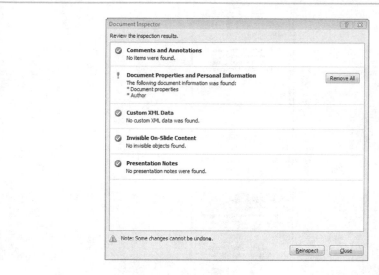

Figure 17.4   *Specify the content you want to remove by selecting Remove All.*

Checking Your Presentation for Accessibility

If you publish your presentation to a general audience or know that people with disabilities will view it, you should check your presentation for accessibility.

 LET ME TRY IT

Checking Accessibility

To check accessibility, follow these steps:

1. On the File tab, select Info to open Backstage view.

2. In the Prepare for Sharing section, click the Check for Issues button.

3. From the menu that displays, select Check Accessibility. The Accessibility Checker pane opens, as shown in Figure 17.5.

4. Review and fix each potential issue based on the comments in the pane. For example, the Accessibility Checker might identify missing alt text or find issues with the reading order of content on your slides, problems that would cause difficulty for someone with a visual impairment who uses a screen reader.

5. Click the Close (x) button to close the pane and return to your presentation.

Figure 17.5   *Verify that your presentation is accessible to people with disabilities.*

Running the Compatibility Checker

If you want to save your presentation as an earlier version of PowerPoint, you could lose features that weren't yet available in previous versions. See Chapter 2, "Creating a Basic Presentation," for more information about saving in a previous version of PowerPoint.

 **LET ME TRY IT**

Running the Compatibility Checker

To run the Compatibility Checker, follow these steps:

1. On the File tab, select Info to open Backstage view.

2. In the Prepare for Sharing section, click the Check for Issues button.

3. From the menu that appears, select Check Compatibility. The Microsoft PowerPoint Compatibility Checker dialog box appears, as shown in Figure 17.6.

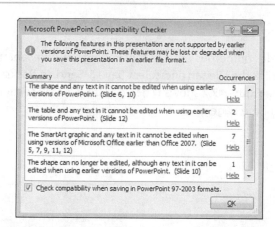

Figure 17.6   *Verify that your presentation won't lose special effects or features if you save as a previous version of PowerPoint.*

4. Review the summary results in the Compatibility Checker and decide either to revise your presentation or accept the limitations of saving in a previous version.

5. Click the OK button to close the dialog box and return to your presentation.

Sharing Your Presentation with Others

PowerPoint offers several ways to share your presentation with others, including several that are new to PowerPoint 2010. For example, on the Save & Send page in Backstage view, you can do the following:

-   Send your presentation to others via e-mail.

-   Save your presentation to the web on Windows Live SkyDrive.

-   Save your presentation to a corporate SharePoint site.

-   Broadcast your slide show on the web.

-   Publish slides to a Slide Library hosted on SharePoint.

 See Chapter 13, "Working with Audio and Video," for more information about broadcasting your slide show on the web.

 TELL ME MORE   Media 17.4—Setting Ground Rules for Successful PowerPoint Collaboration

Access this audio file through your registered Web Edition at
my.safaribooksonline.com/9780132182553/media.

Sending via E-Mail

PowerPoint provides numerous options for sending your presentation to others via e-mail. To do so, click the File tab and select Save & Send. In Backstage view, select Send Using E-Mail. Figure 17.7 shows the Send Using E-Mail section, which displays on the right side of the page.

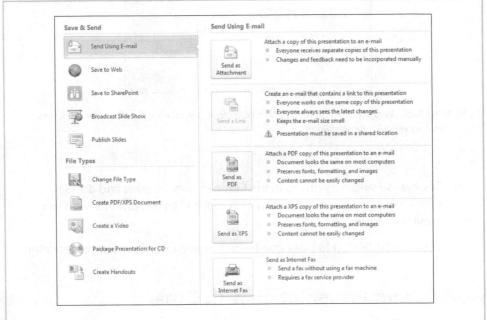

Figure 17.7   *Choose one of several e-mail options.*

Your options include

- **Send as Attachment**—Open your default e-mail application, such as Microsoft Outlook, and attach a copy of the open presentation.

- **Send a Link**—Open your default e-mail application and insert a link to a presentation stored in a shared location, such as a SharePoint site or SkyDrive site. If your presentation isn't stored in a shared location, this option isn't available.

- **Send as PDF**—Save your presentation as a PDF and attach it to an e-mail message. PowerPoint opens your default e-mail application to send your message.

- **Send as XPS**—Save your presentation as an XPS file and attach it to an e-mail message. PowerPoint opens your default e-mail application to send your message.

- **Send as Internet Fax**—Send your presentation as a fax through a fax service provider. If you haven't already signed up with a provider, selecting this options opens a website with a list of potential providers.

See Chapter 2 for more information about saving in PDF or XPS format.

Saving Presentations to the Web

If you use webmail, such as Gmail or Hotmail, or another e-mail client that doesn't open automatically when you click one of the e-mail buttons, you can attach your presentation to an e-mail message manually.

You can save your presentations to Windows Live SkyDrive directly from Microsoft PowerPoint. SkyDrive (http://skydrive.live.com), as shown in Figure 17.8, is a new collaboration option for Office 2010 users, which offers up to 25GB of free online storage that you can use to collaborate with colleagues anywhere in the world. See Chapter 20, "Accessing PowerPoint on the Web and Mobile Devices," for more information about SkyDrive.

Figure 17.8 *SkyDrive enables you to save your presentations on the web for online viewing and collaboration.*

SHOW ME Media 17.5—Saving to the Web

Access this video file through your registered Web Edition at my.safaribooksonline.com/9780132182553/media.

SkyDrive is part of Windows Live and requires a Windows Live ID to access. If you have an existing account with another Windows Live application, such as Hotmail or Messenger, you already have a Windows Live ID. If you don't, you can sign up for a free Windows Live ID by clicking the Sign Up for Windows Live link.

LET ME TRY IT

Saving to SkyDrive on the Web

To save to SkyDrive, follow these steps:

1. On the File tab, select Save & Send.

2. In Backstage view, select Save to Web (see Figure 17.9).

Figure 17.9   *Save directly to SkyDrive from Microsoft PowerPoint.*

3. On the right side of the screen, click the Sign In button to open the Connecting to docs.live.net dialog box, as shown in Figure 17.10.

4. Enter your Windows Live ID e-mail address and password, and click the OK button. Your Windows Live information appears on the right side of the screen (see Figure 17.11).

> Click the New button to create a new folder. (The actual SkyDrive site opens.)

5. Select the folder in which you want to save your document, and click the Save As button.

6. In the Save As dialog box, enter a file name and click the Save button.

Figure 17.10   *Enter your Windows Live ID e-mail address and password to access SkyDrive.*

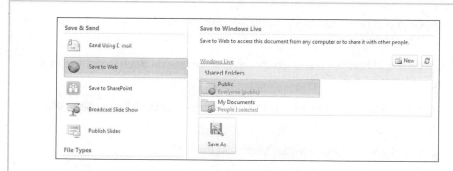

Figure 17.11   *Choose the folder where you want to upload your PowerPoint presentation.*

If you want to share your presentation with the general public on the web, consider saving it to a slide-sharing site such as SlideShare (www.slideshare.net), authorSTREAM (www.authorstream.com), MyPlick (www.myplick.com), SlideBoom (www.slideboom.com), or PowerShow (www.powershow.com).

PowerPoint uploads your presentation to the SkyDrive website where you can collaborate with anyone in the world with web access.

Saving Presentations to SharePoint

If you have Microsoft Office Professional Plus 2010 installed, your Office suite includes Microsoft SharePoint Workspace 2010, formerly called Microsoft Office

Groove. This application is the desktop client for Microsoft SharePoint 2010 (http://sharepoint.microsoft.com), Microsoft's online collaboration platform.

Whereas companies of any size can easily use Microsoft Office Live Workspace or SkyDrive for collaboration, SharePoint enables larger companies to maintain their documents, communications, and team services on a system they control. SharePoint servers are generally located in enterprise environments. These companies have a dedicated IT staff responsible for maintaining, backing up, and controlling access to the server containing the company information. Unlike Office Live Workspace or SkyDrive, a corporate IT staff normally installs and maintains SharePoint and provides access to specific individuals within your company.

SharePoint Workspace 2010 enables you to perform the following collaboration tasks:

- Work simultaneously on your PowerPoint presentations with colleagues in multiple locations using Office 2010's new co-authoring feature. See "Co-authoring in Microsoft PowerPoint," later in this chapter, for more information.

- Check in and check out files, enabling you to securely access and review documents stored on the server.

- Create local SharePoint workspaces to collaborate on documents without access to SharePoint Server.

- Access Microsoft Office Web Apps, such as the Microsoft PowerPoint Web App.

- Save to SharePoint from within Microsoft PowerPoint.

 LET ME TRY IT

Saving to SharePoint

To save a presentation to SharePoint, follow these steps:

1. On the File tab, select Save & Send to open Backstage view.

2. Select Save to SharePoint to display the Save to SharePoint section on the right side of the screen, as shown in Figure 17.12.

3. Select your SharePoint site from the list of recent locations, or browse for a location.

4. Click the Save As button to open the Save As dialog box.

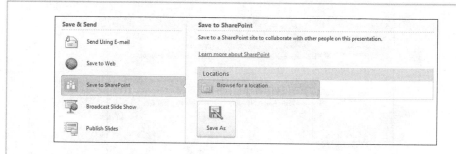

Figure 17.12   *Post PowerPoint presentations for collaboration and sharing.*

5. Verify that the default file name is the name you want to use. If not, edit this field.

6. Click the Save button to save to your SharePoint site.

Publishing Slides to a Slide Library

You can share and reuse PowerPoint presentation content with a group of colleagues by publishing your slides to a *slide library* hosted on a server such as Microsoft SharePoint Server 2010.

You must have SharePoint installed to take advantage of the slide library feature. If you don't, consider sharing your presentations on SkyDrive. You can also publish your slides to an accessible folder on your own computer or to a network share drive.

 LET ME TRY IT

Publishing to a Slide Library

To publish slides to a slide library, follow these steps:

1. On the File tab, select Save & Send to open Backstage view.

2. Select Publish Slides to display the Publish Slides section on the right side of the screen.

3. Click the Publish Slides button. The Publish Slides dialog box opens, as shown in Figure 17.13.

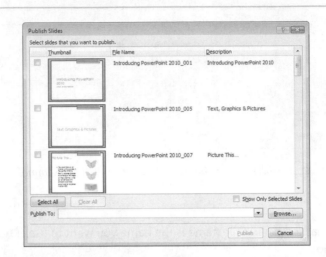

Figure 17.13   *Select the slides you want to publish to a slide library.*

4. Click the Select All button to publish all slides to the slide library. If you want to publish only specific slides, select the check boxes next to their thumbnails.

> To search for the exact pathname, click the Browse button to open the Select a Slide Library dialog box.

5. In the Publish To field, enter the name of the SharePoint folder where you want to publish the slides.

6. Click the Publish button to publish the slides. The system may ask you to enter your SharePoint username and password. Your slides are now available in the SharePoint Server folder you specified.

Other Ways to Collaborate in Microsoft PowerPoint 2010

Depending on what additional technologies your company chooses to deploy and the extensions to Microsoft Office 2010 you use, there are even more ways to collaborate on PowerPoint presentations.

Co-Authoring in Microsoft PowerPoint

Co-authoring is a new Office 2010 feature that enables you to work on the same document simultaneously with other colleagues no matter where they're located. You can also easily identify changes and who is making them. Co-authoring requires either Microsoft SharePoint 2010 or a SkyDrive account accessed with your Windows Live ID.

Co-authoring offers a distinct advantage over sending out documents to multiple people for review and then consolidating their feedback into one master document. It also enables everyone collaborating on a document to view the content, changes, and feedback that others have provided in real time.

To activate this feature, more than one person needs to open the same presentation in either SharePoint or on SkyDrive. See Chapter 20, "Accessing PowerPoint on the Web and Mobile Devices," for more information.

Collaborating with Microsoft Office Communications Server 2007 R2

Part of Microsoft Office Professional Plus 2010, Microsoft Office Communicator Server 2007 R2 (there is no 2010 version) furthers Office 2010 collaboration by integrating instant messaging, video conferencing, telephony, application sharing, and file transfer.

If your company deploys this technology, you can share your desktop instantly while co-authoring with a colleague anywhere in the world or start an instant messaging session with this person.

Collaborating with Microsoft Office Live Workspace

Microsoft Office Live Workspace (http://workspace.officelive.com), as shown in Figure 17.14, is a free web-based tool that offers online file sharing, storage, and collaboration.

With Microsoft Office Live Workspace, you can

- Share up to 5GB of documents in your workspace.
- Collaborate on Microsoft PowerPoint, Word, and Excel documents.
- Maintain versions of your documents for future reference.
- View, edit, and share password-protected documents for added security.

Figure 17.14   *Share and collaborate with a free account on Microsoft Office Live Workspace.*

V

Maximizing the Power of PowerPoint

This chapter shows you how to add interactivity to your presentation with hyperlinks and action buttons.

18

Working with Hyperlinks and Action Buttons

Interactivity can enliven any PowerPoint presentation, whether you present live or let your audience view it online. Fortunately, PowerPoint makes it easy to link to the web, to other slides in your presentation, or to external files.

In this chapter, you learn how to use hyperlinks and action settings in your presentation. You can also watch videos that show you how to insert a hyperlink to the web, insert a link to another slide, and use PowerPoint action settings.

Working with Hyperlinks

Just like on the web, you can create hyperlinks in your PowerPoint presentations. Unlike a typical slideshow in which you must proceed sequentially through your content, a hyperlinked presentation can enable you to move through a presentation in whatever order makes sense for the audience or enable you hide information that you can show only if your audience needs or asks for it.

The first step in creating a hyperlink is to identify the object to link. You can link any object, including text, clip art, WordArt, charts, shapes, and more.

Inserting Hyperlinks

In PowerPoint, you can insert hyperlinks that go to an external website, jump to another location in your presentation, or open an external application.

Inserting Hyperlinks to an External Website

Inserting hyperlinks to external websites is a common use of PowerPoint's hyperlink feature. For example, let's say that you're making a presentation to the board of directors of your company. You suspect some board members will want to know more about current promotions by a rival company. You can create a hyperlink in your slideshow that opens up your web browser, connects to the Internet, and displays your competitor's website. Of course, if no one asks or if time is running short, you don't even need to use the link. But you know it's there, just in case.

When you create a hyperlink for the first time, you use the Insert Hyperlink dialog box. If you change the hyperlink, the Edit Hyperlink dialog box displays. These dialog boxes are identical except for the Remove Link button found in the Edit Hyperlink dialog box, which enables you to remove the selected hyperlink.

 SHOW ME Media 18.1—Inserting a Hyperlink to an External Website
Access this video file through your registered Web Edition at
my.safaribooksonline.com/9780132182553/media.

 LET ME TRY IT

Inserting a Hyperlink to an External Website

To insert a hyperlink to an external website, follow these steps:

1. In Normal view, select the text or object you want to link (see Figure 18.1).

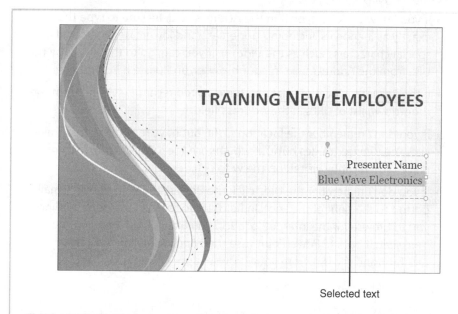

TRAINING NEW EMPLOYEES

Presenter Name
Blue Wave Electronics

Selected text

Figure 18.1 *Select text or any other object to which you want to add a hyperlink.*

2. On the Insert tab, click the Hyperlink button. Alternatively, press Ctrl+K. The Insert Hyperlink dialog box displays (see Figure 18.2).

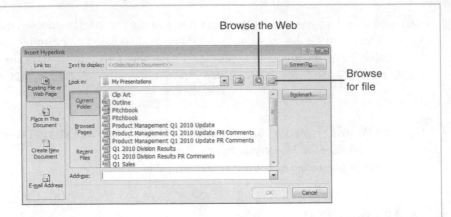

Figure 18.2 *Use the Insert Hyperlink dialog box to specify the location you want to link to the selected text or object.*

3. By default, PowerPoint selects the Existing File or Web Page button and the Current Folder button. This view lets you find the URL you want in several ways:

    - If you know the URL, type it in the Address field. Be sure to type the URL exactly as it appears, including uppercase and lowercase letters and all special characters (such as the tilde ~). If you can, go to the site, copy the URL from the Address field in your browser, and paste it in this field.

    - If the link is to a location that you have visited recently, select it from the drop-down list of URLs in the Address field.

    - If you don't remember the location's URL but have recently visited there, click the Browsed Pages button and choose the location from a list of places you recently visited on the web.

    - If you don't remember the URL, click the Browse the Web button (small button to the right of the Look In field) to go to your browser, enabling you to browse for the Internet location you want. When you find the location, switch back to PowerPoint (use the Windows taskbar or press Alt+Tab), and the URL from your browser appears in the dialog box.

4. Click the OK button.

If you add a link to text, that text now displays underlined and in a different color. The actual color you see depends on the PowerPoint theme you use. If you add the link to any other object, the object's appearance doesn't change, but the object is linked nonetheless.

Inserting Hyperlinks to Another Slide in Your Presentation

In addition to linking to websites, you can also link to other slides in your presentation. Creating links to other slides helps you customize your slideshow so that you can move quickly to the slides you need. For example, after your opening title slide, you might want to include a table of contents slide with hyperlinks from each topic to a specific location in the slideshow. On the last slide for each topic, you can include a link back to the table of contents slide.

 SHOW ME   Media 18.2—Inserting a Hyperlink to Another Slide in Your Presentation

Access this video file through your registered Web Edition at
my.safaribooksonline.com/9780132182553/media.

 LET ME TRY IT

Inserting a Hyperlink to Another Slide in Your Presentation

To Insert a link to another presentation slide, follow these steps:

1. In Normal view, select the text or object on the slide you want to link.

2. On the Insert tab, click the Hyperlink button to open the Insert Hyperlink dialog box.

3. Click the Place in This Document button. PowerPoint displays a list of slides in the current slideshow (see Figure 18.3).

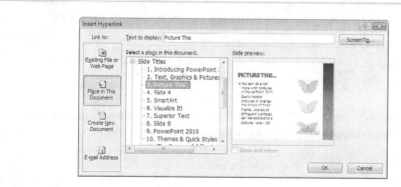

Figure 18.3   *Quickly link to a slide in your open presentation.*

4. Select the slide to which you want to jump.

5. Click the OK button.

Inserting Hyperlinks to Other Files

PowerPoint also enables you to create a hyperlink to another document, either on your own computer or on a network if you're connected to one. When you jump from your presentation to another file, the application displaying that file starts. For example, other PowerPoint files open in PowerPoint, Word documents open in Word, and so on.

 LET ME TRY IT

Inserting a Hyperlink to Another File

To insert a link to another file, follow these steps:

1. In Normal view, select the text or object you want to link.

2. On the Insert tab, click the Hyperlink button to open the Insert Hyperlink dialog box (refer to Figure 18.2).

3. To specify the appropriate file to link to, you can
    - Type the name of the file in the Address field, including its full pathname (for example, **c:\my documents\sales.xls**).
    - Select a file in your current folder.
    - Click the Recent Files button to display a list of recently accessed files.
    - Click the Browse for File button (small button to the right of the Look In field) and browse your computer or network for the file you want.

    If you select another PowerPoint file, you can click the Bookmark button to choose a specific slide to open.

    - Click the Create New Document button to link to a new document that you can create now or later (see Figure 18.4).

4. Click the OK button.

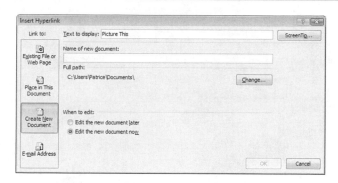

Figure 18.4   *Insert a link to a new document such as another PowerPoint presentation, Excel spreadsheet, or Word document.*

Inserting a Hyperlink to an E-mail Address

Finally, you can insert a link to send an e-mail from your presentation. This is primarily useful if you plan to publish your presentation on the web and want to let your audience contact you after viewing it.

> As a shortcut, just type your e-mail address directly on your slide (for example, type **jsmith@pearson.com**). PowerPoint recognizes common e-mail formats and automatically creates a link for you.

 LET ME TRY IT

Inserting a Hyperlink to an E-mail Address

To insert a link to an e-mail address, follow these steps:

1. In Normal view, select the text or object you want to link.

2. On the Insert tab, click the Hyperlink button to open the Insert Hyperlink dialog box (refer to Figure 18.2).

3. Click the E-mail Address button.

4. Type the address in the E-mail Address field and enter a subject. You can even select the e-mail address from a list of recently used e-mail addresses (see Figure 18.5).

5. Click the OK button.

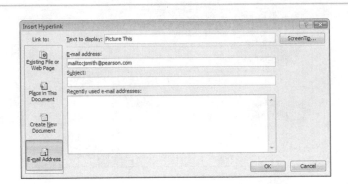

Figure 18.5   *Create a link to an e-mail address, enabling a viewer to send a message.*

Creating Invisible Text Hyperlinks

Linked text looks different from the nonlinked text around it—it's underlined. You might not want the text to look different, but you still want to click that text and jump to the linked page or document. The solution is simple: Cover the text with a shape, link the shape, and then make it invisible.

 LET ME TRY IT

Creating an Invisible Text Hyperlink

To create an invisible hyperlinked object, follow these steps:

1. On the Insert tab, click the Shape button and insert a shape, such as a rectangle, that covers the text you want to link.

2. With the shape selected, click the Hyperlink button on the Insert tab.

3. Type the URL in the Address field.

4. Click the OK button.

5. Right-click the shape and choose Format AutoShape from the menu that displays. PowerPoint opens the Format Shape dialog box (see Figure 18.6).

6. On the Fill tab, select the No Fill option button.

7. Select the Line Color tab and then choose the No Line option button.

8. Click the OK button.

Figure 18.6 *Use the Format Shape dialog box to remove fill color and line color, thus making the shape invisible.*

An invisible linked object now displays over the text you want linked. When you play your slideshow, move the mouse pointer to that text area, and click when the mouse pointer changes to a hand. To the audience, it looks like you are clicking on text, although you are actually clicking a linked invisible graphic shape.

An additional benefit to using an invisible link is that no one but you has to know the link is there. If you don't use it, no one will ever know. Text linked in the normal manner, on the other hand, begs to be clicked because the text looks so obviously different.

Customizing Hyperlink ScreenTips

When you point your mouse at a linked object during a presentation, a ScreenTip displays, detailing the location of the link. You can customize the ScreenTip to make it easier for you (or the audience) to know just where you will go if you click the linked object.

LET ME TRY IT

Customizing a Hyperlink's ScreenTip

To customize a ScreenTip, follow these steps:

1. Right-click the linked text or object and select Edit Hyperlink from the menu that appears.

2. Click the ScreenTip button. PowerPoint displays the Set Hyperlink ScreenTip dialog box (see Figure 18.7).

Figure 18.7 *Customize the ScreenTip that displays when you move the mouse pointer to a linked object.*

3. Type the text you want to display in the ScreenTip in the ScreenTip Text field. The note about ScreenTips in Internet Explorer refers to slideshows viewed in the browser, not to slideshows presented normally.

4. Click the OK button to return to the Edit Hyperlink dialog box.

5. Click the OK button to save your changes.

Modifying Hyperlinks

The Edit Hyperlink dialog box is a powerful tool for quickly and efficiently modifying your hyperlinks.

 LET ME TRY IT

Modifying an Existing Hyperlink

To modify an existing hyperlink, follow these simple steps:

1. Right-click the linked text or object, and select Edit Hyperlink from the menu that appears to open the Edit Hyperlink dialog box, as shown in Figure 18.8.

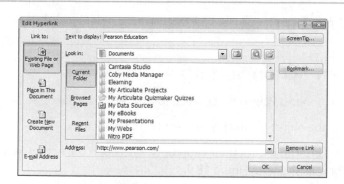

Figure 18.8   *The Edit Hyperlink dialog box lets you update or change an existing hyperlink.*

2.   Make any desired changes, such as entering a new URL or selecting a different PowerPoint slide to jump to.

3.   Click the OK button to save your changes.

Removing Hyperlinks

After inserting a hyperlink, you might decide that you don't want it or that you need to link a different object instead. To remove a hyperlink, right-click a selected object and select Remove Hyperlink from the menu that displays.

Using Action Settings

Action settings are another way to add interactivity and links to your presentation. You can start an action by clicking an object with the mouse or simply by passing the mouse pointer over it. Action settings duplicate some of the functionality of a hyperlink: You can add links to the web or to another PowerPoint slide, for example. They also offer additional interactivity options such as playing a sound file or running a macro.

SHOW ME   Media 18.3—Using Action Settings
Access this video file through your registered Web Edition at
my.safaribooksonline.com/9780132182553/media.

LET ME TRY IT

Adding an Action Setting

To add an action to a PowerPoint object, follow these steps:

1. Select the object to which you want to add an action.

2. On the Insert tab, click the Action button to open the Action Settings dialog box, as shown in Figure 18.9.

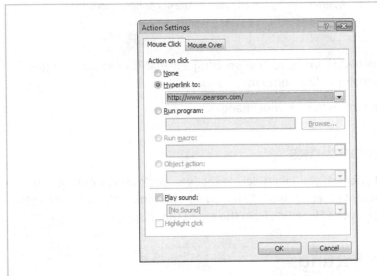

Figure 18.9   *Use a mouse click or mouse over to perform actions in your presentation.*

3. Choose the Mouse Click tab if you want to start the action with a mouse click; choose the Mouse Over tab to start the action by passing the mouse over the object. The Mouse Click and Mouse Over tabs are nearly identical. The only real difference is the method by which you start the action.

> Passing the mouse over an object to start an action is the easier method, but be careful not to get too close to the object too soon or you might start the action before you intend to.

4. Choose the action to take when you click or pause over the object:

   - **None**—No action occurs. Choose this option to remove a previously placed action.

- **Hyperlink To**—Create a hyperlink to a selected slide within your presentation, another PowerPoint presentation, another file on your computer, or a web page.

- **Run Program**—Run the program whose path you specify in the text box. Click the Browse button to open the Select a Program to Run dialog box, where you can search for the program.

You can also use this field to open a file in another program. For example, entering **c:\download\budget.xls** opens Excel and the Budget worksheet that's in the Download folder.

- **Run Macro**—Choose from a list of PowerPoint macros you've created.

- **Object Action**—Open, edit, or play an embedded object. This option is available only for objects that you can open, edit, or play, such as a media clip or something created with another application and embedded into your presentation.

- **Play Sound**—Play an audio file you select from the drop-down list. You can select other sounds by choosing Other Sound from the drop-down list.

- **Highlight Click**—Highlight the selected object when you perform the mouse action.

5. Click the OK button to close the Action Settings dialog box.

To modify or delete an action setting, select the object, click the Action button, and make your changes in the Action Settings dialog box. To remove the action, select None.

Using Action Buttons

Action buttons provide you with another way to use objects to perform certain actions. PowerPoint includes 12 different action buttons:

- Back or Previous
- Forward or Next
- Beginning
- End
- Home
- Information

- Return
- Movie
- Document
- Sound
- Help
- Custom

These buttons function in much the same way as applying an action setting to an existing object. When you place an action button on a slide, the Action Settings dialog box appears. You can then specify mouse actions for the action button. Many action buttons perform common tasks such as moving to a previous slide, so this action is defined by default in the Action Settings dialog box.

To place an action button on a PowerPoint slide, go to the Insert tab and click the Shapes button. Select one of the action buttons that appear at the bottom of the gallery (see Figure 18.10) and then click and drag on the slide to create the button.

Figure 18.10   *The Shapes gallery includes several ready-made action buttons.*

As soon as you finish, the Action Settings dialog box opens, in which you can accept the default action setting or specify the action to attach to this button. Enter the required information and click the OK button. The action button now displays on your PowerPoint slide, where you can resize and reposition it if you like. For further explanation about the options in the Action Settings dialog box, see "Using Action Settings" earlier in this chapter.

To modify an action button, right-click the button, choose Edit Hyperlink from the menu, and make any changes in the Action Settings dialog box. To remove an action button, select it and press the Delete key.

Testing Hyperlinks and Action Settings

Before you present to an audience, test all your hyperlinks to make sure that you set them up correctly. The last thing you want during your presentation is a surprise when you click a hyperlink.

To test the hyperlinks, action settings, and action buttons in your presentation, press F5 to start the slide show at the beginning of your presentation.

If only one slide in your presentation includes a link, go to that slide and click the Slide Show button in the lower-right corner of your screen to start the presentation from the selected slide.

Scroll through your presentation, testing every hyperlink, ScreenTip, action setting, and action button. Verifying that all external links work is particularly important. If you notice any errors, fix them and retest your presentation.

This chapter shows you how to customize
PowerPoint to suit your presentation needs.

19

Customizing PowerPoint

Although many PowerPoint users create outstanding presentations without ever customizing PowerPoint, others prefer making a number of changes to suit their work style and presentation needs. Fortunately, PowerPoint offers numerous customization options.

In this chapter, you learn how to customize all aspects of PowerPoint, including the Quick Access Toolbar, Ribbon tabs, and slide masters. You can also watch videos that show you how to customize the Quick Access Toolbar, customize the Ribbon, and create custom slide layouts on the slide master.

Working with the Quick Access Toolbar

The Quick Access Toolbar is a customizable toolbar that contains popular commands you may use regardless of which tab currently displays. By default, the Save, Undo, and Redo buttons are available from the Quick Access Toolbar, shown in Figure 19.1.

 SHOW ME Media 19.1—Working with the Quick Access Toolbar
Access this video file through your registered Web Edition at
my.safaribooksonline.com/9780132182553/media.

Moving the Quick Access Toolbar

The toolbar's default location is in the upper-left corner of the screen. If you prefer, you can move the toolbar to just below the Ribbon. To move the toolbar, click the down arrow to its right, next to the Redo button, and select Show Below the Ribbon from the menu that displays.

There are only two options for placing the Quick Access Toolbar. You can't move it to any other location on your screen.

Click to modify the toolbar

Figure 19.1   *The Quick Access Toolbar gives you ready access to popular PowerPoint commands.*

Adding and Removing Quick Access Toolbar Commands

To quickly add the most popular commands to the toolbar, click the down arrow to its right and choose from the available options:

- New
- Open
- Save
- E-Mail
- Quick Print
- Print Preview

- Spelling
- Undo
- Redo
- Slide Show from Beginning
- Open Recent File

A check mark is placed before each active command on the toolbar, such as the default commands Save, Undo, and Redo. To add other another command from this menu to the toolbar, click it. To remove one of these commands from the toolbar, click it again, and the check mark disappears.

To add a command button from another tab to the toolbar, right-click it on the Ribbon tab and select Add to Quick Access Toolbar from the menu that displays. For example, let's say that you want to add the New Slide button to the Quick Access Toolbar. To do so, go to the Home tab, right-click the New Slide button, and select Add to Quick Access Toolbar. The New Slide button is placed on the Quick Access Toolbar to the right of the Redo button.

To remove a button, right-click it on the toolbar and choose Remove from Quick Access Toolbar from the menu that displays.

You can perform advanced customizations to the Quick Access Toolbar in the PowerPoint Options dialog box, described in the next section of this chapter.

Setting PowerPoint Options

PowerPoint lets you change many basic options, such as how you edit, save, or print your presentations, and how you view PowerPoint. Changes you make in the PowerPoint Options dialog box become your new default settings until you change them again.

To access the PowerPoint Options dialog box, click the File tab and choose Options (see Figure 19.2).

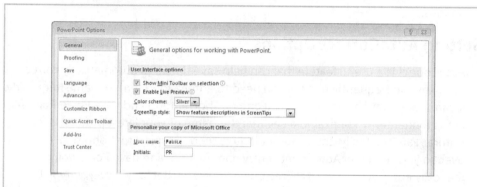

Figure 19.2   *Use the PowerPoint Options dialog box to change many of PowerPoint's default settings.*

Personalizing PowerPoint

On the General tab of the PowerPoint Options dialog box, you can change the most popular options in PowerPoint:

- **Show Mini Toolbar on Selection**—Display the Mini Toolbar when you select text, enabling fast access to common formatting tools, including font style, font color, bolding, and more.

- **Enable Live Preview**—Preview potential formatting changes directly in your presentation before actually applying them.

- **Color Scheme**—Choose between the Blue, Silver, or Black color scheme for your PowerPoint background. Note that this refers to the background of the program, not to the background color of your slides.

- **ScreenTip Style**—Display enhanced ScreenTips with detailed instructions for using a specific command, standard ScreenTips with a basic command identifier, or no ScreenTips at all.

- **User Name**—Whenever you use options that require your name, PowerPoint uses the name found here.

- **Initials**—Whenever user initials are required, PowerPoint uses the initials found here.

Setting Proofing Options

On the Proofing tab, you can specify AutoCorrect and spelling options. Chapter 4, "Working with Text," covers spelling options. This section focuses on AutoCorrect options.

Setting AutoCorrect Options

AutoCorrect is a useful feature that can help save time and automatically correct mistakes you frequently make. If you need to enter a long term or name frequently, it can save you time and effort if you enter a shorter term and have PowerPoint fill in the longer term. For example, say that the name of your latest product is "All-Natural, Fat-Free Chilly Cherry Sorbet." You're tired of typing that phrase over and over, so you set up an AutoCorrect entry named "CCS" and have PowerPoint automatically enter "All-Natural, Fat-Free Chilly Cherry Sorbet" any time you type the letters "CCS."

Be aware that any AutoCorrect entries you make in PowerPoint also carry over to other Microsoft Office applications, such as Word, Excel, Outlook, and so forth.

In addition, if you know that you always misspell a particular word, you can enter the word as you normally misspell it in the Replace field and then enter the correct spelling in the With field.

To open the AutoCorrect dialog box, click the AutoCorrect Options button on the Proofing tab. The AutoCorrect dialog box for your installed language opens, as shown in Figure 19.3.

This dialog box includes four tabs: AutoCorrect, AutoFormat As You Type, Actions, and Math AutoCorrect.

Basic AutoCorrect options on the AutoCorrect tab include

- **Show AutoCorrect Options Buttons**—Display the AutoCorrect Options button after an automatic correction occurs. Pause the mouse over the small blue box beneath the correction, and click the down arrow to view a menu of options (see Figure 19.4). From here, you can revert back to your original entry, stop automatically correcting this type of entry, or open the AutoCorrect dialog box.

Figure 19.3   *You can view and modify automatic correction options in this dialog box.*

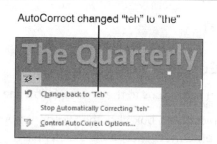

Figure 19.4   *Choose from several options when you automatically correct text entries in PowerPoint.*

- **Correct TWo INitial CApitals**—Automatically correct instances in which you accidentally type two initial capital letters in a row. You can enter exceptions to this rule if you like (such as ID).

- **Capitalize First Letter of Sentences**—Automatically capitalize the first letter of all sentences.

- **Capitalize First Letter of Table Cells**—Automatically capitalize the first letter of text in a table cell.

- **Capitalize Names of Days**—Automatically capitalize days of the week such as Monday, Tuesday, and so forth.

- **Correct Accidental Use of cAPS LOCK Key**—When caps lock is on and you type regular sentences, AutoCorrect turns off caps lock and fixes the capitalization of whatever you typed.

- **Replace Text As You Type**—Automatically replace AutoCorrect entries as you type them.

Customizing AutoCorrect Entries

You can customize AutoCorrect entries. The lower portion of the AutoCorrect dialog box includes a list of existing automatic corrections, where you can do the following:

- Add an AutoCorrect entry by typing the term to replace in the Replace field and its replacement in the With field. Then click the Add button.

- Delete an existing entry by selecting it and clicking the Delete button.

- Change an existing entry by selecting it and entering the new data in the Replace and/or With fields as needed. Then click the Replace button.

 LET ME TRY IT

Specifying AutoCorrect Exceptions

To specify AutoCorrect exceptions to these rules, follow these steps:

1. In the AutoCorrect dialog box, click the Exceptions button. Figure 19.5 illustrates the AutoCorrect Exceptions dialog box.

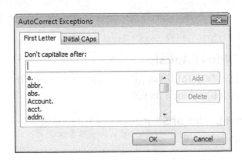

Figure 19.5   *If you want to make exceptions to AutoCorrect functionality, you can do it here.*

2. On the First Letter tab, you can specify abbreviations that end with a period that you don't want to treat as the end of a sentence. PowerPoint ignores standard rules of capitalization here and doesn't capitalize the next letter after the period. Terms such as etc. and abbr. are already included, but you can also add your own or delete any existing entries.

3. On the INitial CAps tab, shown in Figure 19.6, you can enter any capitalized terms that you don't want PowerPoint to convert to lowercase. For example, to avoid having the term ID converted to Id based on the normal rules of capitalization, add it to this list.

4. Click the OK button to return to the AutoCorrect dialog box.

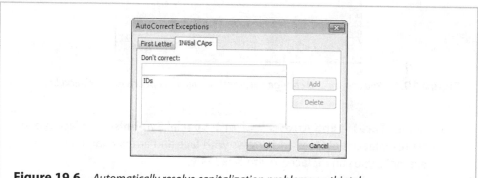

Figure 19.6   *Automatically resolve capitalization problems on this tab.*

AutoFormatting As You Type

The AutoFormat As You Type tab of the AutoCorrect dialog box lets you replace and apply a number of formatting options as you type. You save time because you don't need to format manually. Figure 19.7 shows this tab.

Options include

- **"Straight Quotes" with "Smart Quotes"**—Insert a "curly" quotation mark when you type a quotation mark. If this check box is not selected, you get "straight" quotation marks, a throwback to typewriter days.

- **Fractions (1/2) with Fraction Character (½)**—Replace 1/4, 1/2, and 3/4 with formatted fractions such as ¼, ½, and ¾.

- **Ordinals (1st) with Superscript**—Replace manually entered ordinals with superscript ordinals.

- **Hyphens (—) with Dash (—)**—Replace manually entered hyphens with an em dash. Using two hyphens is a holdover from typewriter days when there was no way to type a proper dash.

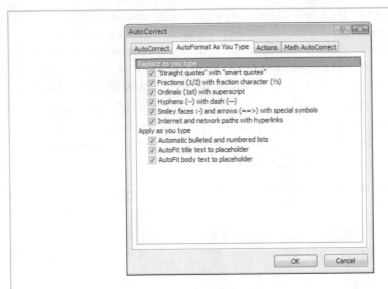

Figure 19.7   *You can see and change automatic correction options in this dialog box.*

- **Smiley Faces :-) and Arrows ==> with Special Symbols**—Replace typed representations of faces and arrows with face and arrow characters. For example, you can replace :-) with ☺.

- **Internet and Network Paths with Hyperlinks**—Apply a hyperlink to an Internet address so that it opens a browser when you click it. For example, AutoCorrect converts www.microsoft.com to www.microsoft.com.

- **Automatic Bulleted and Numbered Lists**—Apply automatic bulleting or numbering when PowerPoint detects that you're creating a list (when you use an asterisk for a bullet, for example).

- **AutoFit Title Text to Placeholder**—Resize text if it won't fit in a title placeholder. For example, if your theme's title text is 44 points by default, you can reduce the font size if your title is too long to fit. When PowerPoint fits title text to the placeholder, the AutoFit Options button appears. Click the down arrow on the right side of the button to display a menu from which you can accept or reject automatic fitting and open the AutoCorrect dialog box.

- **AutoFit Body Text to Placeholder**—Resize text if it won't fit in a body text placeholder. This option works in much the same way as the AutoFit Title Text to Placeholder option.

These options are all selected by default, but you can remove the check mark if you want to deactivate them for any reason.

Setting Up Additional Actions

Actions let you do things in PowerPoint that you'd normally use other programs or Internet services to do. For example, actions can link a date in a presentation to Microsoft Outlook, letting you see your calendar or schedule a meeting for that date. They can also link a stock ticker symbol to financial information at MSN Money.

Use the Actions tab of the AutoCorrect dialog box to enable additional actions such as Measurement Converter, Date, or Financial Symbol. As an example, let's say that you enable the Date action. When you right-click a date on a PowerPoint slide, you can select Additional Actions from the menu that displays to show your calendar in Outlook.

Setting Math AutoCorrect Options

If you include mathematical equations in your presentation, use the Math AutoCorrect tab to enter specific text that PowerPoint converts to the correct symbol. For example, you can type **\Delta** to enter Δ on your slide.

Setting Save Options

Click the Save tab to view and change Save options (see Figure 19.8).

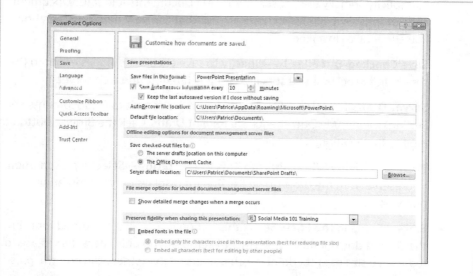

Figure 19.8   *The Save tab of the PowerPoint Options dialog box helps change default file-saving options.*

Save options include

- **Save Files in This Format at**— By default, PowerPoint saves its files in the PowerPoint presentation format (*.pptx).

- If you work in an environment in which some people use old versions of PowerPoint, you might need to agree on a common format for everyone to use. Or you might want to save your presentation in a web format. Other options include PowerPoint Macro-Enabled Presentation, PowerPoint 97–2003 Presentation, or OpenDocument Presentation.

Saving a PowerPoint presentation in an earlier format might result in the loss of certain features available only in PowerPoint 2007.

- **Save AutoRecover Information Every NN Minutes**—This automatic backup provision saves a temporary copy of your presentation (typically in the \Windows\Temp folder) as frequently as you specify with this option. If you exit your document properly, the automatic backup file is erased. If you don't exit properly (for example, because of a power failure), PowerPoint opens this file the next time you use PowerPoint so that you can determine whether it contains changes you didn't save.

- **Default File Location**—PowerPoint saves your presentations in the folder you specify. Initially this is usually your My Documents folder (C:\Documents and Settings\Owner\My Documents), but that can vary depending on how PowerPoint was installed.

- **Save Checked-Out Files To**—Specify to save checked-out files either to the server drafts location you specified on this tab or to the web server.

- **Server Drafts Location**—Save server drafts by default to C:\Documents and Settings\Owner\My Documents\SharePoint Drafts. Click the Browse button to modify this location.

- **Preserve Fidelity When Sharing This Presentation**—Select a presentation to preserve from the drop-down list. The list displays only presentations currently open.

- **Embed Fonts in the File**—Select this option if you want to embed fonts in the current document. Options include embedding only characters in use to reduce file size or embedding all characters so that others can edit the presentation.

Setting Language Options

The Language tab enables you to select languages for editing, display, help, and ScreenTips. These options are most useful if you plan to create presentations in a language other than English or want to enable a different version of English, such as English for the UK or Canada if your default is the United States.

Setting Advanced Options

Click the Advanced tab (see Figure 19.9) to display advanced options for editing, printing, and formatting a presentation.

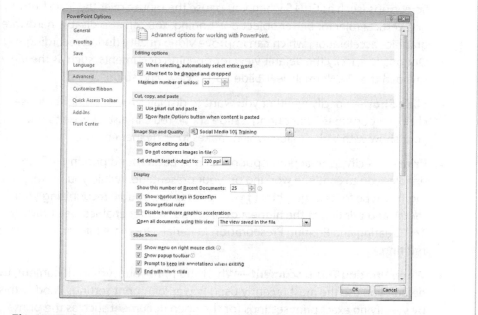

Figure 19.9   *The Advanced tab of the PowerPoint Options dialog box offers advanced editing, printing, and slide show options.*

This page includes the following sections:

- **Editing Options**—Specify text selection, drag-and-drop, and undo options. Be aware that increasing the number of undos enlarges your document and also increases the risk of file corruption. Unless you need more, stay with the default number, or fewer.

- **Cut, Copy, and Paste**—Enable Smart Cut and Paste, which verifies that there's one space before and after the text and that there are no spaces before the end punctuation if you paste the text at the end of a sentence. Also, you can choose to show the Paste Options button that enables you to make choices about how you want to paste a copied object or text, such as whether to keep source or target design template formatting.

- **Image Size and Quality**—Select options that affect image size and quality such as discarding editing data, not compressing images in the file, and setting default target output. Remember that uncompressed images increase file size, which makes your presentation more prone to corruption.

- **Display**—Display a specific number of recent documents, shortcut keys in ScreenTips (such as Ctrl+S when you pause the mouse over the Save button), or a vertical ruler for better object positioning. You can also disable hardware graphics acceleration, which can improve video quality during recording. Optionally, specify the default view for opening documents, such as the view saved in the file, Normal view, Slide Sorter view, and so on.

- **Slide Show**—Specify whether you want to display a menu on right mouse click or a pop-up toolbar during a slide show. You can also choose to end your show with a black slide, which makes for a cleaner ending.

- **Print**—Specify general print options such as background printing (which enables you to continue working on your presentation while you print), printing TrueType fonts as graphics (if your printer has trouble recognizing your fonts), and printing at the highest quality your printer enables. See Chapter 16, "Creating and Printing Presentation Materials," for more information about printing.

- **When Printing This Document**—When you print your current document, by default you use the most recently used PowerPoint print settings. Modify this by specifying exact print settings for the open document such as the print format (full slides, handouts, notes, and so forth) and color (full color, grayscale, or black and white).

- **General**—Add sound effects for screen elements such as menus and buttons, show customer-submitted content when you search Office.com, and set advanced web options.

Customizing the Ribbon

The PowerPoint Ribbon shown in Figure 19.10 is command central for your presentation design activity and offers an easy way to perform common tasks. Although many users are happy to use the Ribbon as it is, PowerPoint also enables you to customize the Ribbon to your exact specifications.

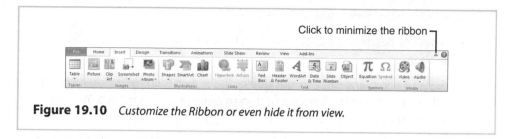

Figure 19.10   *Customize the Ribbon or even hide it from view.*

On the Customize Ribbon tab (see Figure 19.11), you can control which tabs display on the Ribbon and which buttons and groups display on each tab.

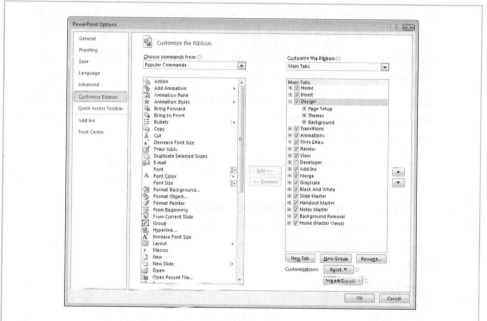

Figure 19.11   *Customize the Ribbon by adding and removing command buttons.*

You can also access the Customize Ribbon tab by right-clicking the ribbon and choosing Customize the Ribbon from the menu.

The left side of the tab lists commands that you can add and remove from the Ribbon. These commands usually display as buttons, such as the New Slide button on the Home tab. The right side of the Customize Ribbon tab lists Ribbon tabs and the commands on each tab.

On the Customize Ribbon tab, you can

- Select or deselect the check box next to any tab to show or hide it on the Ribbon.

- Select a command on the right side of the screen (currently visible on the Ribbon) and click the Remove button to remove it from the tab. You can always restore this later.

- Use the Move Up and Move Down buttons to reposition the placement of any tab or command.

- Rename a tab or command by selecting it and clicking the Rename button.

- Reset the Ribbon to its default by clicking the Reset button. You have the option to reset only a selected Ribbon tab or all Ribbon customizations.

- Export your customizations to an exported Office UI file or import a file you've already exported.

- Create new groups on a Ribbon tab and add new commands to it. Note that you must create a new group to add a command to a Ribbon. You can't add a command on its own.

- Create a new Ribbon tab and add groups and commands to it.

 SHOW ME   Media 19.2—Customizing the Ribbon
Access this video file through your registered Web Edition at
my.safaribooksonline.com/9780132182553/media.

 LET ME TRY IT

Adding Commands to a Ribbon Tab

To create a new group with commands on an existing tab, follow these steps:

1. On the Customize Ribbon tab, select the type of tab you want to add a command to from the Customize the Ribbon list. Options include All Tabs, Main Tabs, and Tools Tabs. The list of tabs below populates based on the category you choose.

2. Select the tab to which you want to add the command.

3. Click the New Group button. PowerPoint inserts a new group at the end of the tab list.

4. Click the Rename button, change the default name to something more meaningful, and click the OK button to close the dialog box.

5. Select the command category you want from the Choose Commands From list. The list of commands below populates based on the command category you choose.

6. Select the command you want to add to the Ribbon.

7. Click the Add button to add it to the selected group. Be sure that you've selected your new group on the right side of the screen. PowerPoint won't add a command to an existing group.

8. Use the Move Up and Move Down buttons on the far right of the dialog box to adjust the location of your new button on the Ribbon.

9. Click the OK button to save your changes and close the dialog box. The Ribbon now displays the new command.

Adding a new tab is similar to adding a new group. Just click the New Tab button instead of the New Group button.

Customizing the Quick Access Toolbar

The Quick Access Toolbar tab (see Figure 19.12) enables you to perform advanced customizations to the Quick Access Toolbar, such as adding commands not accessible from the toolbar and rearranging the order of toolbar buttons.

On the Quick Access Toolbar tab, you can

• Select a command on the right side of the screen (currently visible on the toolbar) and click the Remove button to remove it. You can always restore this later.

• Use the Move Up and Move Down buttons to reposition the placement of any command.

• Reset the toolbar to its default by clicking the Reset button. You have the option to reset only the Quick Access Toolbar or all customizations.

• Export your customizations to an exported Office UI file or import a file you've already exported.

• Add a new command to the Quick Access Toolbar.

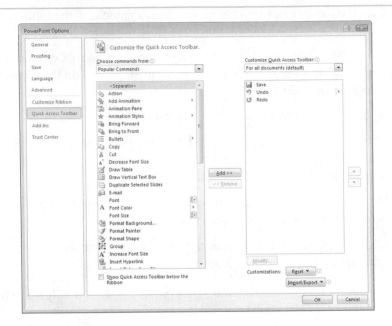

Figure 19.12   *Perform advanced customizations to the Quick Access Toolbar.*

LET ME TRY IT

Adding Commands to the Quick Access Toolbar

To add a new command to the Quick Access Toolbar, follow these steps:

1. Select the command category you want from the Choose Commands From list. Some options match tab names and others reflect the category. The list of commands below populates based on the command category you choose.

2. Select the command you want to add to the toolbar, and click the Add button to add it to the right side of the dialog box.

3. Use the Move Up and Move Down buttons on the far right of the screen to adjust the location of your new button on the toolbar.

4. By default, the toolbar appears the same for all presentations. If you want to specify that the changes you just made should apply to only the current presentation, click the down arrow next to the Customize Quick Access Toolbar list and choose your presentation name from the list.

5. Click the OK button to save your changes and close the dialog box.

Hate the Quick Access Toolbar and want to get rid of it entirely? Remove all buttons and click OK. The toolbar disappears from your screen. If you change your mind, click the File tab, select Options, and go back to the Quick Access Toolbar tab, where clicking Reset restores everything again.

Setting Add-In Options

On the Add-Ins tab, you can view and manage PowerPoint add-ins, which offer supplemental features that enhance your PowerPoint experience. You can also download add-ins from the Microsoft Download Center (www.microsoft.com/downloads). Go to the Add-Ins tab on the Ribbon to access the features of the add-ins you've activated.

Setting Trust Center Options

The Trust Center tab describes security and privacy issues. Click the Trust Center Settings button to open the Trust Center dialog box, where you can specify security and privacy settings.

Setting Presentation Properties

As you create and modify your presentation, you automatically change many of the presentation's properties. To view and modify presentation properties, click the File tab, and select Info to open Backstage view. On the right side of the screen, you can view basic details about your presentation properties. To view more information or edit properties, click the Properties button (it's just the below the thumbnail image), and select Show Document Panel from the menu. PowerPoint opens the Document Properties dialog box, as shown in Figure 19.13.

In this dialog box, the name of the presentation Author displays by default. (Change this by clicking the File tab, selecting Options, and entering a new User Name.) You can also optionally enter a Title, Subject, Keywords, Category, Status, and Comments.

To remove this data from a presentation before sharing, use the Document Inspector (File tab, Info, Check for Issues). See Chapter 17, "Sharing and Collaborating on Presentations," for more information.

For more options, click the down arrow to the right Document Properties and choose Advanced Properties from the menu. A dialog box with the name of your presentation appears. This dialog box enables you to specify file details, enter a custom summary, display details presentation statistics, and create custom properties.

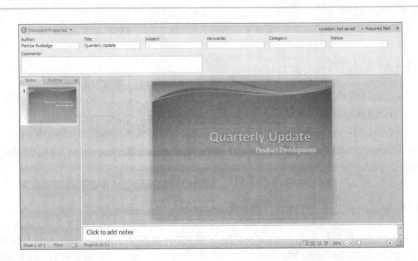

Figure 19.13 *Enter data to identify your presentation in the Properties dialog box.*

Working with Slide Masters

PowerPoint helps you achieve a consistent look in your slide presentations. You want your audience to focus on the message and not be distracted by poor and inconsistent design from one slide to the next.

Slide masters help you achieve this uniformity by storing data about a presentation's theme and slide layouts, such as colors, fonts, effects, background, placeholders, and positioning—and applying it consistently throughout your presentation. Each presentation contains at least one slide master. In most cases, you won't need to do anything to the slide master but can customize it if you choose. For example, you can change the default fonts, placeholders, background design, color scheme, or bullets; reposition placeholders; or add a logo. You can also create additional slide masters.

A template file (*.potx) can contain one or more slide masters. Each slide master can contain one or more sets of slide layouts, including custom layouts.

G See Chapter 2, "Creating a Basic Presentation," and Chapter 3, "Customizing Themes and Backgrounds," for more information about themes and layouts.

Modifying the Slide Master

To modify your slide master, go to the View tab, and click the Slide Master button. PowerPoint displays the slide master layout and editing screen (see Figure 19.14).

Slide master thumbnail   Close and return to presentation

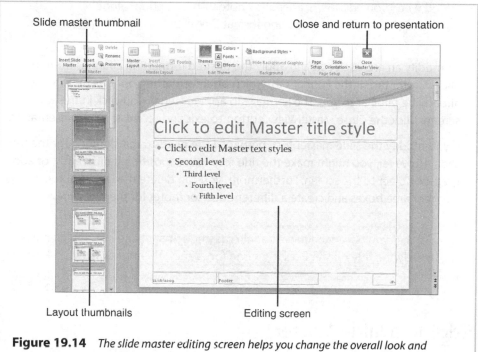

Layout thumbnails   Editing screen

Figure 19.14   *The slide master editing screen helps you change the overall look and layout of your custom design templates.*

You can modify either the slide master, which affects the entire presentation's design, or the master for a specific slide layout, such as the title master or the title and content master.

All changes you make to the title or other text while in the slide master editing screen apply to all slides in your slide presentation except those based on a specific layout master, thus helping you achieve consistency from slide to slide.

Place the mouse pointer over the thumbnails on the left side of the screen to display which thumbnail is for the overall slide master and which is for each layout master. Select the thumbnail to make formatting changes to the desired master.

The master includes several areas you can modify: Title, Subtitle, Text, Date, Footer, and Number.

In the Date, Footer, and Number areas, you normally don't add text but instead format the <date/time>, <footer>, and <#> placeholders. This information is added when you edit the Header and Footer. An exception might be the page numbering, where you can add and format "Page" before the <#> placeholder.

To modify an area, select it and apply the desired formatting changes from the Slide Master tab or the Format tab, which offer formatting options that should already be familiar to you. The Format tab appears when you click in the editing screen. Click the Close Master View button to exit and return to your presentation.

If you modify the slide master first, perhaps little needs to be changed for the title slide. However, you might make the title font larger, position it differently, or add a graphic object to the screen. Furthermore, you can delete the Date, Footer, or Number area boxes and create a different date or footer for the title slide.

Be sure that you have modified the slide master before changing the title master. Initially the title master uses the same fonts and other attributes as the slide master.

Adding a Slide Master

In PowerPoint, a template file (*.potx) can have one or more slide masters.

 LET ME TRY IT

Adding a Slide Master

To add a slide master, follow these steps:

1. On the View tab, click the Slide Master button to open the slide master editing screen.

2. Click the Insert Slide Master button in the Edit Master group on the Slide Master tab. A custom slide master displays. The thumbnails for the slide master and its related layouts appear below the thumbnails for your existing slide master. If you previously had only a single slide master, your new slide master will be numbered as Slide Master 2, as shown in Figure 19.15.

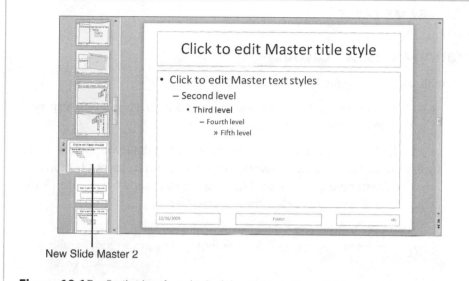

New Slide Master 2

Figure 19.15 *Easily identify multiple slide masters in PowerPoint.*

3. Make any desired changes to the slide master and layouts just as you would with your original slide master. The Slide Master and Format tabs offer many formatting options.

4. Click the Save button on the Quick Access Toolbar to open the Save As dialog box.

5. Accept the default File Name or enter a new name.

6. From the Save As Type drop-down list, choose PowerPoint Template and click the Save button. Your new slide master is now available in the template you saved.

Creating a Custom Layout

PowerPoint offers nine predefined layouts, such as Title Slide, Title and Text, and Title and Content, which you can select by clicking the Layout button on the Home tab. These predefined layouts should be sufficient for most presentations, but sometimes you might need something a little different.

SHOW ME   Media 19.3—Creating a Custom Layout

Access this video file through your registered Web Edition at
my.safaribooksonline.com/9780132182553/media.

LET ME TRY IT

Creating a Custom Layout

To create a custom layout, follow these steps:

1. Go to the View tab and click the Slide Master button. PowerPoint displays the slide master layout and editing screen.

2. Go to the Slide Master tab, select the thumbnail of the layout before which you want to add the custom layout, and click the Insert Layout button in the Edit Master group. A custom layout appears, as shown in Figure 19.16, whose thumbnail is just below the selected layout.

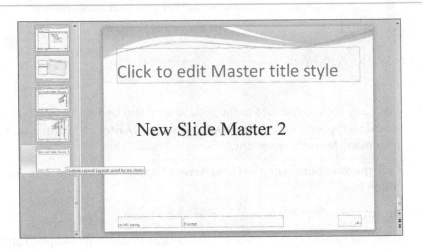

Figure 19.16 *Create a custom layout if none of the standard layouts meets your needs.*

3. By default, the custom layout contains a title placeholder and three footer placeholders for the date/time, generic footer, and slide number. To remove these placeholders, deselect the Title and Footers check boxes in the Master Layout group.

4. To add other placeholders, click the Insert Placeholder button in the Master Layout group. Options include the following placeholders: content, text, pictures, charts, tables, SmartArt, media, and clip art.

5. Select a placeholder from the list, click a location on the slide layout, and drag the mouse to create an appropriately sized placeholder.

6. Continue adding placeholders and formatting your layout with the options on the Slide Master and Format tabs.

7. When you finish, select the thumbnail of the custom layout, and click the Rename button in the Edit Master group on the Slide Master tab. The Rename Layout dialog box displays.

8. Enter a new name for your layout and click the Rename button.

9. Click the Save button on the Quick Access Toolbar to open the Save As dialog box.

10. Accept the default File Name or enter a new name.

11. From the Save as Type drop-down list, choose PowerPoint Template, and click the Save button. Your custom layout is now available when you click the New Slide button on the Home tab.

Renaming a Slide Master or Layout

If you create a new slide master or layout, you'll probably want to rename it.

 LET ME TRY IT

Renaming a Slide Master or Layout

To rename a slide master or layout, follow these steps:

1. On the View tab, click the Slide Master button to open the Slide Master editing screen.

2. Select the thumbnail of the slide master or layout you want to rename on the left side of the screen.

3. Click the Rename button in the Edit Master group on the Slide Master tab. The Rename dialog box opens.

If you're renaming a slide master, the name of this dialog box is Rename Master. If you're renaming a layout, the name is Rename Layout.

4. Enter the new name for the slide master or layout and click the Rename button.

Duplicating a Slide Master or Layout

Sometimes you want to create a slide master or layout that is similar to something that currently exists, yet requires a few small changes. Rather than starting from scratch, you can duplicate the existing master or layout and make your changes from there.

 LET ME TRY IT

Duplicating a Slide Master or Layout

To duplicate a slide master or layout, follow these steps:

1. On the View tab, click the Slide Master button to open the slide master editing screen.

2. Select the thumbnail of the slide master or layout you want to duplicate on the left side of the screen.

3. Right-click the thumbnail and choose either Duplicate Slide Master or Duplicate Layout from the menu. Alternatively, press Ctrl + D on the keyboard to duplicate. A duplicate of your slide master or layout displays, which you can then customize.

Deleting a Slide Master or Layout

If you make a mistake or no longer need a slide master or layout, you can delete it.

 LET ME TRY IT

Deleting a Slide Master or Layout

To delete a slide master or layout, follow these steps:

1. On the View tab, click the Slide Master button to open the slide master editing screen.

2. Select the thumbnail of the slide master or layout you want to delete on the left side of the screen.

3. Click the Delete button in the Edit Master group on the Slide Master tab. The slide master or layout is deleted.

Preserving a Slide Master

If you want to retain a slide master with your presentation even though you haven't applied it to any slides, you can choose to preserve it.

 LET ME TRY IT

Preserving a Slide Master

To preserve a slide master, follow these steps:

1. On the View tab, click the Slide Master button to open the slide master editing screen.

2. Select the thumbnail of the slide master you want to preserve on the left side of the screen.

3. Click the Preserve button in the Edit Master group on the Slide Master tab. The slide master is preserved.

Applying a Theme to a Slide Master

If you want to apply a new theme to a slide master, you can easily do so. When you apply a new theme to a master, the theme also applies to the layouts that comprise the master. Keep in mind that if you have only one slide master, applying a theme creates a second slide master with the chosen theme. If you apply a new theme to a slide master other than your original slide master, the master's theme changes to your new selection.

 LET ME TRY IT

Applying a Theme to a Slide Master

To apply a theme to a slide master, follow these steps:

1. On the View tab, click the Slide Master button to open the slide master editing screen.

2. Select the thumbnail of the slide master whose theme you want to change on the left side of the screen.

3. Click the Themes button in the Edit Theme group on the Slide Master tab.

4. Choose a new theme to apply from the gallery. If you selected a slide master other than the original master, the theme is applied to the master. Otherwise, PowerPoint creates a new slide master with the chosen theme.

⊕ *See Chapter 3 for more information about PowerPoint themes.*

Modifying the Handout and Notes Masters

In addition to the presentation itself, PowerPoint lets you modify the handout and notes masters.

To modify the handout master, go to the View tab and click the Handout Master button. PowerPoint displays the Handout Master editing screen and Handout Master tab (see Figure 19.17).

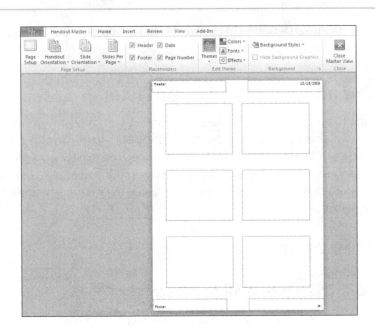

Figure 19.17 *The handout master defines the default layout for your template's printed handouts.*

On the handout master, you can

- Choose the number of slides you intend to include on each handout page by clicking the Slides Per Page button on the Handout Master tab. Choices include one, two, three, four, six, or nine handouts per page.

- Modify, reposition, or delete the Header, Footer, Date, and Page Area text boxes.

> You can easily change the number of slides to be included in the handouts in the Print dialog box when you actually print the handouts, without customizing the handout master.

- Access the Format tab by selecting an object, where you can make edits to the text on the handout master.

To modify the notes master, go to the View tab and click the Notes Master button. PowerPoint displays the Notes Master editing screen (see Figure 19.18).

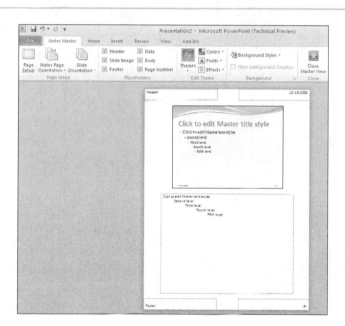

Figure 19.18   *The notes master defines the default layout for your template's printed notes.*

On the notes master, you can

- Reposition or resize the slide area, depending on how much area you want for the text (notes).
- Reposition or resize the notes area.

- Modify, reposition, or delete the Header, Footer, Date, and Page Area text boxes.

- Change the notes page orientation to either portrait or landscape.

- Access the Format tab by selecting an object, where you can make edits to the text on the handout master.

Although you can change the background colors and color schemes for the handout and notes masters, you probably won't want do so. Handouts and notes are usually printed, and background colors aren't necessary or wanted. You can, however, add a graphic element, such as a company logo, which then displays on each printed page.

This chapter shows you how to access PowerPoint through its web application and mobile devices.

20

Accessing PowerPoint on the Web and Mobile Devices

Even if you're away from the computer where you installed PowerPoint 2010—or away from any computer, for that matter—you can still access your PowerPoint presentations.

In this chapter, you learn how to access PowerPoint on the web and from mobile devices such as a Windows smartphone. You can also watch videos that show you how to add files to SkyDrive, create a presentation in SkyDrive, and edit a presentation in the PowerPoint Web App.

Using the Microsoft PowerPoint Web App

Microsoft Office 2010 introduces web-based versions of its most popular applications, including PowerPoint, Word, Excel, and OneNote. To use the PowerPoint Web App, you need either Microsoft SharePoint 2010 (primarily for use in large organizations) or a Windows Live ID and a SkyDrive account (for use by anyone with web access).

With the Web App, you can view and edit PowerPoint presentations from any computer. It's important to note, however, that the Web App's editing features comprise just a small subset of the features available in the desktop version of PowerPoint. You should plan to perform only minor edits in the Web App.

This section focuses on accessing the Web App on SkyDrive with a Windows Live ID. Installing and deploying SharePoint is normally the domain of a corporate IT department, and someone from that department would set up your access rights to the Web App via SharePoint.

Setting Up SkyDrive

SkyDrive offers up to 25GB of free online storage that you can use to collaborate with colleagues anywhere in the world. SkyDrive is part of Windows Live and requires a Windows Live ID to access. If you have an existing account with another Windows Live application such as Hotmail or Messenger, you already have a

Windows Live ID. If you don't, you can sign up for a free Windows Live ID. Be aware that, as a web application, SkyDrive could change or include new features in the future.

To set up SkyDrive, go to http://skydrive.live.com (see Figure 20.1), click the Sign In link, and enter your Windows Live ID. If you don't have an ID, sign up for a free account by clicking the Sign Up button.

Figure 20.1   *Signing up for SkyDrive takes only a few minutes.*

On SkyDrive (see Figure 20.2), you can

- Create new folders by selecting Folder from the New drop-down list. You can share folders with everyone (a public folder), only people in your network, or selected people you have provided access to. Alternatively, you can make your folder private so that only you can access it.

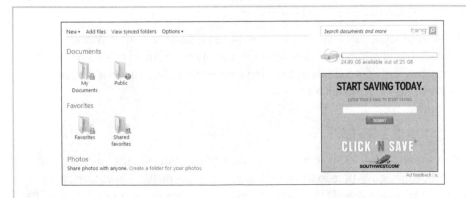

Figure 20.2   *Upload up to 25GB of documents to share with your network.*

- Add files to your folders by clicking the Add Files link. From here, you can browse your computer and select the files you want to upload. You can upload files up to 50MB each. See "Adding Files to SkyDrive" below for more information.

- Open individual files by clicking a folder icon and then clicking the file's icon.

- Create a new PowerPoint presentation by selecting PowerPoint Presentation from the New drop-down list. You can also choose to create a new Word, Excel, or OneNote file.

- View your available storage in the upper-right corner of the screen.

Adding Files to SkyDrive

If you want to work with an existing PowerPoint presentation in the Web App, you must add it to SkyDrive. You can do this directly in SkyDrive or save it from within PowerPoint. See Chapter 17, "Sharing and Collaborating on Presentations," for more information about saving to the web from PowerPoint.

 SHOW ME Media 20.1—Adding Files to SkyDrive

Access this video file through your registered Web Edition at
my.safaribooksonline.com/9780132182553/media.

 LET ME TRY IT

Adding an Existing File to SkyDrive

To add an existing file (such as a PowerPoint presentation) to SkyDrive, follow these steps:

1. In the SkyDrive main window (refer to Figure 20.2), click the Add Files link.

2. Select the folder where you want to store your presentation.

3. Click the Select Documents from Your Computer link to access the Open dialog box, as shown in Figure 20.3.

4. Navigate to the file you want to upload, and click the Open button to return to SkyDrive. Remember that SkyDrive limits individual file size to 50MB.

5. Click the Upload button to finish the upload process.

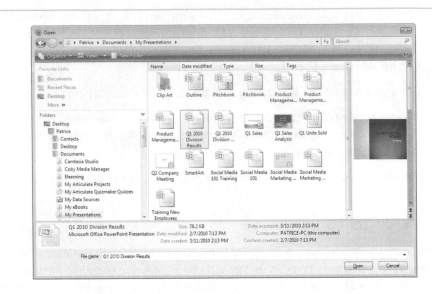

Figure 20.3 *Select the file you want to upload to SkyDrive.*

Creating New Presentations in SkyDrive

Another option is to create a new PowerPoint presentation directly in SkyDrive. You can edit this presentation in the Web App or download it later for use in the desktop version of PowerPoint.

 SHOW ME   Media 20.2—Creating a New Presentation in SkyDrive
Access this video file through your registered Web Edition at
my.safaribooksonline.com/9780132182553/media.

 LET ME TRY IT

Creating a New Presentation in SkyDrive

To create a new PowerPoint presentation in SkyDrive, follow these steps:

1. In the SkyDrive main window (refer to Figure 20.2), select the folder where you want to store the presentation you create.

2. From the New drop-down list (see Figure 20.4), select Microsoft PowerPoint Presentation.

3. Enter a presentation name, and click the Save button, as shown in Figure 20.5.

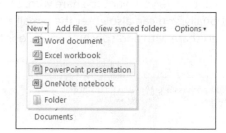

Figure 20.4 *Create a PowerPoint presentation directly in SkyDrive.*

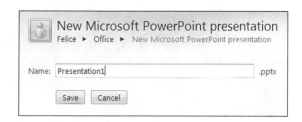

Figure 20.5 *SkyDrive automatically saves your new presentation in the PPTX format.*

The Microsoft PowerPoint Web App opens, where you can add content to your presentation. See "Editing a Presentation in the PowerPoint Web App" later in this chapter for more information.

Setting SkyDrive Permissions

If you want others to view or edit your SkyDrive files, you must give them permission. In SkyDrive, you set permissions at the folder level, not for each individual file.

 LET ME TRY IT

Setting Permissions

To set permissions, follow these steps:

1. In the SkyDrive main window (refer to Figure 20.2), select the folder for which you want to set permissions.

2. From the Share drop-down list, select Edit Permissions.

3. Select the group of people you want to share with, as shown in Figure 20.6. Optionally, you can also enter the e-mail address of an individual you want to share with and specify permissions for this person.

Figure 20.6 *Select the groups or individuals you want to share your presentations with.*

4. From the drop-down list that displays, select one of the following options, depending on the permissions you want to set:

   • Can View Files

   • Can Add, Edit Details, or Delete Files

5. Click the Save button to save your permission settings.

LET ME TRY IT

Editing Presentations in the PowerPoint Web App

You can edit any presentation that you create or save in SkyDrive. If one of your colleagues saves a presentation to SkyDrive, your ability to edit depends on the permissions this person gives you.

SHOW ME   Media 20.3—Editing a Presentation in the PowerPoint Web App

Access this video file through your registered Web Edition at ***my.safaribooksonline.com/9780132182553/media.***

 **LET ME TRY IT**

Editing a Presentation in the PowerPoint Web App

To edit a presentation, follow these steps:

1. In SkyDrive, select the folder that contains your presentation.

2. Select the presentation you want to edit. If you haven't activated the Web App, you're prompted to do so.

3. Click the Edit in Browser button (see Figure 20.7) to open the presentation in the Microsoft PowerPoint Web App. Remember, you must have edit rights for this link to display.

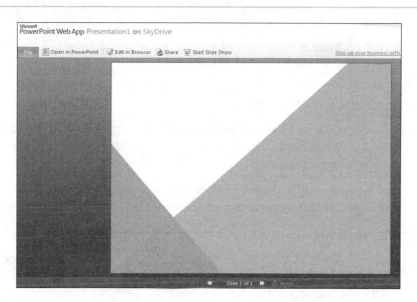

Figure 20.7   *You can choose to edit, view, download, delete, or comment on a presentation.*

From each individual file's page on SkyDrive, you can also add comments, select people to share your presentation with, and download, delete, copy, or rename your presentation.

Figure 20.8 shows the PowerPoint Web App in Edit mode.

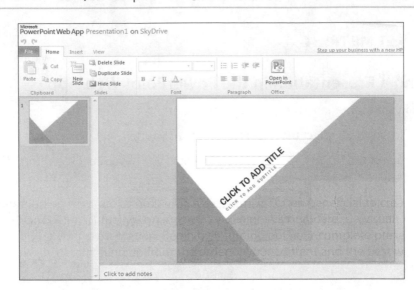

Figure 20.8   *Edit your presentation in the Microsoft PowerPoint Web App.*

This mode includes the following tabs:

- **File**—Display a menu of choices that enables you to open your presentation directly in the desktop version of PowerPoint, provide feedback to Microsoft, or close your presentation.

- **Home**—Cut, copy, and paste objects; create, delete, duplicate, and hide slides; modify and format text; and open your presentation in PowerPoint.

- **Insert**—Insert pictures, SmartArt graphics, or hyperlinks.

- **View**—Choose to view your presentation in one of the following views: Editing, Reading, Slide Show, or Notes. See Chapter 1, "Introducing PowerPoint 2010," for more information about PowerPoint views.

The commands and buttons on these tabs function in much the same way as they do in the desktop version of PowerPoint. The main difference is that you can perform them online on a computer that doesn't have PowerPoint installed.

The PowerPoint Web App doesn't have a Save button because it saves your changes automatically.

Viewing Presentations in the PowerPoint Web App

Even if you don't have edit rights to a presentation, you can still view it if the owner gives you view privileges.

 LET ME TRY IT

Viewing a Presentation in the PowerPoint Web App

To view a presentation, follow these steps:

1. In SkyDrive, select the folder that contains your presentation.

2. Select the presentation you want to view.

3. Click the View link to open the presentation in the PowerPoint Web App.

Figure 20.9 shows the PowerPoint Web App in View mode.

Figure 20.9   *Preview a slide show in View mode.*

This mode includes the File tab, which offers a menu of choices that enables you to open your presentation directly in the desktop version of PowerPoint, provide feedback to Microsoft, or close your presentation.

You can also click one of the following buttons:

- Open in PowerPoint
- Edit in Browser (if you also have edit rights)
- Start Slide Show

Accessing PowerPoint from Mobile Devices

If you want to access your PowerPoint presentations on the go, consider Microsoft PowerPoint Mobile 2010 (http://www.microsoft.com/office/2010/en/mobile/default.aspx). The PowerPoint mobile application isn't part of the standard Microsoft Office 2010 suite but is a separate application available for Windows smartphones running Windows Mobile 6.5 or above. Microsoft Office Mobile 2010 also includes SharePoint Workspace Mobile and mobile versions of Word, Excel, and OneNote. A mobile Outlook application comes preinstalled on these phones.

With PowerPoint Mobile, which is shown in Figure 20.10, you can

- View and edit your presentations, including charts, tables, and SmartArt graphics.

- Share your presentation files with others via email or SharePoint Server 2010 (using the SharePoint Workspace Mobile application).

Figure 20.10 *Access PowerPoint on the go with PowerPoint Mobile.*

- Copy and paste content from within PowerPoint or other applications.

- Control a PowerPoint presentation on your laptop computer from your Windows phone using the Presentation Companion. You can download Presentation Companion from the Microsoft Download Center at http://www.microsoft.com/downloads. An advantage of using the Presentation Companion is that it gives you the ability to use multiple monitors—one for delivering your presentation and another (your phone) for viewing your speaker's notes.

This chapter explores software and tools that extend the power of PowerPoint.

21

Extending PowerPoint with Third-Party Tools

PowerPoint offers a vast array of advanced features, but even the most comprehensive application can't be all things to all people. Fortunately, a number of third-party developers have created unique and useful tools with the PowerPoint user in mind.

In this chapter, you learn about third-party software and tools that make PowerPoint even more useful, creative, and powerful.

Extending PowerPoint with Third-Party Software

With all its powerful new features, PowerPoint 2010 lessens the need for many third-party applications. However, there are still times when you might want to take advantage of the advanced functionality of specialty software. This section covers a trio of options worth considering.

Camtasia Studio

Camtasia Studio (www.techsmith.com/camtasia.asp) is a complete recording, editing, and publishing solution that can convert your PowerPoint presentations to Flash, plus do much more.

The Camtasia Studio add-in for PowerPoint enables you to record your presentation directly in PowerPoint and publish it as a Flash movie (or in another format). You can also enhance your movie by editing the audio and video, inserting title clips, adding callouts and hotspots, and creating picture-in-picture recordings with video. Saving presentations in DVD format for playback on TV is another option.

If you want to create e-learning tutorials, Camtasia Studio also offers interactive quizzes and SCORM (Sharable Content Object Reference Model) compliance. Using PowerPoint with Camtasia is a popular way to create e-learning programs quickly, in an environment that's familiar to any Microsoft Office user.

If you're new to e-learning, some of its terminology might be unfamiliar to you. Most e-learning solutions are SCORM-compliant. This means that they meet the standards specified by SCORM for web-based e-learning systems. Many e-learning solutions, particularly those run by larger organizations, use a learning management system (LMS) to manage their e-learning content and delivery.

Figure 21.1 illustrates the use of Camtasia Studio in PowerPoint.

Camtasia Studio buttons on the Add-Ins tab

Figure 21.1   *The Camtasia Studio add-in enables you to enhance your presentation with even more options.*

Articulate Rapid E-Learning Studio

Articulate Rapid E-Learning Studio (www.articulate.com) offers the following suite of e-learning applications that integrate with PowerPoint, each of which you can also purchase separately:

- **Articulate Presenter**—Create e-learning courses in PowerPoint and convert them to Flash. Advanced features include animation support, voice synchronization, presenter videos, learning game and quiz integration, SCORM-compliance, LMS support, and more.

- **Articulate Quizmaker**—Create custom Flash quizzes and surveys that integrate with Articulate Presenter and offer 21 different question types.

- **Engage**—Engage your audience with interactive content including timelines, media tours, pyramids, guided images, glossaries, labeled graphics, and tabs.

- **Video Encoder**—Convert videos to Flash video format and edit, crop, and format videos.

Figure 21.2 shows the Articulate tab as it displays in PowerPoint.

Another option is Articulate Online, an alternative to a complex LMS system, which provides online reporting and quiz/survey tracking.

Figure 21.2 *Articulate helps you create sophisticated Flash-based e-learning from PowerPoint.*

Adobe Presenter

Adobe Presenter (www.adobe.com/products/presenter) enables you to create Flash multimedia presentations and on-demand and real-time e-learning courses from within the familiar PowerPoint environment. Then, you can extend your presentation with quizzes, surveys, and interactivity before converting to Flash for delivery. Presenter also integrates with Adobe Acrobat Connect Pro web conferencing software for a complete delivery solution. You can purchase Adobe Presenter on its own or as part of the Adobe eLearning Suite of applications.

Getting Creative with Third-Party Templates, Backgrounds, and Clip Art

Even though PowerPoint and Microsoft Office Online (http://office.microsoft.com) offer an extensive array of templates, backgrounds, and clip art to use in your presentations, sometimes you just want something different.

The good news is that numerous third-party providers offer collections of templates, clip art, and more. You're sure to find the exact match for your presentation needs. Here are some interesting places to start:

- CrystalGraphics PowerPlugs (www.crystalgraphics.com) are a series of PowerPoint plug-ins that enhance the quality of PowerPoint presentations. PowerPlugs include video backgrounds, transitions, charts, pictures, Flash animations, templates, TV-style 3-D titles, shapes, presentation shells, photo animations, and music.

- Clipart.com (www.clipart.com) offers a vast collection of more than 10 million objects, including clip art, photos, fonts, and sounds. Clipart.com is available by subscription, with timeframes ranging from one week to one year.

- Presentation Pro (www.presentationpro.com) sells a bundle of 18,000 templates, graphics, and icons suited for PowerPoint presentations and several other PowerPoint tools.

- Ppted.com (www.ppted.com) offers another extensive collection of PowerPoint templates and backgrounds.

Enhancing Your PowerPoint Experience with External Hardware

Software isn't the only option for third-party PowerPoint tools. There are also several unique hardware solutions that solve common problems and make delivering PowerPoint presentations a more productive experience.

Impatica ShowMate

The Impatica ShowMate (www.impatica.com) is a small device that connects your Blackberry handheld device to a projector, enabling you to deliver a PowerPoint presentation without the need for a bulky computer. This plug-and-present solution works with the Impatica for BlackBerry Enterprise Server, which enables you to view PowerPoint presentations on Blackberry devices (including animations, slide transitions, rich text, and hyperlinks). The ShowMate also comes with a Bluetooth USB adapter for wireless use with Bluetooth-enabled Blackberry devices.

Papershow

The Papershow Kit (www.papershow.com) contains a Bluetooth digital pen, USB key loaded with software, and interactive paper that transmits to your screen, all bundled in a case that fits in your pocket. You can import your PowerPoint presentation into Papershow, print it on the interactive paper, and then annotate your presentations on a screen.

TurningPoint

TurningPoint (www.turningtechnologies.com) is a PowerPoint add-in that works with wireless keypads to form an audience response system you can use in real-time during your presentations. Members of your audience receive a credit card-sized ResponseCard keypad that they click in response to an interactive polling slide in your PowerPoint presentation. The results are submitted to a wireless receiver, which you can then share with your audience or analyze for reporting purposes.

Audience response systems such as TurningPoint are popular in both the corporate and education markets. TurningPoint offers several additional features specifically for use in schools and universities, including the ability to integrate special ExamView questions into your PowerPoint presentation.

Laser Mouse

The Laser Mouse (www.lasermouse.com) is a long-range wireless remote mouse with a built-in laser pointer. It's designed specifically with the delivery of PowerPoint presentations in mind, with a navigation disk and slide advance button.

Integrating PowerPoint with Twitter

The use of Twitter during conference and other large presentations is on the rise. Rather than having your audience's commentary take place solely on this backchannel, you can become part of it and integrate Twitter into your presentation. This section introduces you to two innovative ways to do just that.

Poll Everywhere

Poll Everywhere (www.polleverywhere.com) enables you to maximize the use of Twitter during a live presentation by polling your audience.

To start, you ask your audience a question—either a multiple choice question or an open-ended question. They respond via Twitter, SMS text message, a smartphone's web browser, or a computer's web browser. Finally, you can display real-time poll results directly in your PowerPoint presentation.

SAP PowerPoint Twitter Tools

SAP (www.sapweb20.com/blog/powerpoint-twitter-tools) has released a series of free PowerPoint Twitter tools that increase audience interactivity during your presentations. These include

- PowerPoint Twitter feedback slides, which display tweets on PowerPoint slides during your presentation, with the capability to filter spam or any content you don't want to share.

- PowerPoint AutoTweet, which enables you to tweet key points during your presentation.

- PowerPoint Twitter voting, with real-time results displayed in bar charts and pie charts.

- PowerPoint Twitter ticker bar that displays the last 10 tweets at the bottom of your presentation slides.

- PowerPoint mood meter, enabling your audience to communicate their agreement or disagreement with key presentation points.

- PowerPoint crowd meter, to monitor and display the crowd noise in your room.

- PowerPoint zoom text, which zooms text on your screen.

- PowerPoint Twitter update bar.

index